Language and Public Policy   Hugh Rank, editor

NCTE Committee on Public Doublespeak

Clare Barkley, Urbana High School, Illinois
John A. Black, Darien High School, Connecticut
David Burmester, Davis Senior High School, California
Walter A. Buchmann, The Union for Experimenting Colleges and Universities, Ohio
Robert Cirino, Honolulu
Edward P. J. Corbett, Ohio State University
Daniel Dieterich, University of Illinois at Urbana/Champaign
Richard Gambino, City University of New York
Walker Gibson, University of Massachusetts
Nat Hentoff, New York University
D. G. Kehl, Arizona State University
Gerald Kincaid, Minnesota State Department of Education
Donald Lazere, University of California, Berkeley
Howard F. Livingston, Pace University, New York
Ray Liedlich, Contra Costra College, California
William Lutz, Rutgers University, New Jersey
H. Thomas McCracken, Youngstown State University, Ohio
Nancy McCracken, Youngstown State University, Ohio
David Milan, Tacoma Community College, Washington
Catherine Minteer, Southern California School District
Terence Moran, New York University
Richard Ohmann, Wesleyan University, Connecticut
Wayne O'Neil, Massachusetts Institute of Technology
Ernest R. Page, Pennsylvania State University
Neil Postman, New York University
Hugh Rank, Governors State University, Illinois
Bruce Reeves, Acalanes High School, Lafayette, California
Paul Smith, Trinity College, Connecticut
George Solana, Strake Jesuit College Prep School, Houston
Charles Weingartner, University of South Florida
Robert B. Wolk, Washburn High School, Minneapolis
Howard Ziff, University of Massachusetts

Language
and Public Policy

Hugh Rank, editor
NCTE Committee on Public Doublespeak

National Council of Teachers of English
1111 Kenyon Road, Urbana, Illinois 61801

Editor/Susan B. Drake
Designer/David Colley

Library of Congress Catalog Card Number 74-84479
NCTE Stock Number 25733

Acknowledgments

"Words from Watergate" by Stefan Kanfer. Editorial from TIME, Vol. 102, August 13, 1973. Reprinted by permission from TIME, The Weekly Newsmagazine; Copyright Time Inc.

"Watergaters' Forked Tongues" by Sydney J. Harris. From STRICTLY PERSONAL by Sydney J. Harris as published in the *Chicago Daily News* September 26, 1973. Courtesy of Publishers-Hall Syndicate. Copyright 1973 by Publishers-Hall Syndicate.

"Watergate Lingo: A Language of Non-Responsibility" by Richard Gambino. Republished from *Freedom At Issue* (Nov.-Dec. 1973) published by Freedom House, 20 West 40th Street, New York, N.Y. 10018. Copyright 1973 by Freedom House, Inc. Reprinted by permission of the publisher.

"A Watergate Summer" by Don L. F. Nilsen. From *College English,* Vol. 35, No. 7, April 1974. Copyright 1974 by the National Council of Teachers of English. Reprinted by permission of the author and the publisher. Originally titled "Notes from Kalamazoo: From Workshop 15, 'Semantics and Discourse Analysis.'"

"Language and Dramatic Character" and "Beginnings of the Committee" by Walker Gibson. From *College English,* Vol. 35, No. 7, April 1974, and *English Journal,* Vol. 63, No. 5, May 1974. Copyright 1974 by the National Council of Teachers of English. Reprinted by permission of the author and publisher. Originally titled "Seeing Ourselves."

"The Language of Deceit" by David Burmester. Reprinted from *Media & Methods,* May 1973. Used with permission. Copyright 1973, North American Publishing Co.

"Ad" by Kenneth Fearing, which appears in "The Electric Carrot: The Rhetoric of Advertisement and the Art of Persuasion" by D. G. Kehl. Copyright by and used with permission of the estate of Kenneth Fearing.

257424

"Ad-Man, Business-Man, Teacher-Man" by Bruce Reeves. From *English Journal,* Vol. 61, No. 5, May 1972. Copyright 1972 by the National Council of Teachers of English. Reprinted by permission of the author and the publisher.

"Mendacious Messages from Madison Avenue (and a Recommended Remedy)" by Vincent P. Norris. From *Media & Consumer,* September 1973. Copyright 1973 by Media & Consumer Foundation. Reprinted by permission of the author and the publisher.

"*Mad* Magazine—Witness for the People" by Richard Reeves. From NEW YORK Magazine, October 1, 1973. Copyright © by the NYM Corp. Reprinted with the permission of NEW YORK Magazine.

"Plight of the American Language" by Jean Stafford. From *Saturday Review/World,* December 4, 1973. Reprinted by permission of the author and her agent, James Brown Associates, Inc. Copyright © 1973 by Jean Stafford.

"How We Debase the English Language" by Melvin Maddocks. From The Christian Science Monitor, December 6, 1973. Reprinted by permission from The Christian Science Monitor. © 1973 The Christian Science Publishing Society. All rights reserved. Originally titled "The Last Word."

"Semantics, Attitudes, and the Training of Teachers" by Howard F. Livingston. Reprinted from ETC., Vol. XXIX, No. 2, by permission of the International Society for General Semantics. Copyright 1972 by the International Society for General Semantics.

"Let Them Eat Wonderbread" by Peter Klappert. From *Saturday Review,* October 7, 1972. Copyright 1972 by Saturday Review, Inc. Reprinted by permission of the publisher. "The Truth" by Randall Jarrell reprinted from *The Complete Poems* by Randall Jarrell by permission of the publisher, Farrar, Straus & Giroux, Inc. Copyright © 1949, 1955 by Randall Jarrell. "Dear Fellow Teacher" by George Starbuck reprinted from *White Paper* by permission of the publisher, Atlantic-Little, Brown. Copyright © 1966 by George Starbuck.

"Symbols, Language, and Violence" by Rollo May. From *Liberal Education,* Vol. LVIII, No. 1, March 1972. Copyright 1972 by the Association of American Colleges. Reprinted by permission of the publisher.

"The Road to Radicalism: A Semantic Aberration" by E. W. Cardaci. Reprinted from ETC., Vol. XXVIII, No. 3, by permission of the International Society for General Semantics. Copyright 1971 by the International Society for General Semantics.

"Politics and the American Language" by Justus George Lawler. From *College English,* Vol. 35, No. 7, April 1974. Copyright 1974 by the National Council of Teachers of English. Reprinted by permission of the author and the publisher.

On Dishonest and Inhumane Uses of Language

Resolved, That the National Council of Teachers of English find means to study dishonest and inhumane uses of language and literature by advertisers, to bring offenses to public attention, and to propose classroom techniques for preparing children to cope with commercial propaganda.

On the Relation of Language and Public Policy

Resolved, That the National Council of Teachers of English find means to study the relation of language to public policy, to keep track of, publicize, and combat semantic distortion by public officials, candidates for office, political commentators, and all those who transmit through the mass media.

Resolutions passed by the
National Council of Teachers of English
at its sixty-first Annual Meeting, 1971

Contents

Introduction

Hugh Rank

Hugh Rank of Governors State University, Illinois, was the original chairman of the NCTE Committee on Public Doublespeak. He resigned that position in 1973 in order to complete work on this book designed for teachers, on a text designed for students (*Liars in Public Places,* to be published by Scott Foresman in 1975), and on a "Counter-Propaganda" schema intended for general use to replace the old "list" from the Institute for Propaganda Analysis.

During November 1971, in Washington, D.C., the Federal Trade Commission, that agency of our government which has direct responsibility to protect the public from deceptive advertising, was holding its *first* hearing on modern advertising practices. These open sessions had considerable significance, yet very little about them was reported in the press. As Stanley Cohen, the Washington editor of *Advertising Age* reported (November 22, 1971): "For the most part the public had little opportunity to know anything about what was happening. . . . There was only an occasional wire service story on the testimony that took place and—except for the trade press—the press seats in the hearing room were empty most of the time. . . . The broadcast media did even worse. A major government agency was spending 15 days to determine whether our children are being seduced by TV, and whether 200 million consumers are being 'manipulated.' But except for the fragments fed in by occasional reports of the news services, it was 'non-news' for the networks and the broadcasting industries. And the cameras and the tape recorders and the network newsmen were nowhere to be seen. How's that for performance from an industry that likes to impress us with its valiant efforts to 'defend the right to know'!"

These were significant hearings. For the first time, a $26 billion a year language industry was seriously examined. Certainly advertising has been controversial for the past 20 years and it would seem that when the FTC finally decided to organize a systematic investigation, some attention should have been paid. Nearly every major advertising agency and association testified and FTC staffers asked some penetrating questions. But, unless you were a reader of the trade newspaper, *Advertising Age,* unless you read very carefully the issues from October 25 to November 29, you would have known practically nothing about these hearings.

Simultaneously in November 1971, another unpublicized meeting

was taking place in another American fantasy city—Las Vegas—
the 61st Annual Convention of the National Council of Teachers
of English. At that convention, NCTE passed two significant resolutions. One resolution, after the appropriate background rationale, resolved that NCTE *"find means to study dishonest and inhumane uses of language and literature by advertisers, to bring
offenses to public attention, and to propose classroom techniques
for preparing children to cope with commercial propaganda."*

The second resolution, more politically oriented, quoted Orwell's
point that "language is often used as an instrument of social control." The Watergate conspiracy had not yet taken place, so the
background material focused on the manipulation of language by
the government and the military in the Vietnam war. The resolution concluded "Although teachers of English do not make national policy, we should do what we can to free public language
and thought from manipulation by the powerful" and resolved
that NCTE *"find means to study the relation of language to public
policy, to keep track of, publicize, and combat semantic distortion
by public officials, candidates for office, political commentators, and
all those who transmit through the mass media."*

Shortly afterwards, NCTE announced the formation of the Committee on Public Doublespeak, charged with the omnibus task of
combating the advertisers, the politicians, and the major public
manipulators of language in our society. In the initial press release, Robert Hogan, NCTE's Executive Secretary, said: "It isn't
that the interests of NCTE in the mechanics and the structure of
language, as well as its history, are diminishing at all. Behind the
appointment of the committee is a resurgent interest in the content of language. The question is not just whether subjects·and
verbs agree, but whether statements and facts agree."

Hogan's statement recognizes certain common stereotypes that
many people harbor about English teachers: prissy fussbudgets
being sticklers about "grammar rules" or, in the ivory tower myth,
absentminded professors fumbling their way through halls of ivy.
We, who are in the profession of teaching our language, know the
frivolousness of these common stereotypes of English teachers. Yet,
it is significant that at the FTC hearings there were no English
teachers or rhetoricians testifying about the nature of language
manipulation. There *were* academics testifying. But they came
primarily from the business schools: marketing professors, eco-
nomics professors, behavioral scientists, psychologists—the teachers
and trainers of the future *persuaders* of this country.

Oddly, there was no representation from those hundreds of thousands of teachers of English, the teachers and trainers of the future *persuadees* of this country. (This oversight on the part of the FTC has been reciprocated by the English teachers. In my own experience as the original chairman of the Committee on Public Doublespeak, I talked and wrote to hundreds of English teachers and found that few had any awareness of the FTC, its specified responsibilities, and its operations.)

It's very impractical for a small group of English teachers to attempt to "do something" about a $26 billion a year advertising industry and a multi-billion dollar propaganda campaign from our government and diverse politicians. It's very Quixotic. But the fact remains: there are real windmills out there; there are real problems.

Today's generation is experiencing a propaganda blitz unequaled in human history. In our daily, unnoticed environment we Americans are subjected to more ads and more political persuasion than ever generated in the supposedly "classic" propaganda campaigns of Nazi Germany. Granted, it's easy for us to recognize the overt, blatant propaganda machinery of Red China, with its blunt ballets, slogans, and posters. It's more difficult for us to be aware of our own environment, saturated with propaganda urging us to buy this product or that policy. Such use of language has most serious consequences for all people on earth. We, who are language teachers in that nation which has suddenly developed into a nuclear power within the past 30 years, do have obligations. What can we do? There is no panacea, of course. No quick salvation, instant grace. No simple answers. We can't do everything. But we can, perhaps, do something.

In the academic world during the past generation others have shared these feelings and have attempted—or are attempting—to do something. Certainly, one can see that the formation of the NCTE Committee on Public Doublespeak is but a part of a wider general movement of people who have labeled themselves with diverse names: *semanticists, rhetoricians, communications* or *media people*—teachers and scholars in English departments and speech departments who are concerned with the social effects of language. Perhaps in our most skeptical moments we are most aware of the failure of these people to achieve their high goals; but in our optimistic moments, we recognize the impulse that still moves us to reform, to change, to try again, despite the odds.

Language and Public Policy is one of the early products of the NCTE Committee on Public Doublespeak. The intent here is both to inform our colleagues and to persuade them. In the first case, we assume that some colleagues already are interested and committed to this study and that the materials here will further aid them. For example, a number of these excellent essays appeared in small-circulation magazines and were sent in to the committee by NCTE members wishing to share their discoveries. But some of these essays seek to exhort and to persuade. Here, we assume that some of our colleagues may have recently turned their attention to the problems involved in propaganda analysis, semantics, persuasion techniques—in brief, to that complex of related items which we have grouped under the umbrella term *Doublespeak*, with all of its rich Orwellian overtones. We hope to persuade more of our fellow English teachers that such studies are important, that they deserve a more prominent place in the study of "English."

Most teachers are aware of the dangers of parochialism, of adhering exclusively to one of the many groups, cults, and special interest clubs within that amorphous category of people known as "English teachers." One need only go to an NCTE convention to see the supermarket of ideas and attitudes, where each group can make a case for the importance of their own interest, for the primacy or the relevance or the usefulness of their ideas to "mental development" or "liberal education" or so on. Yet, considering the limited amount of time allotted in schools to language studies, teachers are also aware that priorities must be established: some language skills are more important than others.

Rather than get into an unending argument over the *intrinsic* merits of these various special interests, we would like to point out some *extrinsic, external* criteria which make propaganda analysis so vital today—the "Public" of Public Doublespeak.

Since 1945, there has been a quantum change in persuasion. Yes, people have always tried to persuade others. Aristotle, 2500 years ago, outlined the basic patterns. But, since 1945, the money expended (by Madison Avenue, by the Pentagon, by the Democrats and Republicans, by the USSR); the technology used (computers, television, etc.); and the sophisticated, coordinated use of corporate manpower have made a tremendous difference. For example, up until very recently, parents have always acted as buffers protecting their children from the "outside world." No huckster or salesman would ever dare approach a child. But today parents unthinkingly use the TV as a babysitter, allowing the huckster a straight shot at their kids. Something new, and very important, is happening in human languaging today. But most schools plod along, giving more attention to minor 19th century writers than to major 20th century language developments.

The first section of this book centers on the words of Watergate. At present (fall 1974), literally dozens of books and hundreds of articles about the Watergate affair are in print, in addition to the millions of words of official testimony and journalistic reports which have appeared during the past two years. Obviously, Watergate will remain in the American consciousness; the multiplicity and complexity of the issues involved will continue to stimulate political scientists, sociologists, psychologists, and historians. In future years we can expect an ongoing analysis, in books and articles and classrooms, as teachers and scholars continue to reflect on the lessons learned from Watergate. With the sheer bulk of this material available, the brief collection offered here cannot be comprehensive, but it is a good representative sampling of those Watergate articles which focused on language manipulation.

The second section is meant to be a sampler of the many items and interests which cluster around our concerns of countering commercial and political propaganda. Some are specific how-to-do-it articles relating ideas or techniques that can be used in the classroom, particularly to teach analysis of commercial advertisements. Other articles look at the students' life outside the classroom; the *Mad* magazine article, for example, acknowledges the power of that satiric watchdog, which has probably done more to immunize our children from cant and crap than most teachers or educational institutions. Still other essays analyze or excoriate language manipulation in war, politics, or everyday society. The alert reader will recognize that there is no orthodoxy presented here. One must read this anthology critically because of the diverse opinions, the variety of approaches, the differences in degree and of kind, expressed by these writers. Such a spectrum may suggest the diversity within the NCTE Committee on Public Doublespeak, which is essentially a loose confederation of people who have common concerns but different responses.

In the third section, an eloquent exhortation for action from Congressman Robert F. Drinan is followed by speeches concerned with language abuse delivered in recent years by leaders of academic and scholarly organizations such as the National Education Association, Speech Communication Association, Linguistic Society of America, and Conference on English Education. In the final section, the focus narrows to the NCTE Committee on Public Doublespeak. Here, information from those within the committee and commentary from outside observers are presented as a kind of status report.

Thus, the book starts with articles about the most widely known episodes of language manipulation today—those of the Watergate affair—and moves on to consider a variety of ever-present and ever-increasing examples of semantic distortion. Attention is then focused more sharply on teachers' responsibilities in essays that seek to persuade and demonstrate that teachers should and can prepare children to cope with dishonest and inhumane uses of language.

1

Watergate as Watershed

... focused on the words of Watergate ... a representative sampling of articles concerned with language manipulation ...

Watergate and the Language

Hugh Rank

To teach students how to recognize "the strategies of silence, the tactics of omission, evasion, diversion, circumlocution," must be one of the most important lessons that we learn from the Watergate experience, according to Rank's analysis. Here he also discusses Watergate jargon, Nixon's vulgarity, and the inference of character through analysis of language.

Watergate was a watershed in the history of American politics and it may well prove to be such a crucial junction in the history of American education. A generation earlier, the launching of a Russian satellite proved to have an enormous impact on American educational systems, as Sputnik became the catalyst and the symbolic rallying point for a crash program in developing American scientific and technological education. The Watergate experience will hardly be so clear cut: Watergate was an internal agony, not an external threat; Watergate was not a simple dramatic stroke, the affair was complex and drawn out, even beyond the unprecedented resignation, and subsequent "pardon," of an American president. The trauma has been etched deep on our national psyche and we are likely to see the traditional American reforming instinct surface again in educational and curriculum reforms, using "Watergate" as a battle cry. Obviously, the political phenomenon of Watergate will affect the study of history, politics, and government, at all levels from the elementary school classes in "Civics" and "Current Events" to the curricula of the graduate schools and law schools. But it is also likely that the impact of Watergate will be found in the teaching of *language arts*. For millions of Americans who witnessed, Watergate was a war of words, a drama of language manipulation.

After two years of investigation and controversy, two events especially focused public attention on the use and abuse of language: the televised congressional hearings in the summer of 1973, and the release of the White House transcripts in the late spring of 1974. During the televised hearings, the various linguistic issues ranged from random charges of "grammatical errors" to formal charges of legal perjury. Some people were concerned that Standard English Usage was being violated, while others responded to the barrage of clichés and repetitions, the bureaucratic and legalistic jargon, the omissions and circumlocutions of the witnesses.

In the early skirmishes in this war of words, it took only a few days of the Ervin committee televised hearings (May–June, 1973) to alert and alarm the language purists, the legendary fussy Miss Thistlebottoms, who registered their horror that "so-called educated men"—college graduates and lawyers—were violating every rule in the old grammar book. Defenses of "good English," "Standard English," and (quaintly enough) "The King's English" began to appear in newspaper letters-to-the-editor columns. Although such complaints were indeed accurate in most instances—the Watergate witnesses could hardly open their mouths without uttering a solecism per sentence—most observers would agree that these critics had missed the main point.

But such fussiness did not come principally from those who are professionally concerned with language *qua* language: the linguists and scholars and the classroom teachers of English. NCTE, for example, had established, a year earlier, a Committee on Public Doublespeak. At that time, Robert Hogan, NCTE's Executive Secretary stated: "Behind the appointment of the committee is a resurgent interest in the content of language. The question is not just whether subjects and verbs agree, but whether statements and facts agree."

During the Watergate hearings, most members of the NCTE committee listened to TV not for subject-verb agreements but for those techniques of language manipulation which were being used to conceal truth. Many Watergate witnesses were educated men, from the nation's finest schools, who used their skills in language to lie, to evade, to conceal, to confuse. So obvious was their manipulation that citizens who aren't normally interested in language matters recognized, vaguely at least, that language indeed was being used—either as a weapon or as a mask.

Within days after the Ervin committee hearings began on television, certain stock phrases ("at this point in time"), words ("inoperative"), metaphors ("game plan," "laundered money"), and bureaucratic and legal jargon provided source material for political cartoonists, nightclub comedians, TV talk show hosts, and satirists of all sorts and degrees, from the professional to the barroom pundit. Herblock and "Doonesbury," Art Buchwald and Russell Baker, *Mad* and *National Lampoon* had a heyday. It was a cornucopia of cant for satiric recycling.

Even the more solemn Watergate watchers were astonished by the verbal performance. David Wise (*The Politics of Lying*) sent me his "favorite" Watergate quote—a 300-word answer by Ehrlichman (to a "yes-no" kind of question) in which the words simply flowed out, sidetracking, winding back and forth, looping around, eventually ending nowhere, a diversionary bit of rambling non-sense. In my judgment, one of the high spots (low spots?) of Watergate testimony was that of Patrick Buchanan, later described by *Time* as "quick-witted and fast talking. . . . the Administration's most effective witness." A sampling of Buchanan's effectiveness:

Senator Inouye: "Do you think it's ethical?"
(long pause)
Buchanan: "I don't think it's unethical."

Senator Montoya: "Do you think it's proper?"
(long pause)
Buchanan: "I don't think it's improper."

In Orwell's famous essay, "Politics and the English Language," he thought that it "should be possible to laugh the *not-un* formation out of existence." Unfortunately, Orwell was wrong. Nobody laughed.

As Richard Gambino wrote in "Watergate Lingo" (reprinted in this anthology): "The torrent of circumlocutions, mechanical verbal formulas, misplaced technical jargon, palliative expressions, euphemisms, and inflated phraseology indicate that the brains both of speakers and listeners are being anesthetized or stunted. . . . It is often hard to tell whether they are merely dissemblers trying to paralyze the minds of others, self-deceivers who have crippled their own intelligences, or glib dolls whose characters remained undeveloped as their smartness grew." Gambino suggested that the general emphasis on Watergate's sensational *1984* aspects (bugging, spying, etc.) obscured the importance of the ethical and moral irresponsibility which flourishes in the fertilizer of this debased language: "If our political language, and therefore our public thinking, becomes so debauched that moral meanings can no longer be clearly expressed, then all the gadgets, technology and techniques of Watergate will be unnecessary. We will have already slipped into a *1984* nightmare. A society that cannot speak or understand sense is condemned to live nonsensically."

But the dominant language problem of the whole Watergate affair was not what was said, but what was unsaid. Watergate essentially will be remembered as a classic example of concealment and secrecy, in all phases from the initial planning through all parts of the cover-up attempt. The language problem was that of omission, a more subtle kind of lying and deception than the "active" aggressive untruths we normally recognize as lies.

Virtue or vice is not confined to one party. Both of the "landslide" elections in recent years were achieved (as voters found out much later) by deception—by suppressing, concealing, omitting certain key facts from the voters. Lyndon Johnson's promises of peace in Vietnam persuaded many people who feared that Barry Goldwater would bomb North Vietnam; years later, when the *Pentagon Papers* were revealed, the public found out the truth of Johnson's policy in that era. The Nixon/Agnew rhetoric of "law and order" in the campaign summer of 1972 helped them win a lopsided election victory. Here again, the voting public did not know, was not informed, about the abuses of power. The facts about the Watergate affair, the Cambodian bombings, the President's income tax juggling and real estate deals, the solicitation of bribes from big business, the attempts to use the CIA, FBI, and IRS as political tools, were concealed from the American public during the election of 1972. Two years later, many of the White House lawbreakers were in jail, others were in shame. Most citizens are Watergate-weary now, yet some of the basic problems involved are those nonpartisan, enduring dilemmas of a democracy: for example, is there a "consent of the governed" if the citizens are deliberately uninformed, misled? Watergate will be remembered as a classic example of concealment, of omission, of a more subtle kind of deception that the "active" aggressive untruths we normally recognize as lies.

Our society's Judeo-Christian heritage emphasizes the prohibition of active lying: "Thou shalt not bear false witness against thy neighbor." People well understand deliberate falsification, lying under oath, perjury. But very little attention is given by ministers, moralists, or churchgoers to passive deception, sins of omission, calculated silence and secrecy, evasions and half-truths. In fact, our society places high value on keeping quiet. Silence is golden. We make folk heroes out of those (including gangsters) who keep their mouths shut, who "stonewall it." And we label those who reveal the truth as *squealers, informers, tattletales,* and *stool pigeons.*

We grow up with ambiguities: our parents tell us to "own up" to our own errors, sins, misdeeds, mistakes, violations. We are told to "fess up," "be honest," "tell the truth." Yet, at the same time, our parents tell us (and we tell our children) that we are not to tell on others, not to be a tattletale on our siblings, our classmates, our companions (and later) our fellow workers when they err, sin, or commit a crime. Granted, there are problems and distinctions concerning such silence which need to be discussed by our moralists, but some people recognize that these attitudes, learned in childhood, to be "loyal" to our group, to keep our mouths shut, later serve the interests of those adult groups most eager to keep their operations as secret as possible: criminal organizations; inefficient or corrupt bureaucracies; corporations or governments that abuse power or exploit people.

Much of the hatred of the press by Nixon and his supporters was not simply because the press was the messenger, the bearer of bad news, but because it helped expose the situation, it was the tattle-tale. The whole Watergate situation originated in the arrogance of a generation of expanded presidential power and was nurtured by an obsessive concern about secrecy, about plugging "leaks." After two years of exposés, the White House still spent much time trying to divert attention from the substance of the information and focus on the "leaks" and "squealers."

Thus we can see that the language issues in the first year of Water-gate centered around "bad grammar" (deviations from standard usage), clichés, trite expressions, repetition of commonplace met-aphors, parroting of bureaucratic jargon, a bit of outright perjury here and there, and a great deal of evasive circumlocution and un-spoken truth. When the probers learned by accident of the White House tapes, a new phase began for Watergate word watchers. Here, suddenly, the illusions and fabrications, the images of the President and his associates, were devastated by their own words. The release of the transcripts in the spring of 1974 provoked three major controversies concerning language: Nixon's vulgarity; the editing and prior censorship of the documents; and the revelation of character conveyed by the words spoken in the Oval Office.

Nixon's pedestrian vulgarity was no secret among his intimates, nor his enemies. Joe McGinniss's *The Selling of the President 1968* had rather amply exposed what was under the PR image being pack-aged and sold in the 1968 election. But a large audience of true believers, which Nixon so carefully cultivated, did not know these aspects of his personality, or would not believe the critics who pointed them out. To those who had believed in the "morality" of Nixon, who had long seen Nixon as the innocent victim of the slanderous attacks of the villainous press, the (expletives deleted) in the transcripts were shocking. Emmet John Hughes, one of President Eisenhower's aides, commented that ". . . the single word that first came to mind as I read these transcripts was 'vulgarity'—vulgarity of thought and vulgarity of conscience. . . ." Editors at the *Chicago Tribune* noted that the transcripts "provide a cultural shock. Presidents don't talk like city hall hacks, do they? But ap-pearance—the ruffles and flourishes, the prim smile and Sunday services—confronted reality and lost."

Why such an intense reaction? For one thing, Nixon had set him-self up for such a fall from grace through years of preaching and pieties. In Jungian terms, the distance and the tension between the projected *persona* and the repressed *shadow* had been growing dangerously far apart. Just as Agnew's law-and-order speeches would echo back, ironically, after he was exposed as a criminal, Nixon's pious pronouncements would be remembered; in the 1960 TV debates with John F. Kennedy, Nixon attacked the language of Harry Truman, in words which would come back later to haunt Nixon:

> It makes you realize that whoever is President is going to be a man that all the children of America will either look up to or will look down to. And I can only say that I'm very proud that President Eisenhower restored dignity and decency and, frankly, good language to the conduct of the presidency of the United States. And I only hope that should I win this election, that I could [see] to it that whenever any mother or father talks to his child, he can look at the man in the White House and say: "Well, there is a man who maintains the kind of standards personally that I would want my child to follow."

More serious vulgarities were the intimations of ethnic slurs, especially anti-Semitism, in Nixon's informal White House conversation among colleagues. After the initial release of the transcripts, rumors that some of the deletions contained derogatory remarks (such as "Jew boy," "kike," and "wop") were denied by the White House as another example of irresponsible press coverage. But the allegations were substantiated in August when other transcripts were yielded by Nixon in compliance with the Supreme Court order. Although the critical legal evidence from these transcripts was Nixon's early knowledge of the Watergate break-in and approval of a cover-up, magazines and newspapers noted these documents included a Nixon remark that his daughter ought to avoid public appearances at anything concerned with "the arts . . . the arts you know—they're Jews, they're left wing."

Nixon's "jocko-macho" talk (as Nicholas von Hoffman called it) was amply demonstrated; the limited supply of tough-guy metaphors, akin to verbal locker room swaggering of muscle-flexing *machismo* at the beach: "tough it out," "stonewall it," "trade off," "head to head," "zone defense," "let it hang out," "bottomline it." Years earlier, some critics had felt that Nixon's overt enthusiasm for spectator sports (shaking hands with athletes, telegrams and phone calls to coaches) was simply a calculated ploy ("a grandstand play") to win the favor of certain voters, to create the illusion that he was "just one of the guys." It was no illusion. Nixon was not the first politician to use the imagery of athletics (see

"Sports Metaphors" in William Safire's *The New Language of Politics*), but the transcripts reveal that the traditional emphasis on "fair play," "following the rules," and "good sportsmanship" had been replaced by a "win at all costs" mentality.

From the moment that the White House version of the transcripts was originally released, the massive number (almost 1900) of omissions, "expletives deleted," "characterization deleted," and deletions "for national security reasons" or "unrelated material" made the transcripts suspect. If Nixon would release such damning material, how much more damning was that still concealed? Such inferences were widespread at the time. Were they reasonable?

Aristotle, some 2500 years ago, as the first major rhetorician teaching the art of persuasion, pointed out some of the common axioms used in persuasion: "If the less probable of two events has occurred," he said, "the more probable event is likely to have occurred too." Because rhetoric is involved in cases where there is doubt and disagreement (instead of certitude), Aristotle continued with a series of common arguments which people use in order to make reasonable judgments: "If someone had the power and the desire and the opportunity to do something," Aristotle continued, "then he has done it." In other words, people have long recognized the validity of overwhelming circumstantial evidence in cases which will not yield to certitude because the statements or opinions of the various parties involved are in conflict.

The initial mistrust of the edited transcripts was confirmed by subsequent events: two months later, in July, the House Judiciary Committee issued its version of the transcripts, based on a more sophisticated technical analysis of the tapes. Although Chairman Peter Rodino did not accuse the White House staff of deliberate distortion, the evidence indicated that the "errors" and "accidental omissions" benefitted Nixon. (Further evidence of the unreliability of the White House transcripts was provided a month later, August 5, when the President was forced by the Supreme Court to surrender other tapes which, by his admission, were "at variance" with his earlier public statements; three days later Nixon resigned.)

The House version printed Nixon's vulgarities, instead of censoring them with the euphemistic "expletive deleted." Ironically, the media then imposed a self-censorship: CBS-TV, for example, visually showed the vulgarities in an enlarged-print scene, but the reporter's voice-over left blank spaces as he read the text; the *Chicago Tribune*, in a front page box, apologized to its readers for printing "some" (not all!) of Nixon's vulgar language.

The House version also printed the *omissions*. Of special importance here were the fifteen pages of the Nixon-Mitchell conversation which weren't in the original version; the key omissions from the March 21st conversation ("stonewall it"); and the frequent omissions of one-word Nixon responses to Dean. Some key words were recorded differently ("should" instead of "can") and the House version occasionally noted response *laughter* within conversations, thus suggesting some of the tone of the conversation. The House version was a great deal more damaging to President Nixon than the earlier edition, although the impact on the public was less, understandably so, considering the shockwaves of the first revelations.

The primary impact of the transcripts (both the White House version and the more revealing version from the Rodino committee) was that they laid bare the President's character. The May 1974 issues of the nation's newspapers and magazines were saturated with violent and bitter commentary about the transcripts, indicating that a shocked, angered, and sorrowed nation did not hesitate to infer the caliber of Nixon's character from the words which had been revealed. Almost unanimously, the assessment of Richard Nixon's character was rather harsh, even from those who once had been loyal supporters, but who now felt that they had been betrayed. Republican Senator Hugh Scott, who had earlier predicted that the transcripts would vindicate Nixon, was one of the first to express his disillusionment: "shabby, disgusting, immoral." Throughout the country these sentiments were echoed in an intense outpouring of criticism and analysis of Nixon's character as revealed in the transcripts. In the future, one must remember that in May 1974, Nixon was still a powerful protagonist; after his resignation and loss of power, he was seen by many as a pathetic figure, one inspiring *pathos,* and the tone and temper of subsequent criticism against him differed after "this point in time."

In the previous year, at the November 1973 convention of the National Council of Teachers of English, Walker Gibson, delivering his presidential address to that group, pointed out some links between the teaching of literature in the classroom and the analysis of the ongoing Watergate investigation. "When we read *Hamlet,* or *Charlotte's Web,* or whatever it may be," Gibson said, "we infer dramatic character from language. Because Hamlet says the things he says, in the way he is made to say them, we conclude that he is this or that sort of a person, and we have our evidence before us in the words on the page—or stage. Learning to read is learning to infer dramatic character from linguistic evidence." Gibson then made some analysis of the Watergate hearings, of both the witnesses and the senators, and of some of the inferences one could make from their language: "What does it say, for example, about a person's attitude toward law and order if, when describing some clearly illegal act by a White House colleague, he calls the act *inappropriate?"*

At that time, Gibson was speaking about the publicly known Watergate testimony as witnessed on TV. No one knew *then* that the very words of the President in the Oval Office were being tape-recorded, and that they would eventually become public. Gibson's point is even more germane when one considers the impact of the transcripts. Louis Mumford, for example, said that he felt as if Nixon had "committed moral suicide in public" when the transcripts were released. Carey McWilliams, writing in *The Nation* (May 18), ironically commented: "The Nixon of the transcripts is an authentic person. It is refreshing to listen to the real private voice after years of exposure to the public television voice and manner. The transcripts contain *his* words and phrases. This *is* the way he thinks. No PR fakery, no television smirking, no smug self-righteous rhetoric. . . . This is a hard-bitten operator, a political huckster, a man on the make and obsessed with making it." The differences between a person's public and private voices (or *personae*) has long been an intriguing topic for teachers of language and literature. For years to come, it seems certain that the Watergate transcripts will be alluded to in the classrooms as teachers explain and illustrate this practice of inferring character from speech.

Another lesson which should be learned from Watergate, and which can be taught in the classroom, is that language can be manipulated to downplay, to hide, to conceal, to omit. More attention can be given, in a kind of "defensive rhetoric," to teaching students how to recognize the strategies of silence, the tactics of omission, evasion, diversion, circumlocution.

Hopefully, one of the political lessons which can be learned by all citizens is the need for comprehensive disclosure laws, codes of ethics, open information laws by which political groups, commercial corporations, and governments at all levels must reveal full, clear, understandable information about their financing and operations. Citizens and consumers will eventually recognize that all of the various "Truth-in-" laws (lending, packaging, advertising, etc.) are related to this basic concept of full disclosure. At present, the privacy of the individual citizen is being invaded at the same time the secrecy of the corporate structure is being protected; this trend must be reversed. Perhaps, one way to start is in the classroom, by making students aware of these patterns of concealment.

Watergate also revealed a serious, widespread public misunderstanding about the adversary role of a free press in a democratic society. Even after all of the disclosures and confessions of guilt, many Americans still believed that the press, the media, had railroaded Nixon. History teachers might point out to their students that American presidents in the past have had a long tradition of wanting the press to act as a volunteer "public relations" staff, but that the press sees its role more as a "watchdog," well aware that political power can be abused, has been in the past, and probably will be in the future. Perhaps schools ought to re-think their journalism and media programs. Instead of teaching a few kids how to put together a school newspaper, or training a few in the mechanical or electronic aspects of television, it might be more beneficial if we instruct many of our future voters about the issues and problems of the press in a free society.

Hopefully, young people will grow up in this generation with fewer illusions, with fewer romanticized myths about our history and our politics, with a greater awareness of how fragile democracy can be. Hopefully, the schools will recognize that our future citizens need a more sophisticated literacy, a literacy which includes training in the critical analysis of propaganda techniques, language manipulation, and the new media.

Words from Watergate

Stefan Kanfer

Appearing as a *Time* "Essay" in the period of the televised Senate hearings, Kanfer's article incisively detailed some of the jargon and cant of the Watergate witnesses. *Time* reaches, and influences, an extraordinarily large audience in the United States; thus, one would expect that Kanfer's article might have positive results. Unfortunately, however, two years later some people are still seriously using the phrases "at this point in time. . . at that point in time."

Wilson: How do you know that, Mr. Chairman?

Ervin: Because I can understand the English language. It is my mother tongue.

Yes, but Lawyer John Wilson's clients, John Ehrlichman and H. R. Haldeman, are also children of that mother tongue. And so are Caulfield and Dean, Odle and Porter, Mitchell and Magruder, and virtually every other Watergate witness. Those witnesses are a peculiar group of siblings, obedient to every authority except that of their parent language.

Even with the admission of tapes, no one will ever master the entire vocabulary or thought processes of the Nixon Administration. But tantalizing glimpses are possible through the aperture of the Ervin hearings. By now, of course, the Nixonian cadre has turned a few phrases to bromides, notably the sci-fi sounds: "At that point in time," and, "In that time frame." Still, these clichés are excellent indicators of the Administration's unwritten laws of language: 1) never use a word when a sentence will do; 2) obscure, don't clarify; 3) Humpty Dumpty was right when he said to Alice: "When *I* use a word . . . it means just what I choose it to mean." Most of the Watergate witnesses prefer not to answer with a simple yes or no. The vagueness shown last week by H. R. Haldeman has been the motto of the month: "I am not sure whether I was or not. I may very well have been." Other witnesses felt that truth was illusory; facts could only be construed "in their context." The quibbling over nuances would do credit to Henry James—as when Ehrlichman vainly tried to distinguish between "literal" and "actual."

Perhaps because Haldeman has been characterized as a former adman, he avoided any run-it-up-the-flagpole chatter. Still, he introduced some collector's items: "Zero-defect system," for perfection; "containment" for the withholding of information. Throughout the hearings, where precision would help, a file of worn metaphors and similes appears. Usually the phrases smack of the military or sports—two arenas notable for their threadbare lexicons. Porter thought of himself as "a team player," Dean as a soldier who had "earned my stripes." Ehrlichman considered himself proficient at "downfield blocking." J. Edgar Hoover was "a loyal trooper." Mitchell football-coached, "When the going gets tough, the tough get going"; and everybody worried about the chief "lowering the boom."

Responsibility was obviously diffused; in the New Nixon years, power no longer seems to emanate from persons but from real estate. The President rarely appears in testimony. The word comes from "the Oval Office." When Caulfield carried the fragile promise of Executive clemency, said McCord, he spoke of "the very highest levels of the White House"—perhaps the first time that favors were to be dispensed by architecture.

Euphemisms are to the tongue what novocain is to the gums. In the hearings, criminality is given scores of numbing disguises. For "intelligence-gathering operations" read "breaking and entering," for "plumbers" read "burglars," for "stroking" read "cheap flattery," for "puffing" read "expensive flattery," for "White House horrors" read "Government-sponsored crimes." The roster seems endless: "dirty tricks," "laundered money," "telephone anomalies" —all perform the same function: the separation of words from truth.

Sometimes the resonances are poignant: McCord's use of the familiar "game plan" or young Odle's attempt to "make a couple of things perfectly clear." Occasionally they are mystifying, as in the characterization of CBS Newsman Daniel Schorr as "a real media enemy"—as opposed, perhaps, to an unreal media enemy. Often, however, they are terrifying because they illuminate just how much ignorance the functionaries had—not only of the law but of themselves.

To the Ervin committee, for example, Ehrlichman released a clandestine tape recording of a conversation he had had with Herbert Kalmbach. It contains a dazzling example of self-deception. Kalmbach is asked to testify that he spoke to Ehrlichman in California, when in fact the conversation took place in Washington. "I wouldn't ask you to lie," says the former presidential aide.

It was this recording that prompted Mary McCarthy to speculate in the London *Observer:* "[The tape] shows Ehrlichman demanding that his friend commit perjury. That is the only way it can be read. Perhaps this is illuminating. If Ehrlichman cannot realize what his taped voice says in plain English, perhaps Nixon cannot either, and so his own battery of tapes may be produced after all."

Whether or not the President can comprehend plain English, it is certain that many on his staff could not or would not. In their obfuscations they were not alone. Long before the Nixon Administration took office, the military had its "pacification" and "fragging." Radical critics led their own assaults on the English language with the substitution of "offing" for killing, the prating of "fascism" every time an obstacle was encountered. At the same time, business gave its own donation at the office, with the computer talk of "inputs," "software" and "print-outs."

Indeed, every sector has its private jargon meant to mystify the outsider, frequently at the cost of undermining the speaker. Yet, all these linguistic abuses have paled beside the rhetorical revelations of Watergate. With that special gift of hindsight so praised by committeemen and witnesses, the spectator can now perceive that the seeds of the affair were planted long ago, in the first days of Nixon's tenure. Once upon a point in time, Administration spokesmen instructed commentators: "Don't judge us by what we say but by what we do." As the world now realizes, verb and act are in the deepest sense inseparable.

In his classic essay, *Politics and the English Language*, George Orwell spoke for all time: "If thought corrupts language, language can also corrupt thought." Yet even with his innate pessimism, Orwell offered a solution—a method more applicable today than it was in the holocaust of the '40s. "One ought to recognize," he wrote, "that the present political chaos is connected with the decay of language, and that one can probably bring about some improvement by starting at the verbal end."

It takes no feminist to see how much the nation owes its mother tongue. If that tongue is to speak again with clarity and force, alterations have to begin, not in the spirit of litigation but in its opposite: the defense of values. The Watergate evasions will have to be swept away with those who mouth them. Honest politics will not miraculously reappear. But in the absence of bromides and shibboleths, Americans may once again be able to put in some good words for their Government. And vice versa.

Watergaters' Forked Tongues

Sydney J. Harris

In a sense, this column by the syndicated journalist Sydney J. Harris is representative of the many comments made by newspapermen, and in letters-to-the-editor, about the "low level of literacy" of our national leaders. But Harris does not get mired in trivia; he uses examples to support his broader vision of the effects of an inhumane use of language.

Leaving politics quite aside, the most appalling aspect of the whole Watergate inquiry is the low level of literacy it has revealed— among interrogators as well as witnesses.

I have rarely heard such poor English spoken publicly by presumably educated men, most of them lawyers, as I have during the first round of the Senate Watergate hearings. Almost every grammatical and syntactical sin in the book was committed daily— and some of the barbarisms and solecisms were almost painfully repetitious.

Everyone by now has commented on the "at this point in time" and "in that time-frame," and other such obvious phrases of ponderous jargon. But I am not even speaking of such officialese— what shocked me was the lack of rudimentary good English to be heard in those hearings.

"He invited my wife and I to dinner," says a former attorney general of the United States. "It was a meeting between the four of us," says another highly placed official, a graduate of one of America's most illustrious universities. "That memoranda was dated July 20," says still another White House aide, obviously oblivious of the fact that "memoranda" is a plural.

Cases, tenses, moods, agreements, antecedents, all were grossly violated by senator and spy alike. Participles dangled wildly, prepositions were either unattached or redundant, sentences were uttered that made Gen. Eisenhower's prose seem loftily Ciceronian. Nor was it merely that the witnesses were nervous; their interrogators were equally tortuous and ambiguous in their questioning.

Now is all this simply a snide sort of intellectual snobbery on my part? I think not, and hope not. For, when the laws of a language are violated and ignored, when turgid phrases and muddy sentences are condoned, it then becomes too easy to slip from correctness not into incorrectness—but into evasion, half-truth, and eventually the kind of sinister euphemism that refers to bombing of defenseless civilians as a "protective strike" instead of the wicked thing it actually is.

And I am convinced that it is our national indifference to language and its humane use (which is why it is part of the "humanities" in school) that culminates in a White House press secretary being able to dismiss a prior statement as being "inoperative." What this word really meant in that context was, "Don't believe what I told you then—believe what I tell you now."

To permit anyone to get away with such a blatant deception by waving the magic wand of "inoperative" is to abandon our responsibility as guardians of law and morals as well as of language. Once we begin to tolerate, or overlook, sloppy usage in language, our whole system of human communication becomes vulnerable to the vilest manipulation.

It is not the snob who would preserve good form, but the true democrat, who knows, like Confucius, that "corrupt government begins with the use of the wrong word."

Watergate Lingo: A Language of Non-Responsibility

Richard Gambino

Following in George Orwell's tradition, Gambino points out how political language has been so used as to mask reality, to avoid personal responsibility or guilt for the lies and the crimes committed. Our language is being used by politicians "not as an instrument for forming and expressing thought. It is used more to prevent, confuse, and conceal thought." Gambino, a member of the NCTE Committee on Public Doublespeak, then illustrates these manipulations by examples from the circumlocutions, stock phrases, and jargon of the Watergate witnesses.

We operated on what is known in some industries as a zero-defect system. We attempted to get everything right.

H. R. Haldeman

In a now famous phrase, Ron Ziegler and John Ehrlichman have declared White House statements proven false to be "no longer operative." This is a very handy phrase which can mean any of the following:

> It wasn't true in the first place.
> I'm sorry I said it.
> I thought it was true then but I know now it wasn't.

While the public was left wondering what the phrase meant, responsibility for the original lies was shifted from the liars to the lies themselves. The responsibility was not in the people, not even in the stars, but in the statements themselves, which were spoken of as if they had lives and energy of their own.

In ordinary English we speak of employees being fired. In the language of the Department of State, they are "selected out." It sounds as if the fired people are honored. The palliative phrase relieves the employer from responsibility for an unpleasant act. Similarly, at the C.I.A., according to Director Colby, superiors do not fire subordinates. They "arrange a circumstance where employees can be helped to leave government service early." How helpful of them! One is almost led to think that people dismissed might thank their bosses for being favored.

Those involved in Watergate or its cover-up do not destroy evidence of crimes. They "deep-six" papers. This sailor's phrase conjures up colorful salts jettisoning unneeded ballast over the side instead

of political men engaged in criminal conspiracy. The frequent use
of metaphors and similes to sugar-coat questions of culpability
reached a high point when Special White House Counsel J. Fred
Buzhardt waxed poetic about his predecessor, John W. Dean III.
Instead of saying that Dean's testimony was false, Buzhardt spoke
of "the failure of Dean's muse while he was on the mountain. . ."
Now if Dean were lying under oath he would be guilty of perjury
and could be held legally accountable. But it seems cruel and unusual punishment to declare one a liar and perjuror merely because his muse failed while he was on the mountain. After all,
who among us has not known frustration in our creative enterprises?

Whether Dean's muse was reliable or not, he said during his
testimony that those engaged in the cover-up once suggested that
John Mitchell "should be brought forward." Connotations of
going to the head of the class leap to mind. The phrase also evokes
one coming forward with forthrightness, sincerity and even cour-
age. Through the magic of words, those who made the suggestion
that Mitchell take all the guilt and punishment for all the conspirators sound like honest brokers, even like outraged righteous
souls. As long as their language is used, it becomes impossible
to blame them for wanting to make one man the patsy for a conspiracy to obstruct justice.

When Mitchell finally did come forward (in the ordinary sense
of the term), he spoke to the Senate Select Committee about
"White House horror stories." Not criminal conduct or unethical
behavior by White House officials and employees, but "White
House horrors." "Criminal conduct" and "unethical behavior"
are depressingly meaningful expressions. They lead to thoughts of
real acts by real people with real names and faces who really can
be and should be held responsible. But "White House horror
stories" suggests vague, perhaps unreal, events caused by nameless
occult or imaginary powers. The phrase places the Watergate
crimes and other misconduct in the same categories as silly old
wives' tales of haunted houses and Hollywood fantasy. Although
we are frightened by these horror stories, we know our fears are
baseless. It is only gentle, benign Boris Karloff behind the terrible
Frankenstein mask. Don't be scared kiddies.

If Hugh Sloan, Jr. gave money to a convicted criminal one might
suspect him of something rotten. But if as it was said he merely
paid "increments . . . in the form of currency" to G. Gordon
Liddy, why Sloan sounds as if he was merely giving his fellowman
his due. After all, increments are normally thought to be de-
served. And "currency" is what scholarly economists deal with,

a far cry from the filthy lucre you and I covet. Could Sloan be guilty of something illegal or immoral? Why it is unthinkable—because Washingtonspeak makes it literally unspeakable.

The decline of language

Because of the language they use, and in which we are compelled to follow their accounts, Watergate witnesses and the people they favor are never really responsible. Even those seeking the truth are forced into parlance in which moral and legal responsibility is unutterable. Thus Senator Howard Baker, vice-chairman of the Senate Select Committee, asked one of the witnesses "how we might ventilate the structure of campaigning." One who ventilates a structure—presumably one who causes air to flow through a building—is not per se doing anything or concerned with anything of any moral or legal consequence whatsoever. His behavior is morally and legally neither responsible or irresponsible. It is quite different with a person who attempts to reform illegal and unethical political campaigning, a sticky matter for many on both sides of the Senate hearing table. Better to talk about ventilation.

Many commentators on the Watergate actions have ominously linked the events with the society presented in George Orwell's novel *1984*. As I have watched the Watergate hearings on television, I have been reminded not so much of *1984* as of a lesser known work of Orwell, an essay written in 1945 entitled, *Politics and the English Language*. In it, Orwell warned:

> It is clear that the decline of a language must ultimately have political and economic causes. . . But an effect can become a cause, reinforcing the original cause and producing the same effect in an intensified form, and so on indefinitely. A man may take to drink because he feels himself to be a failure, and then fail all the more completely because he drinks. It is rather the same thing that is happening to the English language. It becomes ugly and inaccurate because our thoughts are foolish, but the slovenliness of our language makes it easier to have foolish thoughts.

A significant lesson is emerging from the Watergate hearings, apart from those that the powerful violate laws, subvert the United States Constitution and scorn decent ethics. The testimony of the Watergate crowd demonstrates that a stock political language has evolved which makes it difficult for the powerful and the public alike even to think meaningfully about respect for laws, loyalty to the Constitution or to exercise moral sensibilities. The torrent of circumlocutions, mechanical verbal formulas, misplaced technical jargon, palliative expressions, euphemisms and inflated phraseology indicate that the brains both of speakers and listeners are being anesthetized or stunted. Critical meanings are barred from the beginning in a form of conceptual contraception. Insofar as we become addicted to the corrupt Watergate language, it is nonsense to speak of political or moral responsibility and irresponsibility. Lacking mastery of clear, meaningful language deprives us of the basic equipment required of responsible people. As we abandon meaningful language in favor of blather, we become positively ir-responsible to ourselves as well as to others. In listening to the Watergate witnesses it often is hard to tell whether they are merely dissemblers trying to paralyze the minds of others, self-deceivers who have crippled their own intelligences, or glib dolls whose characters remained undeveloped as their smartness grew.

Whatever the character of the Watergate witnesses, the hearings show that political language has degenerated since Orwell's warn-ing that thought and language decline together. Seemingly more than before in American politics the English language is used not as an instrument for forming and expressing thought. It is used more to prevent, confuse and conceal thought. Thus we have grown accustomed to calling political lingo "rhetoric." This good word has been so debased to stand for anything from propaganda and nonsense to vicious lies. As the pseudo-language takes hold— *even in the process of our determined attempts to regenerate re-sponsibility in political life*—it drags us further into chaotic condi-tions leading logically and inevitably to political nihilism.

In my opinion we have been so concerned with the *1984* aspects of Watergate—the spying, wiretapping and other "dirty tricks" (an-other euphemism that emerged from the hearings) —that we have overlooked something at least as important. If our political lan-guage, and therefore our public thinking, becomes so debauched that moral meanings can no longer be clearly expressed or under-stood, then all the gadgets, technology and techniques of Watergate will be unnecessary. We will have already slipped into a *1984* nightmare. A society that cannot speak or understand sense is condemned to live nonsensically. To put it in Washingtonspeak, clear political meanings and the higher political values that de-pend on them will have become "no longer operative." In plain language, we will have become a nation of politically nonrespon-sible imbeciles "speaking in tongues." Not the inspired Biblical kind but the spurious Watergate sort.

Personal morality inexpressible

Although there are varieties of Watergate talk, there is one quality common to the witnesses: ways of speaking, one very important thread connecting the apparently disparate linguistic styles. Except when they are accusing current enemies, e.g. Mitchell's calling Jeb Magruder's testimony that he (Mitchell) reviewed tapes and documents gained through illegal wiretaps and burglary "a palpable, damnable lie," their language permits no raising of questions of personal responsibility for unethical or criminal conduct on their part or by their colleagues. Issues of moral right and wrong are inexpressible in their lingo. When Senator Weicker asked Herbert Porter what was "the quality of his mind" (Washingtonspeak for "what were you thinking?") while he dealt in improper use of campaign funds, Porter paused, then replied, "Senator, I'm not a moral philosopher." In politics as in ethics what our language prevents us from articulating, it prevents us from thinking. Although the words of the Watergate people indicate that Washingtonspeak is well on the way to becoming a language in which the whole matter of legality, as well as ethics, will also be inexpressible, it has not yet reached that perfect state. Speakers of this odd language must at present rest content with its power to make only *personal* responsibility for illegal acts impossible. Just as it would have been impossible in Periclean Athens to speak of the internal combustion engine, computers or atomic energy, so in Washingtonspeak personal moral responsibility does not exist. To be sure, illegal acts still exist in Watergate glossology, but in the linguistic progress achieved so far, illegalities exist *sui generis*. They constitute a kind of unholy creation from nothing by no one.

Circumlocutions

Several dominant features of Washingtonspeak have been greatly exposed during the Watergate hearings. Circumlocutions and convoluted language are among the foremost instruments of this language of nonresponsibility. Champion among the witnesses in this skill is the voluble Mr. Ehrlichman. His method was to confound critical questions put to him by blanketing them with intense barrages of grape-shot syntax. The Senators questioning him were given time limits and most of them were poor cross-examiners, an opinion confirmed by a recent survey conducted among prominent trial lawyers. Ehrlichman, therefore, as one of my acquaintances put it, "talked the bastards to death" with such phrases as "we (Dean, Mitchell and Ehrlichman) made an agreement to go out and develop additional information if we could." One may seek, compile, file, pursue, fabricate, conceal, alter, reveal and do other things regarding information. But how does one "develop" it? In a darkroom? A chemist's laboratory? Ehrlichman's language leaves us ignorant of precisely what the three men had agreed to do and therefore unable to assess its morality or legality. We

would be left in this quandary even if, as Ehrlichman said of his
associates and himself, "we gathered together to compare igno-
rances." How do you and I compare what I do not know with
what you do not know? If I speak no Greek and you speak no Chinese, how do we compare these tongues? For a comparison to be
achieved, someone must introduce knowledge. But then someone
would know something, and Ehrlichman was asserting he and his
associates knew nothing when they gathered together.

In reply to the question why he had approved Mr. Kalmbach's
mission of raising money for the jailed Watergate burglars, Ehrlichman allowed that his approval was only "perfunctory" and
given because "Mitchell had some interest in making sure the defendants were well defended." Does "perfunctory" mean Ehrlichman was not responsible? What was Mr. Mitchell's "interest"? Was
the payment for a legal defense, was it hush money, or both? Because of Ehrlichman's verbal dexterity in tying up the English
language, it is impossible to know from his testimony who was responsible for what. Events merely happened.

Although Ehrlichman was aggressively or defiantly blunt throughout much of his confrontation with the Senate Committee, he repeatedly became almost incomprehensibly loquacious when questioned about his responsibility and that of others he insisted are
blameless. When asked about the allegation made by both Richard
Helms and General Vernon Walters, formerly the two top men at
the C.I.A., that Ehrlichman and Haldeman suggested that the
agency ask the F.B.I. to limit its investigation into the "laundering"
of Republican money in Mexico on the pretext that the F.B.I.
would endanger some pretended agency operation in that country,
Ehrlichman's diction became inscrutable:

> My recollection of that meeting is at considerable
> variance with General Walters in the general thrust and
> in the details. In point of fact, as I recall it, we informed
> Mr. Helms and General Walters that the meeting was
> held at the President's request for the reasons I stated.
> Mr. Haldeman said that the Watergate was an obvious
> important political issue and that the President had no
> alternative but to order a full allout F.B.I. investigation
> until he was satisfied that there was some specific area
> from which the F.B.I. should not probe for fear of leaks
> through the F.B.I. or dissociated and disconnected
> C.I.A. activities that had no bearing on Watergate.

Ehrlichman displayed extraordinary skill in surrounding an outrageous opinion with tortuous verbiage which gives it a coating of
justification. Thus he glibly took the offensive when questioned
about the burglary of Daniel Ellsberg's psychiatrist's office:

> I think if it is clearly understood that the President
> has the constitutional power to prevent the betrayal
> of national security secrets, as I understand he does, and
> that is well understood by the American people, and
> an episode like that is seen in that context, there
> shouldn't be any problem.

What "constitutional power"? Which "national security secrets"?
By whose definition? "Well understood by the American people"?
"There shouldn't be any problem"? Ehrlichman's crossfire of stock
phrases sends us diving for cover, numbs our minds and almost
makes us sorry the topic was raised.

Washingtonspeak circumlocution is virtually invulnerable. It
smothers any counterattack with more circumlocution. The circumlocution gains strength over each attempt to pierce it with Hydra's
ability instantly to replace any of its serpents' heads which is cut
off with two others. Thus Ehrlichman first explained—in his fashion—the payment of cash to the captured Watergate burglars by
saying, "John Mitchell felt very strongly that it was important to
have good legal representation for these defendants for a number
of reasons—for political reasons, but also because we had these civil
damage suits that had been filed by the Democrats." When pressed
about exactly what were the "political reasons," Ehrlichman set
the Hydra-like prowess of circumlocution upon his questioners.
"Well," he said, "just that if there were to be a trial and it were
to take place before the election, that obviously that trial would
have some political impact and good representation was simply
essential." By this time the numerous heads of Ehrlichman's verbal
monster were overwhelming. No one on the Committee pursued
the question any further.

Similarly, Ehrlichman's response to a query about whether he suspected Jeb Magruder's involvement in the Watergate cover-up and
what he did about his suspicion was so convoluted as to be totally
uninformative. Again no Senator challenged Ehrlichman's con-
founding statement that:

> There came a time when there was a feeling that, at
> least on my part, based on what Mr. Dean was telling
> me about the unraveling of this thing, that Mr.
> Magruder may have had some involvement, and that
> culminated in a meeting with the Attorney General
> (Mitchell) at the end of July, on the 31st of July,
> where Magruder was specifically discussed. But just
> where in there I acquired the information, I can't tell
> you.

Any questions?

Resort to circumlocution was characteristic of others at key points when questions of someone's personal responsibility threatened to surface. Senator Inouye asked Mitchell a pointed question in plain English: "Have you ever considered whether it was fair to the American people to conspire to keep them from the true facts of this matter [of a series of illegal and unethical actions]?" In the words of the old calypso song, Mitchell's reply was clear as mud and it covered the ground. "Yes, I am sure," he said, "that the subject matter crossed my mind many, many times. But I do not believe now, I did not believe then, that the President should be charged with the transgressions of others. And it is just as simple as that." The habit of using inflated blather at crucial points is so strong that John Dean's "I was trying to test the chronology of my knowledge" was typical.

The stock phrase

Another feature of the Watergate language of nonresponsibility is the use of stupefying stock phrases. A private meeting with the President of the United States arouses considerable interest about possibly revealing statements. But John Dean's "one on one with the President" sounds as impersonal as the shuffling of a deck of cards. It is mechanical in connotation, as are other phrases used by Watergate witnesses. They did not approve things but "signed off on them" as when Jeb Magruder said Mitchell signed off on a proposed project. The phrase makes Mitchell appear to casually flip a switch rather than consciously and knowingly make a decision. You, I and most people take orders from our bosses or superiors in our jobs or careers. John Dean "followed a channel of reporting." It sounds more prescribed by circumstances than an act of conscious obedience. The course of a channel is fixed and a good harbor pilot merely follows it. And reporting evokes much less responsibility than giving and taking instructions.

Watergate people never reflect on the past since such an activity would imply that they are capable of understanding elementaries of personal responsibility. They are forever "in hindsight" like so many creatures with eyes imbedded in their behinds. Thus they merely "see" the past in a manner that permits them not to commit themselves about their moral or legal culpability then or their present view whether they were responsible. For example in the following exchange with Samuel Dash, John Mitchell really reveals nothing about his responsibility for past behavior or his current opinion about that responsibility:

Dash: "As Attorney General of the United States, why didn't you throw Mr. Liddy out of your office?"

Mitchell: "Well, I think, Mr. Dash, in hindsight I not only should have thrown him out of the office, I should have thrown him out the window."

Dash: "Well, since you did neither, why didn't you at least recommend that Mr. Liddy be fired?"

Mitchell: "Well, in hindsight, I probably should have done that too."

To describe a series of circumstances surrounding an event implies personal knowledge which in turn might imply personal responsibility. Therefore, Mitchell volunteered—after being asked a direct question regarding a suspicious meeting—"let me play out the scenario for you." He merely starts the movie projector but has no relation to what might appear on the screen.

Incidentally, whereas most people are told of criminal events, thereby raising questions of their complicity after the fact, Watergate people were merely "brought up to speed on" them. After all, the highway signs specify minimum as well as maximum legal speeds, right?

The stock phrase most used during the Watergate hearings was "at this point in time" and its variations, e.g. "at that point in time." At first these expressions sound merely like pretentious, elaborate ways of saying, "then," "now," "at that time," "at this time," etc. But the stock phrases are much more useful. "At that point in time" serves to isolate the event being discussed, to detach it, bracket it and set it apart from all other events and people. It becomes a moment existing by itself. Questionable conduct is thereby voided by being reduced to a mathematical point, a fiction having no dimensions, connections, history or relation to the present. Surgeons prefer to operate in a "clean field" established by isolation of the area of incision through elaborate operating room techniques. Only a swatch of flesh is presented to the surgeon's eyes instead of a whole patient. The surgeon is thus spared the unnerving sight of the patient's face, posture, and general human appearance at the critical time of surgery. "At that point of time" accomplishes an analogous effect. The difference of course is that the surgical procedure serves a legitimate medical purpose, while the Watergate linguistic procedure obscures personal political and moral responsibility. Two of the axiomatic requirements of personal responsibility are motives before the deed and awareness of consequences after the deed. "At that point in time" foils both.

"Pre-situation" and "post-situation" are Watergate phrases which once again sever events from relations, connections, and hence responsibility. They are even more bloodless than the ordinary legal phrases "before the event" and "after the event."

But perhaps the most blatantly robot evoking phrase is John Dean's saying he "dealt with people telephonically." Now, when you call someone on the telephone, or he calls, and you and he talk, human behavior occurs and ordinary responsibilities for it become discussible. But no more comes to mind when one person deals with another telephonically than when we watch the whir of computer machinery. It is totally impersonal, mechanical, inhuman.

Specialized jargon

Another prominent feature of Watergate talk is the frequent misuse of technical jargon taken from specialized areas of life. Jargon used by specialists in reference to their speciality is meaningful and useful. It facilitates communication between the specialists whether it be in football, medicine, seamanship, stock brokerage, etc. But when appropriated for use in politics, technical jargon from other fields serves contrary purposes. Codes produced by misplaced jargon used in politics serve to mask the true nature of what is happening. And the use of jargon which is elsewhere legitimate lends an aura of justification and respectability to morally and legally dubious behavior. The use of appropriated jargon also serves the old priesthood mystique function of jargon. Those privy to the code enjoy a special, privileged, sophisticated status making them superior to us ordinary slobs.

Much of the jargon used by the Watergate people is taken from the fields of police work and cloak-and-dagger activity. The first is a legitimate profession, the second at least is glamorously mysterious. Unethical and illegal conduct becomes dressed up by the borrowed jargon. Thus, those engaged in burglary, malfeasance of office, criminal conspiracy and other evil conduct did not do these things over ordinary periods of time. They functioned "within time frames," a mechanically detached expression legitimately used in the computer field. Illegal domestic spies constitute a "new intelligence unit" and their equipment was said to need "housing," i.e. quarters that do not call attention to themselves. Images of Humphrey Bogart in trenchcoat playing cat and mouse with the Nazis instead of a sleazy group spying on the personal lives of law abiding fellow Americans.

Illegal activity is spoken of as "games." Criminal conspiracy becomes a "game plan." Conspirators are "team players" like so many good halfbacks or third basemen. Thus Caulfield is said to have told McCord he was "fouling up the game plan." And

Herbert Porter said he remained silent about nefarious doings at Nixon's campaign headquarters because he wanted to be a "team player." Criminal wiretappers are spoken of as "wire men," mere technicians like electricians legitimately used by the telephone company or police department.

Another linguistic style heavily favored by Watergate witnesses is the use of the passive rather than active voice. For example, instead of saying "I was curious" or "I thought of it," the witnesses have an infuriating habit of saying things like "it pricked my curiosity," "it crossed my mind," "it dawned on me." The effect of the habitual use of the passive voice is to create an illusory animistic world where events have lives, wills, motives and actions of their own without any human being responsible for them. This effect is enhanced by another tendency of the speakers—the constant use of multi-syllabic words when ordinary shorter ones would do. This old pedant's trick serves to numb independent thought in the listener and speaker. It also puffs up the status of the speaker in the minds of his audience and in his own self-esteem. Thus, the elegant lingo prettifies the sordid facts probably even in the minds of the guilty.

The use of martyred metaphors, similes, and euphemisms serves the same function of obscuring import and responsibility from the guilty, from the victims and from bystanders. Illegally obtained or illegally used money is "laundered." Cleanliness is next to Godliness. Liddy's lengthy presentation to Mitchell, Dean and others of monstrous plans to use "mugging squads," kidnapping teams, compromising prostitutes and electronic eavesdropping against the White House's political opposition is described by use of a kindergarten phrase as a "show-and-tell session." The exposing of criminal involvement is spoken of as "this matter is starting to unravel." Presumably the journalists, Judge Sirica and the Senators and Congressmen searching out the truth are guilty of taking apart a neatly knitted sweater. Haldeman's reference to the exposition makes the obstruction of justice sound even more benign, and those uncovering it as naughty children or semi-vandals. According to Dean, the White House chief of staff said, "Once the toothpaste is out of the tube, it's going to be very hard to get it back in." Spank the brats playing with the tube!

Those who are spied upon by wiretaps are not referred to as subjects, and certainly not as victims. They were called "targets." Subjects and victims have rights, feelings, dignity—they are humans, citizens. But targets are inanimate things whose sole function is to be hit. Should one object? Do targets at a rifle or archery range complain? Don't be absurd.

Dean described a reassuring phone call from President Nixon as a "stroking session." Normally we stroke our lovers, children and pets—loving gestures, thoughts of which stimulate warm feelings in us. Was or was not Dean implying Nixon's complicity by use of this sensual metaphor? Poets use metaphors and similes to heighten meanings. Watergate people use them to blur meanings.

Among the most infuriating euphemisms used by Watergate witnesses is "surreptitious entry," meaning burglary. Thus a crime becomes a game of hide and seek, or at most a naughty prank. Next time you find a burglar in your home don't shout "police!" Say "Oh, you surreptitious devil you!"

What ordinary crooks call "casing the joint" before a burglary is called by the Watergate bunch "a vulnerability and feasibility study." Surely these men were just students and technicians. But criminals? Never.

Illegal wiretapping is evil. Therefore the Watergate people engaged in "electronic surveillance." Spying on a person's activities is "visual surveillance." Evil people cover up, lie and bribe. Watergate people "contain situations" like so many protective dams.

Is this concern with language mere pedantry, a case of academic vanity? I suggest not. When an elaborate language of nonresponsibility becomes current in the federal government, it would be irresponsible for us not to expose and correct it. We have been had. A language of nonresponsibility is being forced upon us to describe a list of crimes, as Washingtonspeak would have it, "at the very highest levels" of the United States Government. It is a list which beggars our conscience when we push aside the elaborate Watergate talk camouflaging it. As Senator Weicker recently stated them, they should be sobering enough to bring us to our linguistic senses:

> Conspiracy to commit breaking and entering.
> Conspiracy to commit burglary.
> Breaking and entering.
> Burglary.
> Conspiracy to obstruct justice.
> Conspiracy to intercept wire or oral communications.
> Perjury.
> Subornation of perjury.
> Conspiracy to obstruct a criminal investigation.

> Conspiracy to destroy evidence.
> Conspiracy to file false sworn statements.
> Misprision of a felony.
> Filing of false statements.
> Interception of wire and oral communications.
> Obstruction of criminal investigation.
> Attempted interference with the administration of
> the Internal Revenue laws.
> Attempted unauthorized use of Internal Revenue
> information.

To these we might add illegal use of the C.I.A., and numerous unethical practices from violation of the doctor-patient privilege to sabotage of a presidential campaign.

An ancient Roman saying has it that the mind is dyed by the color of its thoughts. Since thoughts are formed in language, it follows that the mind is dyed by the tint of language. Could it be that so much outrageous conduct occurred at least in part because too many minds functioned through a language which extracted personal responsibility from consideration? Did addiction to Washingtonspeak facilitate the commission of conduct ordinarily considered unacceptable to the community at large?

It is time to cleanse our minds—and I don't mean launder— from the muck of Washingtonspeak if we still value government of responsible people, by responsible people and for responsible people. Although a more humble goal, this would be preferable to Mr. Haldeman's "zero-defect system."

A Watergate Quiz: Classical Rhetors for the Modern Student*

Fill in the Blanks—Identify Speaker.

———————————— 1. "It is grievous to be caught."

———————————— 2. "They who mutually injure the state, mutually support each other."

———————————— 3. "The task was a laborious one because eyewitnesses of the same occurrence gave different accounts as they remembered, or were interested in the actions of one side or the other."

———————————— 4. "None love the messenger who brings bad news."

———————————— 5. "A liar will not be believed, even when he speaks the truth."

———————————— 6. "The man who is just and firm of purpose can be shaken from his stern resolve neither by the rage of the people who urge him to crime nor by the countenance of the threatening tyrant."

———————————— 7. "I have found it!"

———————————— 8. "Democracies are most commonly corrupted by the insolence of demagogues."

———————————— 9. "When there is an income-tax, the just man will pay more and the unjust less on the same amount of income."

———————————— 10. "There is also a sure reward for faithful silence."

———————————— 11. "Put not thy faith in any Greek."

* By Hugh Rank, with apologies to Ed Corbett, author of *Classical Rhetoric for the Modern Student* (Oxford University Press) for almost stealing his title. The authors of the quotations: 1. Horace; 2. Herodotus; 3. Thucydides; 4. Sophocles; 5. Aesop; 6. Horace; 7. Archimedes; 8. Aristotle; 9. Plato; 10. Horace; 11. Euripides.

A Watergate Summer

Don L. F. Nilsen

In July 1973, as the televised Watergate hearings revealed the secrets of the conspiracy to millions of American viewers, the College Section of NCTE was holding a summer conference in Kalamazoo, Michigan, where teachers concerned with the problems of doublespeak, propaganda analysis, and semantics were meeting. Don Nilsen's report, from "Workshop 15," illustrates how some teachers were responding to the Watergate hearings, adapting and analyzing that which would be common knowledge to their students.

In order that each participant in the workshop might have an appropriate technical vocabulary for discussing discourse, each participant read a manuscript entitled *Semantic Theory,** which outlines the basic principles of the major approaches to linguistic semantics—interpretive semantics, generative semantics, and case grammar; and which investigates some of the problems which become significant in a semantically oriented grammar. It was not a purpose of our workshop to develop a definitive statement on how discourse should be analyzed, but rather we had the much less ambitious aim of determining what insights the various linguistic models can provide in analyzing (or possibly in generating) discourse. Following are some of the activities of the group.

Because the conference took place at the same time as the culmination of the first stage of the Watergate hearings, the timing for consideration of this particular discourse was excellent. Case grammar provided many insights into the roles that various people played as innovators (Agents), as workers (Instruments), and as pawns (Experiencers), and how these various human roles related to each other and related to the roles of the setting such as place (Location), objects or props used (Object), and chronology (Time). For the human roles we coined the term "First-Person Roles" to refer to the senate committee since they were the speakers, "Second-Person Roles" to refer to the witnesses since they were the persons spoken to, and "Third-Person Roles" for President Nixon and possibly Vice-President Agnew since they were the persons spoken about. Then for each of these persons we discussed the semantic features which had an effect on the discourse. Con-

* By Don and Alleen Nilsen, to be published in spring 1975 by Newbury House, Publishers.

sidering the first-person roles, for example, it was significant that Dash was the Chief Counsel, that Inouye was Japanese, that Gurney was pro-administration, and that Ervin was old, a southerner, chairman of the committee, a constitutional scholar, religious, and humorous. Obviously, the political affiliation, position on the committee, degree of conservativeness, etc. all had an important effect on the kinds of statements that each person made.

We did the same thing for second-person roles. We decided, for example, that the semantic features which affected the discourse of John Mitchell, for example, were that he was an Attorney General which meant that he was part of the White House staff (two features), and that he was a member and chairman of the Committee to Re-Elect the President (two features). We decided that witnesses varied not so much in what they said as in the types of terms they used and in their level of abstraction. John Dean, for example, tended to concentrate on details, while the other members of the White House staff tended to talk in generalities. There was an interesting correlation between the degree of presidential support and the badness of the memory and therefore the vagueness of the statements. In addition to the semantic features mentioned, it was also significant which persons were attorneys, which had been indicted, which had been most directly involved, and of course their various positions both in the administration hierarchy and in the various Watergate incidents.

We decided that the discourses of the third-person roles were basically the same as those of a particular subset of the second-person roles—those that were pro-administration. Of course the semantic features associated with a particular person controlled not only his type of answer, but also the types of questions that he was asked. Depending on the relationship between the first-person speaker and the second-person speaker, there were probing questions, trick questions (used on hostile or reluctant witnesses to attempt to get them to make contradictory statements which could later be explored), and confirmation questions (used on friendly witnesses merely to help them get their point across). The semantic features associated with a person seemed more important than the relationship between first- and second-person speakers involved. Certainly Mr. Baker's humor was not like that of Mr. Ervin and neither of these senators could top Mr. Ulasowicz's humorous forays.

Going from the human roles to the setting roles, in Case Grammar the Object Case is used to cover inanimate manipulated objects; it is what traditional grammar calls the receiver of the action (usually the Direct Object). In the discourse under consideration, there were a number of Objects (or props) that related to the discourse, including the $100 bills in brown paper bags that Ulasowicz delivered, the telephones and bugging equipment, the files that were rifled, the cameras, the receiving equipment across the street in the Howard Johnson's, etc. In this particular discourse there are two chronologies and two locations involved—those of the original incident and those of the investigation. Scenes which were significant in the original incident were the Democratic National Headquarters (especially O'Brien's office), the Howard Johnson's across the street (where there was a listening device), the White House (especially the Oval Office), and the Republican offices where the information was distributed. The first chronology included the first and second break-ins of the Democratic National Headquarters, etc.

Some very interesting linguistic facts came into view in reference to the second chronology—the one related to the unravelling of events by the committee. One of our major considerations in the workshop was the importance of context. In tracing the investigations of the committee, we were constantly aware of the distribution of old and new information as it affected the discourse. The presuppositions and the assertions of each question or statement were determined largely by the particular point in time at which it occurred in the discourse. We could take isolated statements and fairly accurately determine where they would fit into the discourse by knowing the chronology and by knowing the effect of this on the discourse. In general, the later an utterance occurred in the discourse, the more information was available (more old and less new information) and the closer to the Presidency the involvement reached. There were two other discourse chronologies that happened simultaneously with the Watergate break-ins and that bear a relationship to it—the university demonstrations across the United States and Muskie's running for the Democratic nomination.

This brings us to one of the major problems of the workshop: that of defining discourse. We decided that the most relevant consideration in this definition was a term provided by Robin Lakoff, "common topic." We decided that the various parts of a genuine discourse are related to each other not only chronologically but also in terms of cause and effect, etc., and that "common topic" helps us see this relationship. But "common topic" is always determined from a particular point of view; therefore, what is defined as common topic by the administration was not necessarily the same as what was defined as common topic by Senator Ervin, and vice versa. For example, the administration felt that the Watergate incident related to such other "discourses" as national security, separation of powers, executive privilege, the constitutionality of requiring the release of the White House tapes and other documents, university demonstrations, bombing of the White House, etc. Those who were not pro-administration would fail to see the common topic of the above listed items with the Watergate, but rather would see a common topic with an entirely different set of discourses, including the enemies list, a girl taking off her clothes in front of the Democratic Headquarters, campaign finances and disclosures, previous Nixon politics, freedom of the press, the people's right to know, the coverup, and the possibility of impeachment. Some people felt that the Watergate discourse included the bombings in Cambodia, the San Clemente improvements, charges being made against Vice-President Agnew, the McCarthy hearings, the break-in at Ellsberg's psychiatrist's office, the Ellsberg trial, and the bugging of various embassies. In support of this view, they pointed out that there are a number of semantic features that are common to the Watergate discourse and these other discourses—such features as "unilateral decisions," "national security," "coverup of information," "illegality," "clandestine activity," "destruction of evidence," etc. The final conclusion of the workshop was that discourses tend to have fuzzy borders.

We also talked about how the choice of vocabulary is determined by the discourse, the context (the time and place in the discourse), and the role of the speaker. There is a great deal of highly subjective and emotional vocabulary related to the Watergate; each person chooses to use those terms which reinforce his particular position. They include: paranoia, criminal activities, tax audits, perjury, destroying evidence, hush money, bugging, wire taps, psychological profile, lack of ethics (or situational ethics), paid demonstrators, executive clemency, obstructing justice, political dirt, kingly powers, fascist outlook, dirty tricks, laundering of funds, the plumbers, CREEP, White House horrors, enemy list, right to burgle, little Jap, secret tapes, pressuring of the CIA and the FBI, the equation of Democrats and Communists, and the Ehrlichman-Haldeman mentality. None of these words is new to our English language; we had all of them before Watergate, but I would venture to say that the new connotations that have been added to these words through the Watergate hearings will take a long time vanishing.

We also discussed body language, reference, "emic-etic" distinctions, and motivations as they related to the Watergate discourse. Probably the most significant delving we did was into the relationship between a discourse and the real world which it represents. We

were not afraid to discuss truth, falseness (lies), vagueness, misleading statements, equivocation, contradiction, corroboration, and
such elevated concepts as legality, constitutionality, diplomacy, and
morality. We know more about these things than we did before the
workshop and hope to transmit to our students in the classroom
some of the techniques we learned for analyzing discourse and the
real world it represents.

Language and Dramatic Character

Walker Gibson

Extracted from Gibson's Presidential Address at the NCTE convention in Philadelphia (November 1973), the following paragraphs focus attention on a literary skill—the analysis of fictional characters—in which most English teachers have been well trained, and relates this skill to the analysis of contemporary political language.

If we are to survive as a profession, if we are to serve our society in a useful way, it will not be because we've refined our teaching of Walter Scott or even William Faulkner. It will be because we've directed our attention, as experts in symbol systems, to the ways language works in the society.

For a current illustration of how the "new" or "expanded" English teacher might operate, let me allude to Watergate. A number of people, including me, have pointed out that the Watergate Hearings, even during summer vacation, were an English teacher's dream, a wonderful rich laboratory-display of bureaucratic language in action. But it hasn't been so clear what an English teacher ought to do about it, or what a teacher can do about it. Let's think about that for a moment.

A month or so ago, Bob Hogan at our [NCTE] Urbana head-quarters received a letter from an English teacher addressed to this subject. "The major aggravation," the teacher wrote, "of watching Watergate was underlined by a constantly recurring irritant. Some of the most highly educated participants were guilty of breaking the grammatical rule that the subject of the gerund must be in the possessive case, i.e., 'I didn't know about *his* (not him) going.' English teachers, here's your chance to capitalize on Watergate and teach correct grammar."

I would dearly like to believe that that letter was a put-on. If that teacher was pulling our leg, it's a masterful job. But on the whole, I doubt it. I'm afraid we really are being appealed to on the grounds of a frozen and formal "correctness" that could hardly be wider of the mark. And I trust it's obvious that if *this* is to be the English teacher's response to Watergate, we are indeed a doomed profession.

Complaints about the Watergate witnesses' conversational grammar are surely trivial, even though I too marvel when the former attorney general says "He invited my wife and I to dinner." A Chicago columnist is outraged when somebody testifies, "It was a meeting *between* the four of us," surely a construction that you and I might easily use. "That memoranda was dated July 20." Surely it's just a matter of time before *memoranda* becomes a singular noun, in virtually all contexts, and it's silly for columnists or English teachers to get very excited about that.

Nor am I suggesting that classroom bull sessions on the morality of Watergate, the dirty tricks and the enemy lists, are the English teacher's major response, though I should think such discussions might be appropriate in any class. No, I too believe, like Bob Hogan's gerund-conscious correspondent, that an attention to details of language represents our best foot forward. But I would go at it, needless to say, another way.

When we read *Hamlet,* or *Charlotte's Web,* or whatever it may be, we infer dramatic character from language. Because Hamlet says the things he says, in the way he is made to say them, we conclude that he is this or that sort of person, and we have our evidence before us in the words on the page—or stage. Learning to read is learning to infer dramatic character from linguistic evidence. All of us in this room are very good at this. Do we become political propagandists if we simply use this skill of ours to ask the same kinds of questions of the Watergate witnesses?

What does it say, for example, about a person's attitude toward law and order if, when describing some clearly illegal act by a White House colleague, he calls the act *inappropriate?*

What does it say about a person's habits of mind if, when referring to the need to get some people going on a particular job, he uses the phrase *to accelerate the concern of those involved?*

How do we feel about a person's contact with reality if he repeatedly uses the *would* construction, and if he never reports that anybody *said* anything, but only that he *indicated* it? "At this point in time I would indicate that. . . ." The peculiar tentative vagueness of *would* surely tells us something about the speaker's unwillingness to grasp the concreteness of his action. ("Utopia," says Fowler, "the realm of non-fact or the imaginary.") And the choice of *indicate* over more definite alternatives is a similar cop-out, a flight from responsibility.

Finally, what can we learn about dramatic character by observing the witnesses' non-verbal behavior, from the cut of the clothes to the mannikin spouse in the background? What do these tell us about the intended performance?

And all this, of course, has to be applied as well to those on the other side of the interrogation. From Weicker to Montoya, those senators dramatized themselves (as we all do and must) in widely different roles, and it is surely the job of the intelligent TV viewer to *see* these distinctions with all the critical skill he can muster.

There's a great deal that's still mysterious in this kind of endeavor. We don't know enough about kinesics, or about camera point of view, to name just two areas of my own ignorance. But we do know a lot about the dramatic power of language, and in the decades to come we can—if we will—apply this knowledge of ours in ways that may actually help our students survive into the 21st century.

The 21st century, of course, is indeed unknown to us, but we can say that in that century the processes of communication are not going to get any simpler. We can safely bet that *one* criterion for survival or success will be a capacity to change symbol systems, to invent new ones, and adapt old ones for unpredictable situations. The print medium may be dead, for all I know—so be it. But what we can tell our students today, about *any* medium of communication, is sure to be of use if it can be applied to any *other* medium of communication. As I've tried to suggest, for example, a person trained in making literary discriminations can, if he is willing to try, use this skill to make discriminations about the language of bureaucracy in Washington.

2

In and Out of the Classroom

. . . articles about teaching in the classroom and related activities. . . no orthodoxy presented here. . . diverse opinions, a variety of approaches, differences in degree and of kind. . .

The Language of Deceit

David Burmester

"I am convinced that there is a need in school curricula for courses concerning persuasion. Moreover, there are implications in the attempted manipulation of young people which suggest that the study of persuasion must not be put off until high school." Thus, David Burmester, who teaches at Davis Senior High School, California, recognizes the need for classroom material and here offers specific suggestions which can be adapted at many grade levels. Burmester is a member of the NCTE Committee on Public Doublespeak and has a special interest in the persuasion techniques of television.

Even the most jaded media teachers—those who had, for years, quoted John Culkin's figure that the average high school graduate has watched television for 15,000 hours and who had used the figure as evidence for the need to incorporate media study into the curriculum—must have done a double-take when the American Academy of Pediatrics was given an update on this and other television statistics. Addressing the Academy's 1971 Convention in Chicago, Gerald S. Looney, Physician-In-Chief at the Kennedy Memorial Hospital and an instructor in pediatrics at both Boston University School of Medicine and the Harvard Medical School, imparted a startling array of evidence concerning children's viewing habits.

The figures, which also appear in an article, "The Ecology of Childhood," in the Avon paperback *Action for Children's Television,* included such hair-raising items as these: By age 14 a child has witnessed the violent assault on or destruction of 18,000 human beings on television. The Culkin 15,000 hour figure has been updated by almost 50% to 22,000 hours. Perhaps most significant of all, during the 22,000 hours of viewing, this same average young person has been an audience of one for approximately 350,000 commercials.

Sister Ann Christine Heintz of St. Mary's Center for Learning in Chicago prefaces her excellent text, *Persuasion,* by writing: "When people communicate, things happen. Both those who send messages and those who receive them are changed in the communication process. Any attempt one person makes to change another's values, ideas, his ways of acting, or buying practices is a type of persuasion. Persuasion is a fact of modern life; it is a part of the environment."

This recurring theme of the media environment has fascinated me as a teacher and as a person for some time. When I first began my explorations of the language of deceit, however, it was in the character of an English/Media teacher looking for ways to make the study of language more pertinent to contemporary students. What began as a simple classroom investigation of the relationship between perception and bias came, at length, to be a full-scale program of study concerning the use of language to sway, persuade and deceive.

Whether we like it or not, much of the persuasion to which we are subjected is deceitful, if only because it is insidious. FCC Commissioner Nicholas Johnson tells us in his book *How to Talk Back to Your Television Set,* that the mere mention of a product on a television show is almost inevitably responsible for an increase in sales. When "Laugh-In" made "Look that up in your Funk and Wagnall's" a coast-to-coast catch-phrase, the dictionary had to go into extra printings to satisfy a 20% rise in sales. Such items as these argue for a better educated audience; but better educated not in the traditional sense, for traditional skills are not always applicable to the demands of the new media. Audiences of the future must be educated to cope with the language of deceit.

Program content may, indeed, exert tremendous influence on viewers. It is, however, the commercial "messages" which merit particular attention if for no other reason than their staggering frequency. Dr. Looney suggests that the average high school graduate has seen 350,000 of these messages. William Kuhns, in his text *Exploring Television,* sets this figure at 600 per week for the average viewer, or over 400,000 by age 18! Jeffrey Schrank (a frequent contributor to *Media & Methods*), informs us that tests show people have the ability to replay mentally the video portion of a commercial when the audio is broadcast over the radio. Television and radio conspire to saturate our sensibilities with images we ourselves have retained. Mason Williams, songwriter, poet, and late sage of the "Smothers Brothers' Comedy Hour" once told the FCC that "Television is not a salesman with a foot in your door, it's a salesman with a foot in your head."

It is important to emphasize the frequency and abundance of commercial messages. The successful commercial does more than inform. It conditions. The Alka-Seltzer people came up with a successful formula with commercials such as the one in which an actor repeats the statement "Try it. You'll like it." This statement and others like it have entered the mainstream of American language through simple repetition. Hence, when George

McGovern, exultant over his victories in four primary elections on the same day in June of 1972, told a nation-wide television audience "I can't believe we won the whole thing," he was unconsciously plugging Alka-Seltzer by paraphrasing a slogan coined and popularized in one of that product's commercials.

I emphasize television because it is, indeed, the most persuasive of the media. Nicholas Johnson points out that commercial television, sustained by advertising, is able to attract over $2.5 billion annually from advertisers. Politicians are well aware of television's power too. Again according to Commissioner Johnson, most politicians spent more than half their campaign budgets on television spots in 1968. If this trend held through the 1972 campaign—and the chances are that it not only held but escalated—it is reasonable to estimate that the television bill to political advertisers during the recent election was somewhere in excess of $200,000,000 or roughly one dollar for every man, woman and child in the United States, voter or non-voter! This sum is only one half of a larger amount—$400,000,000—which it is estimated was spent at large for the same purpose. Even larger sums will be spent on political campaigns in the future—assuming that controls are not enacted—and political advisers are opting for a larger concentration of funds in television advertising.

At issue here is more than the possibility of graft and corruption implicit in the soliciting of enormous sums of money from private contributors. The media themselves are becoming a party to an extremely unhealthy political atmosphere by providing as a matrix for political campaigning the established pattern for commercial advertising. The media, rather than providing a forum for the public airing of views, are providing exposure time for the politician as product. The public, once able to judge a man on his merits, must now make its decision on the basis of which candidate projects the best image. Image politics may even lead to the situation which seems to have occurred in the 1972 Presidential race where the inaccessibility of the President led many voters to base their decision on what they felt to be a negative image projected by Senator McGovern.

Persuasion is indeed a part of our environment. I am convinced that there is a need in school curricula for courses concerning persuasion. Moreover, there are implications in the attempted manipulation of young people which suggest that the study of persuasion must not be put off until high school. Action for Children's Television (ACT), a Boston-based organization hoping to reform children's programming on television, has taken some important steps toward regulating advertising aimed at children and has done the nation a service by pointing out that advertising during prime children's viewing hours accounts for a much greater percentage of the total on-screen matter than it does during adult "prime time." In response to citizen pressure, last fall the National Association of Educational Broadcasters (NAEB) established guidelines reducing commercial minutes-per-hour from 16 to 12 during children's weekend-morning programming. But as ACT points out, these guidelines affect only subscribing stations (60% of the total) and do not affect after-school programming during the week, when commercials may still account for more than 25% of the broadcast hour. Moreover, incredibly, the 12 minutes commercial time recommended by the NAEB is still 3 minutes more per hour than the 9 minutes of commercial interruptions aired during adult prime time.

Students must be allowed to come face to face with the persuaders of our society. I do not mean only that we must help our young people to become more critical viewers of television. The language of deceit has a much wider use than that. My own first tentative classroom explorations of the language of deceit centered around the use of euphemism and, in particular, its proliferation at the military and governmental level during the Vietnam war. According to San Francisco *Chronicle* columnist Charles McCabe:

> Vietnam, which of all things is the thing we Americans most want to hide from, has corrupted our language almost as much as it has corrupted our spirit. . . . To shell your own troops by mistake is "accidental delivery of ordnance equipment." A shovel is a "combat replacement evacuator." A parachute is, unbelievably, "an aerodynamic personnel accelerator." And there is that lulu of them all, "protective reaction." This means starting a war, as in Laos or Cambodia.

There are other military euphemisms which have been used to disguise the truth: "pacification," "free-fire zones," "incursions." Even the old War Department has become a euphemism, the "Defense" Department.

The current media-aware national administration has been known to dip into the language of deceit on occasion. One remembers a large-scale education bill which was vetoed as "inflationary": at a time when billions of dollars were being squandered on an unpopular war abroad. Even the recent veto of a funding bill for public television had its moments of high linguistic deception. According to official sources, the measure was blue-penciled because it put too much emphasis on national programming at the expense of "adequate emphasis on localism." Ignored in this decision was the fact that the bill actually increased the aid to local public television stations, allocating a two-year sum of $155,000,000 for this purpose.

Euphemism is not, of course, employed solely by governmental agencies. *Time*'s excellent essay, "The Euphemism: Telling It Like It Isn't" (reprinted in Joseph Littell's *How Words Change Our Lives*) provides an excellent springboard into the study of euphemism. Students, most of whom have never really thought about the notion that some language is used merely to cover up something "improper," are quick to provide examples from many different areas of interest—never has the candor of today's youth been made manifest more explicitly than during our study of euphemism!

Euphemism can eventually alter the lexicon of an entire profession. Take, for instance, this classic account from Jessica Mitford's *The American Way of Death:*

> Lastly, a whole new terminology, as ornately shoddy as the satin rayon casket liner, has been invented by the funeral industry to replace the direct and serviceable vocabulary of former times. Undertaker has been supplanted by "funeral director" or "mortician." (Even the classified section of the telephone directory gives recognition to this; in its pages you will find "Undertakers—see Funeral Directors.") Coffins are "caskets"; hearses are "coaches"; corpses generally are "loved ones," but mortuary etiquette dictates that a specific corpse be referred to by name only—as, "Mr. Jones"; cremated ashes are "cremains." Euphemisms such as "slumber room" and "calcination—the *kindlier* heat" abound in the funeral business.

A hidden factor in the art of persuasion—one most often found in advertising—is The Assumption, either founded or unfounded. It is a commonly held assumption among advertisers—and, hence, among many customers—that anything old is good, while any*one* old is not. And there are other assumptions upon which advertising relies. Appeals to sex are the most abundant, but it is interesting to note just how these appeals are directed. A recent magazine ad directed at young women states: "We make our pantyhose for Joe Namath. . .they're worn by women, of course, but they're made for men." In a magazine directed at a general women's audience, the same ad substitutes the word "men" for "Joe Namath." In a major men's magazine we found the following advertising copy: "Joan Daly says she likes it when guys wear Old Spice. Girls like it. Is there a better reason to wear Old Spice?" The hard, sex-oriented sell is clearly a product of our era. A study of older advertisements indicates that while sex has always been a fellow-traveler with free enterprise, it has never been as blatantly obvious as it is now.

Teaching kids to deal with the language of deceit is really an exercise in becoming a resourceful and critical media consumer while directing students to become the same. Most of the raw material for any course of study is available daily in the press and on radio and television as well as in conversation. You will find that an opaque projector—almost every school has one hiding away in some storage closet—can be the most useful piece of equipment available. With it you can project news stories, magazine advertisements, political pamphlets and other printed material which you and your students bring to class. If you have any budget at all, you can make 35mm slides of the better examples for future use.

Television commercials on 16mm movie film are often available free from local television stations. These, though usually outdated, are almost invariably of use in discussing the particulars of persuasion. If you can't get free commercials, you can often buy them in dozen lots from Gaines "16" Films for next to nothing. If none of these resources are open to you and you don't have videotape equipment in your school, there's still one excellent source, probably the best of all: your students. Ominously—in the context of what I have been writing—many students are able to repeat commercials verbatim.

There are a number of projects currently underway throughout the country dealing with the language of deceit, though most of them don't use that term. One center of activity is New York University where, in the late 1960's, critic and author Nat Hentoff started having students monitor the media under the assumption that while the press may act as a watchdog of a free society, no one is keeping an eye on the press. More recently, the NYU School of Education has offered a doctorate in Media Ecology and publishes the *Media Ecology Review* which contains some interesting writing by doctoral students.

Springing up in various larger cities are journalism reviews whose primary purpose is to keep an eye on the local press. The two most influential of these, both concerned with national press, are the *Columbia Journalism Review* and *(MORE)*, both located in New York City.

In *The Dimensions of Change,* Don Fabun quotes an article in *Technology III:* "The limits of our language mean the limits of our world. A new world is the beginning of a new language. A new language is the seed of a new world." If the language of deceit and all its spin-offs and sub-categories are at the heart of the language of the media environment of the future, it is essential that those who must live in that environment be helped to discover the necessary survival skills.

Learning Activities

1. Choose a particular assumption in advertising (e.g. *Children are always "cute"*) and see how often it crops up during an average week's viewing.

2. Borrow an armed forces training film (check with your local recruiter) and try to determine what assumptions are implicit. Also check the film for possible deceptive uses of language. Does the narrator refer to an "enemy"? Who *is* the enemy?

3. Borrow an industrial documentary or free-loan film from the business community (the *Educators Guide to Free Films* lists thousands). Are there "subliminal" messages? If the sponsor is an automobile manufacturer, what cars are driven? (A very good Shell Oil Company film, "Paint," concerns the history of paint-making. All the natural pigments are mixed in sea shells.)

4. Collect advertisements from magazines directed at special audiences (men, women, children, farmers, sports fans, etc.). How do the ads approach their intended audiences? Are there special assumptions made about special audiences? Do certain audiences attract politically-oriented advertisements?

5. Find ads for the same product in magazines geared to various audiences (for example, *Esquire, Seventeen, Sports Illustrated, Newsweek, Vogue*). Do the ads change their tone? Does the language change? Is there a different pitch depending on the audience?

6. Compile a "User's Guide to Euphemisms." Divide the class into research groups, each investigating a different area: politics and government, the military, the human body, the schools, etc.

7. Try to determine where euphemisms come from. When is a word slang and when is it euphemism? Can slang be euphemism and vice versa?

8. Audiotape a television commercial. Write a description of the visual content but keep it to yourself. How many people can describe the visual after hearing the audio?

9. Is the language of deceit intentional at higher echelons of government or is it merely an occupational hazard? Discuss.

10. What is the advertiser's view of America? Using magazine advertisements, construct a collage entitled "The Great American Dream." What is pictured in the collage? What's missing?

11. How is bias important in advertising? Spend some time on bias and its influence on people. Why do Japanese enjoy squid while most Americans blanch at the thought? (Jeff Schrank has some excellent material on hidden assumptions in *Teaching Human Beings, 101 Subversive Activities in the Classroom.*)

12. Product names are not chosen capriciously. Some are merely labels in dictating use or nature of the product (Head and Shoulders, Cool Whip). Others seem to go beyond the labeling process to imply value or quality (Imperial Margarine, Zest). Collect the names of products to determine the motivation behind the naming process.

13. Automobile names are intriguing. Some styles are named after weapons (Dart, Javelin, Sabre) while others are named after animals (Impala, Pinto, Cougar). What psychological impact do these names have on potential consumers? Do other product names work in the same fashion?

14. During the last years of cigarette commercials on TV and radio the FCC allowed equal time to anti-smoking commercials. Now that neither type is on the air any longer, cigarette smoking has increased. Critics blame this on the absence of anti-smoking commercials. The Federal Trade Commission is considering the idea of "counter advertising" in which critics would be allowed to answer claims made in regular ads. Proponents argue that such counter advertisements will help balance fraudulent commercials. Opponents claim that counter advertising would doom commercial advertising. Where do you stand?

15. Produce a periodical newsletter criticizing local press and broadcast media. Don't restrict yourself to local media in all matters, however. The national media are more in need of criticism than all the journalism reviews together could possibly handle.

16. Suggest to your school newspaper that it incorporate a regular column dealing with the language of deceit.

17. Find out if your city has ordinances concerning the size and content of outdoor advertising. If it does, get a copy and find out if they are strong enough. If there are none, organize a committee to study the matter and make recommendations to the city council.

18. Make a poster which attempts to convince someone to do something. Make it very persuasive. Test it on the class.

19. Film a commercial for an idea or an ideal.

20. Compile a list of expressions which have entered the language because of saturation exposure on television ("Try it. You'll like it."; "Sorry 'bout that," etc.).

21. What happens to a politician when he attempts to "adjust" his image to appeal to a broader based electorate? There are examples in real life (discuss what happened to Senator McGovern between the primaries and the general election) and in the media (Michael Richie's film *The Candidate* deals with a senatorial candidate who allows himself to be re-shaped by the media).

22. During the 1972 general election, Californians voted on twenty-two ballot propositions. Of these, all but three of the losing propositions had received the majority of the financial backing (one losing issue had ten-to-one financial support). Have the people finally gotten wise to the big political spenders or did big money uniformly back repugnant issues? Discuss.

23. Write a letter to the FCC urging them to set up minimum guidelines for advertising during prime time children's viewing hours. Make certain you are able to explain what you think these guidelines should be.

24. A while back, ad agency Batten, Barton, Durstine, and Osborn ran an advertisement for themselves describing fourteen products they had invented, products which had names and descriptions but which had yet to be produced. The point of the ad was that people at BBD&O are geniuses at dreaming up products which will sell. All that is needed is a manufacturer. Should products be manufactured merely because they will sell? What are the implications of ad agencies creating products just because there are possible markets for them? Discuss.

25. A quote for discussion: "A feature film made with the same kind of care as a commercial would have to cost $50 million." (Stanley Kubrick)

Resources

Sources for Commercials

Gaines "16" Films usually has commercials for sale. Write to them for a complete catalog which includes old television programs, travel films, film previews, and so forth.

Gaines "16" Films
15207 Stagg St.
Van Nuys, Ca. 91405

The American Television and Radio Commercials Festival rents reels of award-winning commercials for past years. These are the cream of the crop, however, and probably not representative of the worst.

American Television and Radio Commercials Festival
30 East 60th St.
New York, N.Y. 10022

A Baker's Dozen Good Books for Reference or Student Use

1. *Action for Children's Television* (Avon, $1.25)
2. *How to Talk Back to Your Television Set,* Nicholas Johnson (Bantam, $.95)
3. *The Selling of the President 1968,* Joe McGinniss (Pocket Books, $1.25)
4. *How Words Change Our Lives,* Joseph Littell, ed. (McDougal Littell, $2.40)
5. *Coping with the Mass Média,* Joseph Littell, ed. (McDougal Littell, $2.67)
6. *Persuasion,* Sister Ann Christine Heintz (Loyola University Press, $3.00)
7. *Exploring Television,* William Kuhns (Loyola University Press, $3.20)
8. *Mass Media,* Sister Ann Christine Heintz, *et al.* (Loyola University Press, $3.20)
9. *Culture is Our Business,* Marshall McLuhan (Ballantine, $3.95)
10. *Critiques of Contemporary Rhetoric,* Karlyn Kohrs Campbell (Wadsworth, $3.95)
11. *Mass Media: Forces in our Society,* Francis and Ludmila Voelker (Harcourt Brace Jovanovich, $5.25)
12. *Teaching Human Beings, 101 Subversive Activities for the Classroom,* Jeffrey Schrank (Beacon, $3.45)
13. *The American Language,* H. L. Mencken (Knopf, three volumes $38.85 or Raven McDavid's one-volume abridgement, $12.95)

Other Print

The Educators Guide to Free Films is an 800-page listing of free loan films from numerous sources. Every school library should have a copy. Naturally, there are a number of poor films included, but for our purposes this makes little difference. The *Guide*, by the way, is *not* free.

Educators' Progress Service, Inc.
Randolph, Wisconsin 53956

Graphis magazine is an international publication specializing in graphic arts. It generally features at least one article about advertising, and entire issues often are devoted to the subject. The magazine is lavishly illustrated and well worth the rather steep subscription rate.

Graphis
P.O. Box 320
New York, N.Y. 10005

Here are the addresses of *Media Ecology Review* and the two most influential journalism reviews.

Media Ecology Review
New York University
School of Education
23 Press Annex
Washington Square
New York, N.Y. 10003

Columbia Journalism Review
700 Journalism Building
Columbia University
New York, N.Y. 10027

(MORE)
P.O. Box 2971
Grand Central Station
New York, N.Y. 10017

Other Places to Write

Action for Children's Television
46 Austin St.
Newtonville, Mass. 02160

Federal Communications Commission
1919 M Street NW
Washington, D.C. 20554

National Association of Broadcasters
1661 N Street NW
Washington, D.C. 20036

American Broadcasting Company
1330 Avenue of the Americas
New York, N.Y. 10019

Columbia Broadcasting System
51 West 52nd St.
New York, N.Y. 10019

National Broadcasting Company
30 Rockefeller Plaza
New York, N.Y. 10019

Film

There really aren't any films specifically intended for use in the study of the language of deceit. Most films intended to "sell" a "product" will work. The afore-mentioned *The Candidate* is an excellent example of the image-making process in action. At the time of this writing, the film has not yet been released in 16mm. ACT has a short film, "But First This Message," which contains clips from children's television accompanied by comments from TV experts and children themselves. The film sells for $100 and rents for $25; available from ACT.

The Electric Carrot: The Rhetoric of Advertisement
and the Art of Persuasion

D. G. Kehl

Rich in literary allusions and practical examples from current ads, Kehl's
article was first delivered at the 1974 Conference on College Composition and Communication convention in Anaheim. Kehl, who teaches at
Arizona State University and is a member of the NCTE Committee on
Public Doublespeak, explains and defends analysis of contemporary advertising as a means of teaching writing.

"Wherefore do ye spend money for that which is not bread?" The
answer to the prophet Isaiah's interrogative caveat emptor of the
8th century B.C. is perhaps also, to a large degree, the answer to
the success of John the hostler in Fielding's *Joseph Andrews:* "She
was long deaf to all the sufferings of her lovers till one day, at a
neighboring fair, the rhetoric of John the hostler, with a new straw
hat and a pint of wine, made a second conquest over her."[1] John
the hostler, today become John the huckster, John the adman,
John the subliminal seducer hawking the new straw hat and the
pint of wine, continues his conquests. For as Will Rogers put it,
"Advertising persuades people to buy things they don't need with
money they ain't got." Whether in Isaiah's 8th century B.C., in
Fielding's 18th century, or in Rogers' 20th, the means of forceful
persuasion is essentially the same: the effective use of rhetorical
strategies to sell images and attitudes. Such is *Admass,* what J. B.
Priestley has called "a consumer's race with donkeys chasing an
electric carrot."[2]

Whether one regards advertisement as "fat, juicy, sugar-coated lies
for our great Boob public to swallow," as Thomas Wolfe expressed
it in a letter to his mother,[3] or as "the most exciting, the most
arduous literary form of all, the most difficult to master, the most
pregnant in curious possibilities," as Aldous Huxley expressed it,[4]
this cogent form of persuasion offers almost limitless possibilities
in the teaching of composition.

If, on the one hand, it is true that "advertising is a racket. . . , its constructive contribution to humanity exactly minus zero" (F. Scott
Fitzgerald[5]), that advertising is a "sell-out" in which "the
main thing is to be as profitably crooked as you can" (James
Dickey[6]), that "without ability to translate words into verifiable
meanings, most people are inevitably victims of both commercial

and literary fraud" (Stuart Chase[7]), then it is part of the composition teacher's job to help dispel this semantic illiteracy upon which advertisers, as well as demagogues, thrive. If, on the other hand, it is true that "some of the cunningest American literature is to be found in advertisements of soap-suds," as D. H. Lawrence has observed,[8] then it is part of the composition teacher's job to help students understand the effective artistry of words in advertising copy and beyond.

Both sides of advertisement—the tyranny and the artistry, the inanity and the cogency—can and should be stressed in the composition class. For every Auden, who warns, "Thou shalt not be on friendly terms/With guys in advertising firms" ("Under Which Lyre: A Reactionary Tract for the Times"), there is an L. E. Sissman, vice-president of Kenyon and Eckhardt advertising firm and one of the good poetic things to happen in America since Wallace Stevens. For every Thomas Carlyle, who reportedly called advertisement "something against nature," there is a Joseph Addison, who in *The Tatler* (No. 224, September 14, 1710), admired "the great art in writing advertisements"—"the finding out a proper method to catch the reader's eye, without which a good thing may pass over unobserved, or be lost among commissions of bankrupt" (Addison only regretting the "uncleanly" impropriety of reference to "Carminative Wind-expelling Pills" in the "works of polite writers"). One might note, too, Samuel Johnson's observation in *The Idler* (No. 40, January 20, 1759) that "the trade of advertising is so near to perfection, that it is not easy to propose any improvement." (Cf. William Dean Howells' discussion of "The Art of the Adsmith" in *Literature and Life,* New York: Harper, 1902.)

With the intent, then, of helping students discern the subtle manipulation, the linguistic hidden persuasion, as well as to appreciate effective rhetorical strategies, the composition teacher might begin with the basic nature of persuasion, of "propaganda" in both its pejorative and its honorific sense. A propagandist is simply a specialist in *selling* attitudes and opinions. "Everyone lives by selling something," Robert Lewis Stevenson wrote.[9] The *effective* writer "sells" his ideas; his reader says, consciously or unconsciously, "I'll *buy* that." The secret of effective, responsible writing is essentially the secret of effective, responsible advertising: "to crack the shell, to talk to the man inside the man," as a recent ad, "The Secret of Advertising," for the Campbell-Ewald Company expressed it. Effective writing, like effective advertising, demands "an uncommon understanding of people, great sensitivity and skill, and the discipline to use them every single time," thus making the difference between an essay or ad someone skips over and an essay or ad someone reads all the way to the end.

Once the class gets to thinking and talking about the overall effect, the tóne, of an ad, they are ready to consider the question: "What specific techniques contribute to the effect?" In the process of answering this question, the students can learn about virtually every compositional/rhetorical strategy.

Perhaps it is desirable, then, to begin with the whole and work to the parts, to consider, first, the purpose, the dominant impression, the controlling idea, the thesis commitment. Analysis of the coherent relationship between the copy and the art work, showing how each reinforces the other in conveying a dominant impression, can be highly instructive. For students who are visually but not necessarily verbally sensitive, one can discuss the implications of Philip Wylie's remark (in a letter to me, December, 1968) that "a picture is worth a thousand words only if we have words for everything in the picture"—and many ads illustrate just that.

A recent ad for Old Grand-Dad whiskey clearly illustrates controlling idea or theme—art for every taste—, successful ordonnance, and highly effective coherence. It has, for example, an arrangement of two paintings—one abstract modern and one nostalgic traditional—juxtaposed with two bottles of bourbon and with the bust of Old Grand-Dad himself, the "Head of the Bourbon Family," in the center. Similarly, a recent ad for Chivas Regal Scotch illustrates a carefully structured tripartite "essay," the controlling idea of which is, "What is light scotch?" The copy develops the idea through the strategy of definition by negation: "Light" scotch is *not* always light in color; "light" scotch is *not* weak; "light" scotch *is* light on the palate, smooth. Then, using the strategy of cyclic return, the ad concludes with a pun: "You'll see the light," reinforced by a sunrise effect in the bottle itself.

These ads and others like them, all readily available to the composition teacher and his students, illustrate what Swift said a poem should do: develop, *use up,* the metaphor. Ads serve effectively to illustrate modes of development, methods of exposition. For example, the Chivas Regal ad mentioned above effectively illustrates identification. A recent Calvert Whiskey ad employs definition: "What should Soft Whiskey be? According to the dictionary definition of *soft,* Soft Whiskey should be a whiskey having a soothing or quietly agreeable taste; lacking harshness or coarseness; affecting the senses in a gentle or pleasant manner." The Old Grand-Dad ad mentioned above uses comparison-contrast to convey the idea that even contrasting tastes can be satisfied by this "bourbon masterpiece." Further, students can be asked to write an analytical essay based on an ad; or a classification essay based on several ads; or a comparison-contrast essay based on, say, two ads for the *same* product appearing in periodicals directed toward *different* audiences (for example, *Newsweek* and *Harper's*), on ads for the *same* product but *different* brand-names (for example, a Cadillac ad and a Volkswagen ad), or on a recent ad and an older ad for the same product (for old ads see Frank Rowsome's *They Laughed When I Sat Down*, New York: McGraw, 1959; Leonard de Vries' *Victorian Advertisements*, Philadelphia: Lippincott, 1968; et al.).

Ads also work well in teaching something about discovery, invention, the whole pre-writing process of abstracting ideas and formulating thesis commitments. For example, after examining a current Lucky Strike ad, the class could discuss Merrill Moore's poem "Lucky Strike," noting how the poet has abstracted his ideas from advertisement. Or one might use Josephine Miles' poem "Government Injunction, Restraining Harlem Cosmetic Co.," e. e. cummings' "Poem, or Beauty Hurts Mr. Vinal," Vachel Lindsay's "Rhyme About an Electrical Advertising Sign," or Robert Bloch's "Nightmare Number Five." (See also an interesting book by Richard Payne and Robert Heyer, *Discovery in Advertising*, New York: Paulist Press, 1969.)

The transition from a consideration of discovery to logic, evidence, authority, is smooth and natural. Advertisement, including TV commercials, outdoor displays, and magazine ads, is an effective medium for teaching about critical thinking. George Santayana referred to advertisement as "the modern substitute for argument," its function being to make the worse appear better. Ads are characterized by what Jules Henry has called "pecuniary logic": "a false statement made as if it were true, but not intended to be believed. No proof is offered for a pecuniary pseudo-truth and no one looks for it. Its proof is that it sells merchandise; if it does not, it is false."[10]

Virtually all of the logical fallacies, common propaganda devices, can be illustrated in advertisement. For example, ads make frequent use of Glittering Generalities (the reverse of Name Calling), a device to make us accept and approve without examining the evidence (usually nil). What of a substantive nature is offered, for example, by Revlon's popular Pango Peach ad: "From east of the sun . . . West of the moon. Where each tomorrow dawns . . . 'Pango Peach' the new color creation by Revlon. A many-splendoured coral . . . pink with pleasure. What a *volcano* of fashion color! It's a full ripe peach with a world of difference . . . born to be worn in big juicy slices. Succulent on your lips. Sizzling on your fingertips. (And on your toes, goodness knows!) *Go* Pango Peach . . . *your* adventure in paradise." Every plain Jane, by using Pango Peach, is invited to become a voluptuous Cleopatra with all the allure of a sensual Garden of Earthly Delights; every *femme de chambre* can become a *femme fatale*. The reverse of Guilt by Association, this is Glory by Association.

Each of the traditional propaganda devices can be re-examined in terms of what advertisement actually does: *advert* (call or turn attention to) in order to *convert* (change from one mode of behavior to another or from inaction to action). Advertisement, in seeking to advert and convert, *averts* and *diverts,* turns attention *from* the unpleasant—for example through euphemism, Red Herring, etc.—and turns attention *to* the pleasant—for example through Glittering Generalities, "Purr Words," Transfer, Plain Folks Appeal, etc. Further, advertisement seeks to *invert,* to turn upside down, creating an opposite effect, as in Card Stacking and Band Wagon appeals. The attempt to invert leads easily to the tendency to *subvert* (turn under, undermine, corrupt) and to *pervert* (twist, distort, misapply), as in the use of False Generalizations, etc.

Ads also lend themselves to discussions of inductive and deductive reasoning. (See, for example, Walker Gibson's analysis of the syllogism in a Rheingold commercial, Chapter 6, "Sweet Talk: The Rhetoric of Advertising," *Tough, Sweet, and Stuffy,* Bloomington: Indiana University Press, 1966.) Students can be asked to analyze the validity and soundness of the reasoning in selected ads, formulating the syllogisms when possible.

> Bothered with gasid indigestion? Make this simple test and prove to yourself that Alkaheist is the best antacid you can buy. Drop a single handy Alkaheist tablet in a glass of water. See how quickly it dissolves? It gets to work fast, fast, fast in your stomach—faster than any other tablet! Get Alkaheist today!
>
> Major premise: The tablet that dissolves faster relieves acidity better.
> Minor premise: Alkaheist dissolves faster.
> Conclusion: Therefore, Alkaheist relieves acidity better.

While this syllogism is *valid* (the conclusion following logically from the premises), it is not necessarily *sound,* for in order to be so, the major and minor premises must be true in every case. Or note the syllogism, again producing a valid but not necessarily sound conclusion, implied in this ad for Pall Mall:

> I'm particular. Millions are. If you, too, are particular about taste, you don't have to wear a button to prove it! Simply smoke Pall Mall. . . . Be particular. . . . Pall

Mall, famous cigarettes. "Wherever particular people congregate."

Major premise: *Particular* people will smoke Pall Mall cigarettes.

Minor premise: You certainly wish to be a *particular* person.

Conclusion: Therefore, you will smoke Pall Mall cigarettes.

Such is the strategy of selling death (see Thomas Whiteside's *Selling Death: Cigarette Advertising and Public Health,* New York: Liveright, 1971) .

One can, if he or she wishes, teach a great deal about paragraph and sentence rhetoric from selected ads. The copy of the Old Grand-Dad whiskey ad mentioned above can be analyzed according to the Christensen generative rhetoric:

1 Old Grand-Dad has the art of pleasing every taste.
  2 In *either lighter 86 Proof or 100 Proof Bottled in Bond,* Old Grand-Dad is *universally recognized* as a bourbon masterpiece *because of its flawless flavor.*
    3 *It* is a mellow, rich flavor born of the finest, perfectly aged Kentucky whiskey.
      4 *Your first taste tells you/*
1 /that Old Grand-Dad is an outstanding example of the bourbon distiller's art.

The caption functions as the "top" sentence of the paragraph, conveying its controlling idea and that of the entire ad. Sentence 2 adds three details concerning the "art" of Old Grand-Dad: (1) that both the 86 and 100 Proof are considered "masterpieces," (2) universally, (3) because of the "flawless flavor." Sentence 3 shifts to yet a lower level, specifically describing the flavor mentioned in Sentence 2. Sentence 4, although the relative clause merely repeats on a number 1 level what has been said, actually gets down to a number 4 level of generality in its main clause, *"Your* first taste tells *you."* This concluding sentence is highly effective in that it combines the allegedly universal with the individual and personal. The paragraph's subordinate sequence is effective because it leads by steps to the crux of the ad, where everything in the ad is intended to lead: *"your* first taste."

The Calvert Whiskey ad mentioned above effectively uses a leading question—"What should a Soft Whiskey be?"—, followed by a long sentence using parallel participial phrases, and then an arrestingly different, staccato concluding sentence: "It is." In a Ballantine Ale ad (*Life,* November 5, 1951; September 8, 1952) , there appeared the following Hemingway endorsement, which, though it reads like a mediocre parody of Hemingway's style, makes for interesting analysis, especially of sentences:

> Bob Benchley first introduced me to Ballantine Ale. It has been a good companion ever since.
>
> You have to work hard to deserve to drink it. But I would rather have a bottle of Ballantine Ale than any other drink after fighting a really big fish.
>
> We keep it iced in the bait box with chunks of ice packed around it. And you ought to taste it on a hot day when you have worked a big marlin fast because there were sharks after him.
>
> You are tired all the way through. The fish is landed untouched by sharks and you have a bottle of Ballantine cold in your hand and drink it cool, light, and full-bodied, so it tastes good long after you have swallowed it. That's the test of an ale with me: whether it tastes as good afterwards as when it's going down. Ballantine does.

Advertising copy also provides examples of effective use of the sentence fragment, that long-standing taboo of some composition teachers. Those who are interested in the grammar of advertisement, especially those who may feel that ad-grammar is spreading ad nauseam, would do well to examine Geoffrey N. Leech's book *English in Advertising: A Linguistic Study of Advertising in Great Britain* (London: Longmans, Green, 1966), as well as such studies as Richard Tobin's "In Praise of the Subjunctive" (*Saturday Review*, August 8, 1970), the interchange on "Grammar in the Marketplace" (which appeared in the *New York Times*, 1963), et al. One ought to begin such a study, however, with the good common sense of the late Francis Christensen, who wrote: "We might try paying less attention to the medium (that is, the mere propriety of the medium) and more to the validity of the message; we might try out the idea, that is, that the important question about the Winston ad is not about *like* but about the truth of the proposition asserted. Do Winstons really taste good?"[11]

Perhaps it is in teaching the rhetorical strategies of diction that advertisement has the most potential. Certainly, as Richard Altick has observed, "if advertising copywriters were less skillful masters of word connotation, we should spend far less money than we do on products they recommend."[12] David Ogilvy, in his book *Confessions of an Advertising Man*, lists these highly connotative words that "work wonders": *free, new, how to, suddenly, now, announcing, introducing, it's here, just arrived, important development, improvement, amazing, sensational, remarkable, revolutionary, star-*

tling, miracle, magic, offer, quick, easy, wanted, challenge, advice to, the truth about, compare, bargain, hurry, last chance.[13] To this list might be added: *chic, fashionable, sociable, jumbo, guaranteed, refreshing, special, mild, exclusive, top, long-lasting, satisfying, sparkling,* suggested by Mario Pei in *Words in Sheep's Clothing.*[14] One could also make a list of taboo words, those avoided because of their pejorative connotations: not "cheap" but "economy sized," not "fat" but "mature" woman, not "smell" or "odor" but "fragrance" or "aroma." Aren't you glad *you* use euphemism? Don't you wish *everybody* did?

Students can be asked to discuss why particular words were chosen rather than others which have generally the same denotation. For example, note some of the verbal options available to the copywriter in the Old Grand-Dad advertisement:

> Old Grand-Dad has the *art* (skill, artifice, ability, knack, know-how, capacity, craft) of *pleasing* (satisfying, gratifying, indulging, refreshing, flattering) every *taste* (thirst, palate, customer, drinker). In either lighter 86 Proof or 100 Proof Bottled in Bond, Old Grand-Dad is *universally* (generally, widely, extensively) recognized as a bourbon *masterpiece* (success, accomplishment, chef d'oeuvre) because of its *flawless* (exquisite, remarkable, impeccable, perfect) flavor. It is a *mellow* (mild, prime, soft, delicate), *rich* (savory, palatable, delectable, deep-down-good) flavor *born of* (owing to, typical of, peculiar to, emanating from) the *finest* (superlative, excellent, best) *perfectly* (meticulously, faultlessly, impeccably, superbly) aged Kentucky whiskey. Your first *taste* (sip, nip, swig, shot, dram, glass, drink) *tells you* (lets you know, alerts' you, indicates) that Old Grand-Dad is an *outstanding* (unique, superb, matchless) example of the bourbon distiller's *art* (business, work, brew, product, whiskey, craft).

Such an exercise gets down to the basis of writing: the stylistic options available and the criteria for choosing one over others—purpose, audience level and appeal, voice, tone, context, connotation, imagery, etc.

Brand names themselves, such as "Old Grand-Dad, Head of the Bourbon Family," are chosen for their connotative, imagistic appeal. "Old Grand-Dad," besides personifying whiskey, connotes a sense of roots, the best of the old combined with the best of the new—tradition, authority, security, domestic bliss and nostalgia. The correspondence between Ford Motor Company and poet Marianne Moore in 1955-56, when Ford was seeking a name for a new car, is illuminating. Ford wanted "this name to be more than a label"; they wanted it "to have a compelling quality in itself and by itself. To convey, through association or other conjuration, some visceral feeling of elegance, fleetness, and advanced features and design. A name, in short, that flashes a dramatically desirable picture in people's minds."[15] But something went wrong, it seems, for out of some six thousand suggested names, including several dozen by Miss Moore, Ford chose what the Manager of Marketing Research considered a name "with an air of gaiety and zest"—Edsel!

Even to *suggest* the almost limitless possibilities of language analysis in advertisement would consume reams of paper and hours of time. One can discuss examples of virtually every aspect of language: coinages, neologisms, including what Strunk and White call "the language of mutilation";[16] language change of other kinds; both hackneyed and fresh diction, including arresting versions of old forms; usage and levels of diction, slang; euphemism, "weasel words" (the phrase popularized by Theodore Roosevelt in a speech in 1916), jargon, gobbledygook; solecisms; linguistic stock response; what George P. Elliott calls "the language of ecstasy";[17] both verbosity and restraint, the impeccable succinctness which Barzun and Graff have noted;[18] objectivity and subjectivity; the way language establishes tone, reveals voice, and is geared to its audience; sensory imagery; figurative language; etc.

A linguistic study of advertisement can be concluded with a consideration of the relationships between advertisement and poetry, or between "sponsored" and "unsponsored" poetry, as S. I. Hayakawa had called it in "Poetry and Advertising" (from *Language in Thought and Action*, originally an article in *Poetry*, January, 1946). It may be true, as Louis Kronenberger has said, that "the trouble with us in America isn't that poetry of life has turned to prose, but that it has turned to advertising copy."[19] Or it'may be true, as Aldous Huxley insisted, that "it is far easier to write ten passably effective sonnets, good enough to take in the not too inquiring critic, than one effective advertisement that will take in a few thousand of the uncritical buying public."[20] In any case, it is highly instructive to discuss advertisement as "the poeticizing of consumer goods."[21] It is interesting to discuss a current Buick ad vis-à-vis Karl Shapiro's poem "Buick."

Some ads, such as a recent one for Seagram's VO, can be analyzed as poems:

> One whisky has
> a special kind of taste.
> IMPORTED V.O.

> One whisky has combined
> lightness and a brilliance of taste.
> IMPORTED V.O.
> One whisky
> most people like the very
> first time they taste it.
> SEAGRAM'S IMPORTED
> VO
> Known by the company it keeps

Note, for example, the ad's prosodic, but not prosaic, appearance on the page. Note its stanzaic structure, its design, its "inscape" leading to a climax, a crescendo: VO. Noteworthy also are its use of refrain, its parallelism, its effective repetition with variation, its sensory imagery and highly connotative language, its word play ("lightness," "taste"), its synesthesia ("brilliance of taste"), its personification through an epigrammatic reapplication of a hackneyed expression; its rhythmic movement; its masculine endings, including the effective use of spondee in VO; its simplicity and succinctness; its linguistic and grammatical plurisignation in stanza two, perhaps approximating William Empson's first and second types of ambiguity.

Advertisement, of course, is not limited to commercial propaganda, to the selling of goods and products. "Man does not only sell commodities," Erich Fromm has written, "he sells himself and feels himself to be a commodity."[22] The composition teacher, having discussed commercial advertisement with the students, can then move easily to "political advertising," Hitler's definition of *propaganda* in *Mein Kampf*, where he discusses, interestingly enough, many of the techniques widely used by Madison Avenue. Aldous Huxley, in "The Arts of Selling," discusses the similarity between the methodology and effect of commercial advertising and that of political propaganda. His assertion that "the personality of the candidate and the way he is projected by the advertising experts are the things that matter,"[23] can lead to a discussion of the points made by Joe McGinniss in *The Selling of the President 1968* (New York: Trident, 1969) and from there to "The Selling of the Pentagon" (based on J. William Fulbright's book *The Pentagon Propaganda Machine*, New York: Liveright, 1970).

Useful also is Hanson Baldwin's discussion of "Madison Avenue War" in "The Information War in Saigon" (*The Reporter*, Feb. 24, 1966). One might discuss a current Armed Forces recruiting ad (Truman said in 1950 that they had "a propaganda machine

almost equal to Stalin's," *Time*, Sept. 18, 1950) and then Kenneth
Fearing's poem entitled "Ad" (in John H. Bens, ed., *Some Shapers
of Man*, New York: Holt, Rinehart & Winston, 1968).

WANTED: Men;
Millions of men are WANTED AT ONCE in a big new field;
NEW, TREMENDOUS, THRILLING, GREAT.

If you've ever been a figure in the chamber of horrors,
If you've ever escaped from the psychiatric ward,
If you thrill at the thought of throwing poison into wells, have
    heavenly visions of people, by the thousands, dying in flames—

YOU ARE THE VERY MAN WE WANT
We mean business and our business is YOU
WANTED: A race of brand-new men.

Apply: Middle Europe;
No skill needed;
No ambition required; no brains wanted and no character allowed;

TAKE A PERMANENT JOB IN THE COMING PROFESSION
Wages: DEATH.

Cultural propaganda or "institutional advertising" can be examined next. "You can tell the ideals of a nation by its advertisements," Norman Douglas has written.[24] Assuredly ours is "a packaged society," as Russell Lynes has called it: one in which
"everything in America, including people, comes packaged and
the package, by and large, is designed to conceal and not to reveal
its contents or at least to make the contents look a great deal better than they are."[25]

We have, for example, packaged news: "Despite all its pretenses of
representing the public, the average newspaper is simply a business
enterprise that sells news and uses that lure to sell advertising space"
(Otto Friedrich, "A Vivacious Blonde was Fatally Shot Today, or
How to Read a Tabloid," *The American Scholar*, Autumn, 1959).
We have packaged erudition—read the blurb on your paperback
books—or this paragraph from a recent undergraduate bulletin of a
prestigious university (in this case, the University of Southern
California):

> The program as a whole is designed to give the student
> a better understanding not only of the basic skills—
> language as a factor in thought, emotion, and behavior;
> independent reflection and judgment based on the crit-
> ical evaluation of facts and evidence; the methods of
> systematic inquiry and how they may vary with different

fields; and the interrelation of the various fields of
knowledge—but also, and perhaps more importantly, of
the meaning and significance of values and the criteria
of evaluation; of moral, religious, and aesthetic experiences and the role they play in the life of the individual and a culture; of the goals of self-realization,
personal integration, maturity, creativity; and of the nature and meaning of freedom in a democratic society.

Humanitarianism is also professionally packaged—read the ads for
Foster Parents Plan, Vista, and Red Cross. Life itself is packaged:
"Put a life in your life with milk"; "Live modern: Join the Pepsi
Generation." And so is death packaged—read the euphemistic ads
for "memorial parks," especially for California's "most cheerful
graveyard in the world."

Perhaps the ultimate packager is not the mortician but the re-
ligionist, who packages peace now and security beyond the grave:
"All the king's horses and all the king's men . . . The Humpty-
Dumpty peace of the world crumbles easily. Only the peace of
Jesus is shatter-proof" (Campus Crusade for Christ magazine *Collegiate Challenge*) . (See also James W. Carty's book *Advertising
the Local Church,* Minneapolis: Augsburg, 1965.)

"Ultimately we are all busy buying and selling one another."
D. H. Lawrence said it (in his poem "The Root of Our Evil"),
and perhaps Norman Mailer has most clearly exemplified it. In
his *Advertisements for Myself,* Mailer writes: "The way to save
your work and reach more readers is to advertise yourself. . . ."[26]
Even the Devil's "business is self-advertising," according to W. H.
Auden ("New Year Letter"). "The devil keeps advertising," says
a character in *The Exorcist,* "the devil does lots of commercials."

Advertisement—artful packaging and poeticizing; commercial, political, cultural wordmanship—influences us all. Each of us both
entices and is enticed by that electric carrot. But to those who may
still question the value of using advertisement to teach composition,
perhaps dismissing it as inane pop culture, may I simply echo Winfield Townley Scott's remark about Gertrude Stein's writings:
"Mostly crap, yes, but so is fertilizer."[27] Some of the best student
writing I have read has been fertilized, fecundated, fructified by
and based upon advertisement. Both teachers and students who
have worked with advertisement in composition, considering both
the artistry and the tyranny or inanity, not only consider it highly
instructive but also concur with Jerry Della Femina's remark that
"advertising is the most fun you can have with your clothes on."[28]
Or to put it another way, "They laughed when I sat down with my
ad—but oh when I started to write!—"

Notes

1. Henry Fielding, *The History of the Adventures of Joseph Andrews and of His Friend Mr. Abraham Adams* (New York: Rinehart, 1948), p. 72.

2. "The Writer in a Changing Society," *Thoughts in the Wilderness* (New York: Harper, 1957), p. 219.

3. *The Letters of Thomas Wolfe to His Mother,* ed. C. Hugh Holman and Sue Fields Ross (Chapel Hill: University of North Carolina Press, 1968), p. 119.

4. "Advertisement," *Essays New and Old* (London: Chatto and Windus, 1926), p. 126.

5. In a letter to his daughter, Scottie, August 24, 1940, *The Crack-Up* (New York: Macmillan, 1956), p. 300.

6. *Self-Interviews,* ed. Barbara and James Reiss (New York: Doubleday, 1970), p. 44.

7. *The Tyranny of Words* (New York: Harcourt, 1938), p. 27.

8. *Sex, Literature and Censorship,* ed. Harry T. Moore (New York: Twayne, 1953), p. 71.

9. "Beggars," *Across the Plains* (London: Chatto and Windus, 1892), p. 263.

10. "Advertising as a Philosophical System," *Culture Against Man* (New York: Random House, 1963), p. 286.

11. "Between Two Worlds," *Word Study,* October, 1962.

12. *Preface to Critical Reading* (New York: Holt, Rinehart, 1960), p. 18.

13. New York: Atheneum, 1963, p. 105.

14. New York: Hawthorne Books, 1969, p. 11. See also Joseph J. Selden's "The Language of Madison Avenue" in *The Golden Fleece,* New York: Macmillan, 1963, and William H. Whyte Jr.'s "The Language of Advertising," *Fortune,* September, 1952.

15. *A Marianne Moore Reader* (New York: Viking, 1965), p. 215.

16. William Strunk, Jr. and E. B. White, *Elements of Style* (New York: Macmillan, 1959), p. 68.

17. *Conversions: Literature and Modernist Deviations* (New York: E. P. Dutton, 1971), p. 86.

18. Jacques Barzun and Henry F. Graff, *The Modern Researcher* (New York: Harcourt, 1957), p. 307.

19. "The Spirit of the Age," *Company Manners* (Indianapolis: Bobbs Merrill, 1954), p. 25.

20. Huxley, "Advertisement," *Essays New and Old,* p. 127.

21. S. I. Hayakawa, *Language in Thought and Action* (New York: Harcourt, 1963), p. 263.

22. *Escape from Freedom* (New York: Holt, Rinehart, 1941), p. 4.

23. *Brave New World Revisited* (New York: Harper, 1958), p. 57.

24. *South Wind* (Chicago: Argus Books, 1929), p. 90.

25. "The Packaged Society," *Harper's* (August, 1966), p. 18.

26. New York: G. Putnam's Sons, 1959, p. 21.

27. *"A Dirty Hand": The Literary Notebooks of Winfield Townley Scott* (Austin: University of Texas Press, 1969), p. 73.

28. *From Those Wonderful Folks Who Gave You Pearl Harbor,* ed. Charles Sopkin (New York: Pocket Books, 1971), p. 256.

Ad-Man, Business-Man, Teacher-Man

Bruce Reeves

For several years, Bruce Reeves has experimented at Acalanes High School, Lafayette, California, with classroom techniques in the analysis of advertising. The following article describes one of these experiments in the testing of ad claims. Although other members of the NCTE Committee on Public Doublespeak may not share his premise of "increasing trust" in advertising as expressed in this essay, Reeves has been an active member of the committee, contributing to the ongoing dialogue within that group. This was presented as a paper at the NCTE convention in Las Vegas in November 1971.

"You can trust advertising to mess with words. You can look to business and advertising together to play a word game with the consumer, for the benefit of the ad-man and business-man, and the detriment of everyone else"—so wrote one of my students at the beginning of a semester elective called Mass Media and Propaganda.

Over the past three years, I have seen my students in this course come into the classroom distrusting the package on the shelf, the prices on the rack, and almost all the advertisements that bombard them from TV and radio and the printed media. Yet somehow, during the semester, their attitude shifts dramatically in the direction of increasing trust that the products they purchase will turn out to be as advertised. A description of the course unit that leads to this shift—including a proposal to English teachers and advertising-men and business-men in the United States based in part on that shift—is the subject of this talk.

The course looks closely at newspapers, television, and advertising. We try to determine, for example, if the *Chronicle* is more or less biased than the *Examiner,* or whether they both offer the same stuff. We mailed out requests to over one hundred newspapers all over the country, and the seventy or so which came back are being compared first for regional variations in reporting the news, and second for the treatment—or mistreatment—of wire-service copy. Our work with advertising and advertising claims—about which I'll tell you more shortly—got the Breck shampoo people so turned on that they're putting up $700 in a competition between Acalanes and two other high schools (University High School in Urbana, Illinois, and High School of Art and Design in New York) to encourage our teenagers to create their own full-page Breck ad which will run in the spring issue of a number of teenage magazines. The kids conduct attitude surveys in their neighborhoods, analyze short-wave radio propaganda broadcasts from places like Russia, Holland, and Cuba, and from the Voice of America, write storyboards for and produce TV ads, and—they test advertising claims.

Acalanes Mass Media Classes

Study of Effect on Students' Attitudes of Testing the Claims of Advertisements

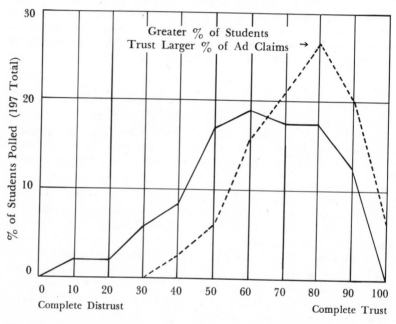

% of Products Purchased Which Students Feel Will Be "As Advertised"

The question: "What per cent of the goods you purchase will turn out to be 'as advertised'?"

Response at start of course: _____
Response at end of course: - - - - - - - -

Verification: Written evidence of above statistics will be produced on request. Above chart is for all courses, 1969–Fall '71.

On the first day of school I ask the students to fill out a questionnaire, one part of which reads: "If you went into a store and bought one hundred items, what per cent of those items would turn out to be 'as advertised'?" The results, to me at least, were predictable, and have remained pretty much the same at the start of each new semester. Some of the kids don't trust anybody, most distrust the larger part of what they hear—and a few are gung ho trusters of everything. But this profile (see chart) undergoes quite a change during the course, largely, I believe, because of the claim-testing project which each student embarks on. The project works this way:

1. The student finds a testable advertising claim from any medium.

2. He works out a procedure for testing the claim, using the scientific method, and submits the claim and testing procedure to me.

3. I verify that the ad is testable (and not something like "Yummy Dog Biscuits are better than ever"), and the procedure a rational and safe one.

4. The student then runs his test, makes his observations, and concludes the product is *as advertised, somewhat misleading,* or *not as advertised.*

5. At this point he presents his results to the class orally, and gets a thorough going-over. What he is about to do next is a bit cheeky, and both student and teacher want the report to be logical, clear, and honest.

6. Regardless of the results of the testing, the student then writes a covering letter for the report and sends both to the manufacturer and ad agency. The letter states clearly the nature of the class and the results of the test; and it asks for a response to the whole process, promising that any such response will get the complete attention of the class.

7. And then the wait. If we are lucky, about half the letters are answered. But those that do arrive are a great conclusion to the process.

Here are some examples of projects, including portions of the correspondence evolving from them:

ZEREX ANTI-FREEZE: Dana Giles tested Zerex's claim that "Zerex is guaranteed not to run out on you. " This test was run, by the way, on October 27 of last year—it is not the current ad. The can is punched, and liquid spurts out, only to stop within seconds. Her observations: "One of the holes stopped squirting out after a minute and a half, but the other two holes took over two and three minutes to stop squirting. Even after the squirting stopped, liquid continued to dribble out slowly. After five minutes, all liquid had stopped leaking, but would readily start dribbling again if the hole was touched."

Dana went on to observe that "the television commercial had more to it than met the eye. Photographic techniques altered the reality of what happened. On the basis of my test, I would conclude that this ad is somewhat misleading in its presentation. It is true that Zerex seals leaks; however, it does not do so as quickly or as completely as the public would be given to believe."

Soon after Dana's letter went to DuPont—but not, I hasten to add, as a result of it—the Federal Trade Commission clamped down on this can-stabbing commercial. Recently you may have seen the ad, saying "We're back!" And in small print you can now read the words "Contents 50 per cent Zerex, 50 per cent water under pressure."

Dana had mixed reactions to DuPont's response. The letter read in part: "I have read your data and conclusions and there are several questions that arise. I think when you answer them and make the necessary adjustments, you will want to reconsider your conclusions. (1) What size was the puncture you put in the can? (2) What form did the puncture take? A round hole or was it a slit? (4) How much pressure did you use? (6) How did you control the puncture for reproducibility?

"I can assure you there were no photographic techniques used to alter the reality that occurred. The conditions used to make the commercial reproduce that of an operating, circulating, pressurized automobile.

"I would be interested in your results after you rerun your test with some small refinements: (1) Circulation—30 G.P.M., (2) Pressure—15 P.S.I., (3) Puncture—20-30 mils wide slit. A slit is the most common radiator opening and not a round hole. You can use a modified automatic center punch. (4) Concentration—50 per cent with water.

"Thank you again for your interest in our product. Sincerely, etc."

Not an offhand reply. Defensive, to be sure. But can we expect anything else? Informative. Perhaps impatience suppressed. Instructive, too, since Dana had obviously overlooked some things.

IVORY LIQUID: Sandy Young tested Ivory Liquid's claim that it is so rich and thick, "it even whips." She indeed found that it whipped. But she took this a step further. As she writes:

"To find out if there was any particular value or significance involved with soap being able to whip, or that any type of soap is able to do it, I selected two other brands of liquid soap, Trend and Brocade. I then made the same test for these two types of soap. . . . Each type of soap was whipped for two and one-half minutes. The results were as follows:

"Ivory Liquid's claim was proved true. One cup of liquid was whipped for two and one-half minutes and grew stiffer and thicker and formed peaks. I found no real value or significance in the fact that Ivory Liquid could whip because the other two dishwashing liquids I used also whipped and proved actually to whip better than the Ivory Liquid."

Proctor & Gamble Company replied: "As you discovered, Ivory Liquid does, indeed, whip as mentioned in our advertising. Today's Ivory Liquid is the creamiest-feeling, mildest Ivory Liquid ever and our advertising was designed to emphasize that creamy Ivory Liquid can help the hands to the creamy complexion of youth. In this connection, we know, of course, that Ivory Liquid is not the only dishwashing detergent which whips, but we simply were equating its creamy consistency to its mildness by way of a visual, memorable demonstration."

It was signed by W. S. Carter of Public Relations who, by the way, will sign all letters to consumers from the PR department. It's a pseudonym used by the people whose job it is to answer letters like Sandy's.

DENNISON'S CHILI: Four students ended up working on the claim that "there are 106 chunks of beef in every can" of Dennison's Chili. They worked separately, and came up with different conclusions, a fact which led to an extra step which I thought put some zing into their report. After sieving and separating the chili sauce and beans from the "chunks," three of the students stated that they came up with far less than 106 chunks. One had many more. The problem, of course, lay with the definition of "chunk." How big did a piece of meat have to be—or how small—before it could be called a "chunk"?

The four of them took to the masses, and conducted a survey among one hundred students asking what size came to mind when people thought of a chunk of wood, meat, and rock. Using the rather clear-cut results, the students concluded that nothing smaller than a cube of meat, $1/4''$ on a side, could be called a chunk. Armed with this, then, they wrote American Home Products, the manufacturer, and stated that they felt the claim was somewhat misleading.

The gist of a thoughtful letter from the company's president, Mr. J. B. Shortlidge, was as follows: "What consumers . . . receive is meat in the form of chunks—we can't think of a more descriptive term—as distinguished from minute meat particles, and, because of our advertising, at least 106 of them. Your students may feel these chunks are small but we can only say that, given the nature of the product and the size of the can in which it is packed, they are appropriate. . . . The slogan with which your students take issue has been in use for five years and no consumer has ever asserted to us that she was misled by it. . . . We hope this letter clarifies the picture. If your students need additional information, please have them contact us. And, while we reach a different conclusion with respect to our advertising from that expressed by your students in their letter, we do wish to congratulate them for their efforts . . . in consumer advertising."

There have been others, too: one boy tested the claim that Zip-coded mail arrives faster—it didn't; another tested the money-back guarantee of five firms—each returned his money; another tested the ketchup claim, "comes out slowest"—it did! And another, a bit desperate for a project, counted to see whether there are indeed over six hundred tiny time pills in each capsule—(there are) .

This business of testing claims and telling an advertiser that he passed or failed the test involves exposure to words with people behind them. And even more important, the student, by writing to someone in the heretofore faceless world of big business, gets to know what it's like to compose for someone who might just snap back to him "Go to hell" instead of "John, you can do better than this. Work on your gerunds." The return communication is the most revealing part of the whole project: there *are* the words, addressed to *him,* the student, in all their sincerity or hypocrisy or vagueness or excitement. And the student *knows!* He knows right away whether he is being taken or sloughed off or listened to.

Many ad claims are untestable at the high school level, either because they indulge in what my students now so easily recognize as "puffery," or because we don't have the technical facilities or know-how to assess the claim. About 80 per cent of the ads tested turned out to be "as advertised"; about 15 per cent turned out to be "somewhat misleading"; and about 5 per cent are found "not as advertised." The fact that the *students themselves* reach these conclusions on the basis of their own tests and find 80 per cent of the ads tested "as advertised"—plus the gratifying response to the project from business and advertising—results in a shift in attitude (based on the earlier questionnaire administered towards the end of the course) , which shows that the students' attitude toward business and advertising is one of increased trust.

I would like, therefore, to urge English teachers in courses similar to this one, to start introducing their students to the semantics of advertising by testing ad claims and sending the results to business and advertising agencies.

Mendacious Messages from Madison Avenue
(and a Recommended Remedy)

Vincent P. Norris

Norris, Pennsylvania State University, accurately points out that few
ads are blatant lies and most deceptive advertising is subtle, difficult
to prosecute. Because the advertisers show little sign of self-regulation,
and the media are not noted for their reforming instinct (in areas from
which their money comes), Norris suggests that consumers take up their
pens as weapons.

"The market," said Anacharsis more than 2000 years ago, "is a
place set apart where men may deceive one another."

Although market mendacity is probably as old as the profit motive,
the contemporary denizens of Madison Avenue have honed the ancient skills of deceiving one's customers to a state of perfection un-
dreamt of in earlier times.

Defenders of advertising insist that only a tiny fraction of advertising is found by the Federal Trade Commission to be false, and
that this tiny fraction is the work of a few fly-by-night operators.
But as *The Nader Report on the Federal Trade Commission* amply
demonstrated, the FTC is underfunded, too many of its too few
personnel are political hacks, it is so subject to a variety of pressures that its posture toward business is characteristically supine;
even at its most aggressive it can act only within the confines of an
outdated law written under the influence of business lobbies. Even
so, a list of the recipients of the agency's cease-and-desist orders
reads, as Commissioner Paul Rand Dixon said, like a Who's Who of
American Business.

Years ago an advertising man said that only a very small portion of
national advertising (that done by manufacturers rather than re-
tailers) could be considered truthful in the sense that a scientist
uses the word. There is no persuasive reason to believe the situation
has since improved. Although the most blatant lies may have dis-
appeared (on second thought some of the current ones are pretty
blatant) the amount of less-than-honest advertising has no doubt
increased. As parity products (all brands of which are identical or
very nearly so) have proliferated, the need to lie has increased. It
is in those consumer-goods industries in which parity products are
the rule rather than the exception that the most intensive adver-

tising efforts are made, and logically so. If one's task is to convince an audience that a circle is different from a square, not much effort, ingenuity or deceit is required. It is when one sets out to prove that two circles of the same diameter are different from each other that he must make a herculean, hyperbolean effort.

That task is precisely the one so frequently assigned the advertising copywriter. "Our problem is," said Rosser Reeves, head of a large advertising agency, "a client comes into my office and throws two newly minted half-dollars onto my desk and says, 'Mine is the one on the left. You prove it's better.'" Surely anyone with a logical cast of mind will agree that such a task must require not only great effort and expense but a cavalier disregard for the truth.

Admen do not think of this as lying but merely harmless puffery: "It doesn't hurt anybody," said the advertiser quoted by Samm Baker in *The Permissible Lie* (obviously a book about advertising). That frame of mind has also been observed by Nicholas Samstag who, like Samm Baker, writes from years of experience in advertising. In *Bamboozled* (obviously another book about advertising), Samstag explains that after years of spending most of their waking hours dealing in half-truths, admen lose their ability to know where the truth is. Howard Gossage, a most unusual advertising man, once made the same point. Admen are innocent, he said, in the Biblical sense of the word: they are utterly incapable of distinguishing between good and evil.

A few other advertising men and ex-advertising men have tried to tell the public about the falsehoods and gimmickry in advertising. Two fairly recent examples are Edward Buxton's *Promise Them Anything* and Paul Steven's *I Can Sell You Anything*. It is nevertheless the case that nothing else which so incessantly intrudes into our lives goes so unexamined by the mass media as advertising.

Only half the adults in this country read even one book per year, according to surveys, and we spend annually a relatively paltry $3 billion on them, yet books are regularly reviewed by numerous periodicals.

Even fewer of us attend even one play per year, spending less than half a billion dollars for tickets. Nevertheless many newspapers and magazines review each season's offerings, telling even those of us who dwell far from the bright lights which plays to see, and which to avoid, on Broadway.

Nearly every American, on the other hand, is a consumer of ads. Television alone thrusts ads into 95 per cent of American homes, rich and poor alike; radio, into nearly 100 per cent. They appear to be free but they are not. We consumers pay for those ads every time we buy advertised products. In fact we pay not only for the ads, but for the monopoly profits made possible by the ads.

All told, ads cost us in 1972 more than $23 billion—which comes to more than $100 for every man, woman and child, or about $320 per household. That is almost seven times as much as we spent for books and plays, and it does not include the higher prices we are charged for advertised products, but only the cost of the ads themselves. If the higher prices (and monopoly profits) made possible by advertising were included, the cost per household would be much higher.

Let us take a moment to clarify that: The public believes, generally, that the purpose of national advertising is to inform us about products, or to "sell more." That is what Madison Avenue wants us to believe, for it sounds harmless enough if not downright beneficial. But it is a valid explanation of only a small amount of national advertising, such as that seen in the "Shopping Mart" section in the rear of the *New York Times Magazine*. The primary purpose of the great bulk of national advertising is certainly not to inform us or even to "sell more," but to create a degree of monopoly power for the manufacturer so that he can sidestep competition. So that Bayer, for example, can dominate the market and thus set a price for its aspirin which it could not possibly obtain if it were compelled to sell that aspirin as a fungible commodity (which it is) in a freely competitive market. This higher price not only covers the large advertising expenditures but goes well beyond that to provide the firm with monopoly profits. As the president of Alberto-Culver said, "The investment will virtually always return a disproportionately large profit." The FTC agrees, pointing out several years ago that in those industries which make heavy advertising expenditures, profits run 50 per cent higher than for American industry as a whole.

To return now to those $23 billions spent last year on advertising (one-fourth of which was spent by a mere handful of firms), further perspective may be gained by noting that it is more than was spent on all of higher education throughout the land. In every recent year, ads cost us five times as much as the space program. More, or perhaps slightly less, than the Vietnam war—depending on which Pentagon announcements are to be believed.

What did we get for our money? Who knows?

A few media make intensive efforts to answer that question for us and to make us better-informed consumers of ads, but they are lonely voices crying in the wilderness. Or crying, I should say, in the green (as in money) pastures of suburbia where reside not innocent lambs but those who least need protection. *Consumer Reports* and *Media & Consumer,* for example, give their readers valuable guidance but the people who read them are not the ones who most need to. In large part they are well-educated and affluent business and professional people who are not easy to con. That they read such media is evidence that they view advertising with a flinty eye. And, should they occasionally be gulled, they can afford it.

It is not the well-to-do but the poor, as recent studies have shown, who pay more. Unlearned in the wiles of the marketplace, they believe, as Warren Magnuson concluded after years of chairing the Senate Commerce Committee, that someone "up there" is looking out for them. They believe that people are not allowed to lie to them in newspapers and on television. (My own classroom inquiries indicate that most college students also believe that.) In their innocence they believe that if "it says on television" that Geritol is good for you and Bayer is better, they must be.

The national news magazines and better newspapers often report the FTC's actions against the more scandalously illegal advertisers but again, they reach comparatively few people, generally those who least need the help. More media could report such news, more thoroughly, to more people. They need not hire a Washington correspondent or even depend on the wire services. The FTC issues a steady stream of news releases, sometimes three or four a day. Any publisher or broadcaster can get on the FTC's mailing list and freely use the releases in his publication or over the air, as a service to his audience. Perhaps many of them don't know that. (Why don't *you* phone your local publishers and station managers and tell them about this free source of news. Tell them to write Arthur L. Amolsch, Director, Office of Public Information, FTC, Washington, D.C. 20580. Tell them you'd like to be kept fully informed about the FTC's activities. What do you suppose they'll say?)

But merely keeping the public informed about FTC actions, although helpful, would not be enough. The FTC cannot do everything that needs to be done, even if it were so inclined. It cannot act against ads which are false or misleading, but only against ads which are *illegal*. The name of the game on Madison Avenue, then, is to bamboozle the American public without quite breaking the law. To invent a permissible lie. To prove that the half-dollar on the left is better than the one on the right. And to get away with it.

To that end, the tricks in the ad agency's bag include weasel words, glittering generalities, the *suppressio veri,* the deceptive differential, the irrational appeal, bandwagon, the *non sequitur,* the veiled threat, and a number of exploitations derived (validly or not) from Sigmund Freud, J. B. Watson, and others. Cleverly used, all these devices are legal, being euphemistically termed "puffery." Also legal are inanity, tastelessness, crassitude, vulgarity, tawdriness, soft-core pornography, silliness, repetition *ad nauseum* and other offenses too numerous to mention.

Against all these the FTC must remain silent. As perhaps, in a free society, the government should.

But the media should not. If the public is served by being told that some books and plays, though within the law, are entirely without merit, does it not deserve to be equally informed about the ads which reach so many more people and cost them so much more money?

We are told this is unrealistic, that the media dare not bite the hands that feed them. That since advertisers pay two-thirds of the cost of publishing newspapers and magazines and the entire cost of commercial broadcasting, the media must dance to their tune. Instead of complaining we should be grateful to advertisers who make possible our low-priced publications and who provide us with radio and television programs absolutely free.

That may be the biggest lie of all. Although the money may pass through the hands of advertisers it is ultimately the consumer, as we have already said but wish to emphasize, who pays for all the advertising and who provides, in one way or another, every cent of revenue received by the media. A company that cons us into paying 98 cents for a 19 cent bottle of aspirin, spends a fraction of that inflated price on television advertising to con us further, and then tells us it is subsidizing our free television, has the *chutzpah* of the fellow who murdered his parents and then asked the court for mercy on grounds he was an orphan. The American people, however, have fallen for that line.

We know that it is possible for ad-carrying media to tell us about advertisers, their ads and their products, because some of them have been doing so. The same publications which carry the most incisive criticism of books and plays also seem to attract the greatest amount of book and theatre advertising. The *Wall Street Journal* provides excellent and critical coverage of advertisers, including its own. *New York* seems bent on outdoing *The New Yorker,* which has long delighted its readers with pungent commentary on admen and their works while at the same time almost reluctantly raking in their money. (Its salesmen do not call on you, grumbled an agency space buyer, they grant you an audience.)

Although totally dependent on the advertising business for advertisers *and* readers, *Advertising Age* sets a courageous example. Flouting the rule that trade publications are little more than centralized flackery, *Ad Age* takes advertisers by the scruff of the neck and gives them a shaking whenever, in *Ad Age*'s view, it is called for.

So far as most publishers and broadcasters are concerned, however, the past century could well be called the Age of Divine Right of Advertisers. But as Louis XIV's "L'état, c'est moi" eventually gave way to more egalitarian notions, it is high time the same fate befell Madison Avenue's "L'économie, c'est nous."

It would be unrealistic to expect the media in general, overnight, to begin commenting on ads as regularly and frankly as they now comment on the arts and other aspects of society. But it should not be a vain hope that eventually, if given sufficient prodding, a few more might venture diffidently into the field, perhaps to start a trend.

The most effective prod available to consumers is probably the letter-to-the-editor, which editors faithfully read as the best source of feedback about their readers' wishes. Editors not only read, they print for all to see, the most devastating letters about their publications' *non*-advertising content. But when have you seen a letter criticizing an ad?

Perhaps one reason we don't see such letters is that we don't write them. Have *you* ever written one?

If enough of us stopped merely fuming to ourselves whenever we are offended by meretricious ads and began writing to the media about them, it might be a first step. Futile as our individual efforts might seem to us, if editors began receiving letters criticizing the ads in their publications, they might get the idea that we consumers—their audiences—do not believe that ads are sacrosanct. And although we may not now directly supply the bulk of their salaries, they know that without us they have no salaries at all.

Bias in the Mass Media: A Student-Consumer Approach
to Analyzing News Products

Robert Cirino

By emphasizing the basic selection/omission process in all communication,
Cirino attacks the myth of "objectivity" in reporting. While some of
his stipulative definitions (e.g. *censorship, propaganda*) differ from those
of other writers in this collection, his context clearly explains his use
of these terms. Cirino, author of *Don't Blame the People* and *Power to
Persuade: Mass Media and the News,* is a member of the NCTE Committee on Public Doublespeak. This article was delivered as a paper at
the NCTE convention in Philadelphia in November 1973.

In order to have a common ground for talking about bias in the
mass media, please put yourself in the following executive or editorial position (but maintaining your own values and judgment)
and make the required decision as quickly as possible:

1. You are the president of a network television news department.
Who will you hire to give commentaries on a regular basis on your
evening news program: one or two commentators with established
names, or a number of different qualified commentators representing a wide spectrum of political viewpoints? (If there is more
than one, their turns would be rotated so that there would be only
one commentary each evening.)

☐ one or two with established names
☐ numerous, representing a wide spectrum

2. You are the copy editor of a large daily newspaper. On what page
will you place the following wire service story:

> A team of psychologists sponsored by the Surgeon Gen-
> eral has found that at least under some circumstances,
> repeated exposure to televised aggression can lead chil-
> dren to accept what they have seen as a partial guide
> for their own actions. As a result, the present entertain-
> ment offerings of the televised medium may be con-
> tributing, in some measure, to the aggressive behavior of
> many normal children.

Page_____

3. You are the general manager of a large wire service. You have
just received a story from your Saigon office written by one of your
most reliable and respected reporters who was on the scene in Cambodia. Part of the story covering military actions reveals how some
American troops were looting stores and houses. You feel that if

this information is sent out over the wires it might cause violent or hostile responses from different anti-war groups, and it might displease the Administration. Will you delete that part of the story telling of the looting, or leave the story intact?

☐ delete
☐ leave intact

4. You are the president of a national television network. The National Organization of Women (NOW) has presented you with the results of their extensive study showing that the commercials your network is carrying are sexist in nature—demeaning to women and depicting them in a limited number of roles compared to men. They are asking you to run—free—commercials that contest and counter this alleged stereotyped and demeaning depiction of women. They claim it is your ethical duty as well as your legal obligation under the Fairness Doctrine (the doctrine requires that broadcasters present all sides of controversial issues). Will you grant NOW any free time so they can air their "counter commercials"? If so, in what proportion to the offending commercials?

☐ no counter commercials will be allowed
☐ yes, in a proportion of _____ counter commercials to every _____ offending commercials

5. You are the president of a national network. Which *one* of the following events will you afford live coverage to:

☐ the fifth manned space trip to the moon
☐ a large anti-war demonstration in Washington, D.C. with an estimated 500,000 attending
☐ a pro-Administration Vietnam policy demonstration with an estimated 100,000 attending
☐ a U.S. Senate committee hearing on prison conditions and brutality
☐ a White House Conference on Hunger in America
☐ the installation of an archbishop

6. You are the president of a national television network. You have just given the President of the United States prime time to address the nation. In his speech, he defends his policies, attacks his critics and defines patriotism and loyalty in a partisan manner. Will you make prime time available to an opposing political party or parties for the purpose of responding to the President's speech?

☐ no
☐ yes, but only to the major opposition party
☐ yes, to all national opposition parties

7. You are the copy editor of a daily newspaper, and have decided

to use a photograph to go along with the day's coverage of the Watergate hearings. You have decided to use one of the many photographs of Chairman Sam Ervin from among many that have been made available to your newspaper. Some show him in an aggressive stance while others show him bored, alert, arrogant, attentive or dozing. Which one will you select? (Circle your choice.)

Regardless of how fair you tried to be, or what your viewpoints are, the decisions you made would produce a biased communication product—one that favors one viewpoint over another. This is no shortcoming on your part; even the best of editors or media executives, using professional journalistic criteria, could not make these decisions without producing a decidedly biased product. This being the case, a consumer will solve little by finding media executives with good motives; the consumer will still be relying on biased information products. Similarly, the buyer of a new car might find automobile executives with good motives, but the car might nevertheless be unsafe. With this in mind, the news consumers might better spend their time examining the final information product rather than the producer's motives, and establish an approach to judging and coping with biased information products.

This does not suggest that we, as consumers of news products, should ignore the producer's rational, professional standards or intentions. But it means we should develop the capacity to analyze mass media products apart from the motives and standards of the producers.

If the consumer judges the product rather than the intentions or performance of the producer, he will find it necessary to expand the meaning of censorship to cover more than the deliberate suppression of information. Censorship, as the term is used here, would include *any* decision, practice or assumption that results in the people being deprived of differing points of view or information. Under this definition, even "unquestioned" editorial decisions might be seen as censorship. For example, ABC, NBC and CBS refused to show a documentary, produced by a presidential commission, on population growth and the American future. The networks rejected it for professional reasons, saying it was too biased and it took a position on a controversial issue—something documentaries should not do, according to their policies. As a result, millions of people were not able to see this documentary.

Knowing that even a conscientious news agency can't avoid some degree of censorship in the routine editing and selecting processes that are required daily, the consumer would be wise to be concerned with whether one censorship decision by any single agency of the mass media is offset by the non-censorship of another. If it is offset, the consumer will have a chance of discovering the information from another agency, and the censorship (honest or dishonest) will be exposed and nullified.

The consumer approach also requires expanding the meaning of bias to deal not only with bias that results from deliberate slanting of information to favor a viewpoint or person, but also the bias that can result from professional, economic, technical or time considerations. In short, any information product that is affected by such considerations is biased. Since all information products are affected, all are biased. Thus the consumer does not ask whether or not there is bias, but asks the more significant questions of what kind of bias exists, who it favors and whether the public is being exposed to countervailing biases that can offset or expose existing bias.

This brings us to a definition of propaganda that evolves from the consumer's approach. Since all information products are biased to some extent and thus favor one perspective as opposed to others, the consumer views all *single* information products as being propaganda. They may include honest bias or seemingly justifiable censorship, but they are still propaganda.

Propaganda by itself is not anything for the consumer to be worried about, but a situation of propagandizing is. This can occur when a person or the public is being exposed to propaganda that comes from a single or limited number of viewpoints, unchallenged by competing propaganda in a comparably potent medium. In short, propagandizing occurs when the consumer is not being exposed to a real competition of viewpoints and information. Propagandizing not only restricts the consumer's choice, it prevents him from being made aware of the dishonest bias and censorship. Uncontested communicators are tempted to resort to blatant lies and deceptions because they are sure such practices won't be exposed. On the other hand, when there is a competition of viewpoints, opposing communicators are quick to point out each other's use of dishonest bias and censorship.

The type of bias created by decisions such as you just made can be differentiated from that produced by the selection of *words* or style of *writing*. Thus far, we have been discussing a non-verbal bias, the type that is created by the visual and audio decisions in advertising or broadcasting. Selectivity and association of images, sounds, tone of voice, inflection, and facial expressions are elements of advertising, but they are also elements of news products as well.

Going over the decisions you just made, you can see they involved selection of images and information, the emphasis of one aspect over another and the exclusion of negative or positive information. Take just one choice—your commentator for the nightly news. If you choose just one or two commentators (as the networks do), you are unavoidably choosing a person with a certain attitude that is communicated by style of dress, facial expression, posture and vocal characteristics. Uncontested, this person can communicate a strong bias completely outside of, or in addition to, what is said. Walter Cronkite's gestures and expressions of approval of manned space exploration serve as an obvious example.

These subtle non-verbal elements of bias are invariably integrated with the choice of words. Further, they have an emotional impact that is often greater than that of words. Since this is the age of television, it is essential that the teacher of English deal with this non-verbal bias as much as with verbal bias since it is our job to help students develop the capacity to analyze, understand and use the media through which society communicates.

How does the teacher of English help the student deal with the non-verbal bias in the mass media? First, it is essential that the teacher allows the student to be placed in the position of making the various decisions that create bias—just as you were a few moments ago.

Secondly, the teacher should encourage participation in the kinds of activities that will develop a student's ability to use non-verbal elements of mass media in communicating a message or describing people and events. For example, as an exercise to learn about the bias that can be intentionally or unintentionally produced by the selection of a photograph to go with a news story, students can select from among four or five photographs the one they think best characterizes an event or person that is the topic of the story. (Ideally, it would be a story both written and photographed by the student.) Next, the student can select a single photograph that will visually most *discredit* the event or person. Next, the student can select one that *exalts* the event or person.

Third, the teacher can request students to compare and analyze their own decisions with those of other students who did the exercise.

Fourth, the teacher can encourage the student to analyze critically cases, patterns, and possible effects of photograph selection by the mass media.

What can students gain from engaging in the above exercises and analyses? Stated in terms of "objectives," the student should be able to:

1. Explain why "objectivity" in producing and presenting information is impossible.

2. List the many decisions that were involved in the production of any mass media product, and describe alternate decisions that could just as well have been made, but weren't.

3. Detect and explain the elements of bias as they are evidenced in information products.

4. Distinguish, in many cases, between bias that is intentional, deceptive or dishonest and bias that is unintentional, unavoidable and honest.

5. Communicate ideas and describe people and events in a wider variety of non-verbal modes; to produce a more persuasive and, at the same time, more honest information product, and have an awareness of the elements that make it persuasive and honest.

6. Explain why exposing the use of intentional or dishonest non-verbal bias will tend to discredit the practitioner and thus inhibit the use of, or render less effective, such bias.

7. Explain how people are, or are not, being exposed to biases from all contrasting viewpoints.

8. Explain why equal competition among contrasting viewpoints is society's most effective way of exposing and reducing the dishonest use of bias.

Hopefully, the student may realize why it is of benefit to each individual and society at large to have the mass media offer a true marketplace of ideas featuring offsetting biases from all representative viewpoints. Ideally, it would be desirable to have the student:

1. Respect and support the honest rather than dishonest use of non-verbal elements of bias;

2. Support the right of the people to make up their own minds and oppose those who would restrict an individual's choice or take it upon themselves to present to the consumer "the responsible viewpoints";

3. Appreciate and take the risk of competing fairly and honestly with verbal and non-verbal bias, even if it means public or classroom rejection of cherished ideas or perceptions.

In ending, let me emphasize that it is especially important for teachers of English to so conduct themselves and their classroom activities in a way that demonstrates their own willingness to reveal their own bias, and to take the risk of allowing students to communicate and to accept whatever ideas they think best, even if the teacher feels that such choices are "dangerous" or "irresponsible."

Mad Magazine—Witness for the People

Richard Reeves

In our generation, *Mad* magazine has done more—more than any English teacher, any textbook, any association of English teachers, or any association of academics, reformers, or miscellaneous do-gooders—to inoculate young people against the daily propaganda blitz they experience. Without pretension or pomposity, the writers and artists at *Mad*—"the usual gang of idiots"—have been fulfilling the satirist's traditional role as society's gadfly. The *Mad*men are not the only satirists on the scene; certainly the advocates of Buchwald, Herblock, and Heller can make a case for their favorite's quality or sophistication. Nor is *Mad* always a masterpiece, each page a gem. But, overall, *Mad* reaches a greater audience, has a greater impact, and does a better job than any of its imitators or competitors, detractors or admirers. As Richard Reeves says, in the following essay, "*Mad* may be the most influential magazine in the United States— if you assume teenagers and other children are worth influencing."

My son is a wiseass. He answers the telephone with cracks like "Do you know where your children are tonight?" He answers most questions with questions—"How was school today?". . . "School?"— half the time you laugh, half the time you want to kick his teeth in.

He thinks Richard Nixon is a crook and a clown—and he does a fair Nixon imitation, for an eleven-year-old. He thinks George McGovern is just a clown and Teddy Kennedy should become a swimming coach. He suspects "Exxon" is the Greek word for rip-off. His favorite work of art is a photograph of the White House with a huge "Nixxon" sign in front and the caption, "But it's still the same old gas!" That was in *Mad* magazine's April issue.

He doesn't just read *Mad*—he memorizes, quotes, collects, and fondles it. So, he tells me, do all but one of the boys in Miss Piper's sixth-grade class at Main Street School in Denville, New Jersey. As far as I can tell, *Mad* is all he reads except for the TV schedule.

And, as far as I can tell from an informal but intensive survey of friends, so does every kid in the country. Certainly more kids than ever are, even though *Mad* has been an adolescent phenomenon since I was fighting acne and surging hormones twenty years ago. Not only has it gotten bigger, much bigger, but its circulation has suddenly begun surging up again in the past year.

Mad may be the most influential magazine in the United States—

if you assume teenagers and other children are worth influencing. Assume it or not, Jeffrey Richard Reeves gets his information from television and his viewpoint from *Mad,* and he and his friends will start voting and doing other things in 1980.

The people at *Mad*—they call themselves "*Mad*men"—are not in the influence business. They are out of the comic book business, out of Brooklyn and the Bronx and Music and Art High School, mostly Jewish with New York strains of street-tough Irish and Italian; the same people who gave you Sid Caesar's lines and, hero of heroes, Neil Simon. *Mad* may be New York's most successful export.

"We don't really know who our audience is," said William M. Gaines, the publisher who describes himself, accurately, as "a maniac." "We kind of publish for ourselves. We publish things because we like them."

Knowing something about the magazine business, I cleverly asked about market research. "Oh!" said Gaines, a huge rumpled man who looks like a fat Karl Marx and plans to vote for John Marchi for mayor, reaching into a desk drawer for a maroon leatherette folder. The pages were literally yellowed: it was the statistical breakdown of answers to four questions tacked onto a Hires Root Beer survey done in 1957 by Eugene Gilbert Youth Research. The sum total of the information was that twice as many boys as girls were then regular *Mad* readers, and thirteen- and fourteen-year-olds read it more often than fifteen- and sixteen-year-olds.

This time *I* said, "Oh!" But Gaines had more: a six-inch-wide sheet of dirty graph paper recording the sales figures for each issue since *Mad* was first published in 1952. Following the bouncing ballpoint dots, I figured out that the latest issue of *Mad* sold more than 2.4 million copies, a jump of more than 300,000 over the year before. From 1968 through 1972 circulation averaged under 2 million. (The circulation of *National Lampoon,* a satirical monthly, is also growing—from 486,000 last year to about 750,000 recently. *Mad*men call it the *Mad* of "the iconoclast crowd.")

Who are the new readers? "I think we're reaching a younger group," said Gaines. "I think we're holding onto young readers longer and getting back some old *Mad* readers, adults," said Al Feldstein, the editor, a Flatbush boy who got into comic books at Music and Art when he found out you could get $18 a page for drawing strips.

Gaines and Feldstein are 20 per cent of the *Mad* staff, ten people working in an eight-room suite at 485 Madison Avenue. That's publisher, editor, art director, production manager, two associate editors, three women handling subscriptions, and a stockboy. Gaines doesn't like to talk exact money figures, but suffice it to say that *Mad* makes a couple of hundred thousand dollars in profit per employee per year.

There are also "the usual gang of idiots," as the masthead calls them, the twenty or so free-lance writers and artists who are each paid $300 a page for their words and drawings in the eight regular issues *Mad* publishes each year. The artwork in the magazine is superb and *Mad* artists—especially Jack Davis and Mort Drucker whose *Time* and *Newsweek* covers often compete—are not doing it for the cash. Part of the attraction is the yearly trips—comic caravans to Europe, Africa, and Japan—that Gaines takes with his staff and regular contributors because he thinks it's good for morale and because he likes traveling and loves the best food and wine with his best friends.

Gaines's friends produce 48 pulpy pages every 45 days under the steady control of Feldstein—the publisher says he's not "the creative type," but he's the dominating type and Feldstein says he edits to make Gaines laugh—and inside a slick cover almost always graced by the grinning face of Alfred E. Neuman. The *Mad* symbol, ("What, me Worry?") Neuman, is a lop-headed, jug-eared, gap-toothed idiot boy—on the current issue he's sitting on the beach, building an elaborate sand castle when a large wave hits; when the wave goes down, the castle is still there and Neuman has been reduced to a pile of wet sand.

Besides the 2.4 million copies sold here for 40 cents each, the staff and usual gang of idiots produce seven foreign language editions, three 75-cent "Super Specials" a year with a mix of old features, and collect royalties on eight "Best of Mad" paperbacks. That's it, conglomerate fans, no advertising and no spin-offs—no posters, sweat shirts, records, key chains or Madboy clubs.

One conglomerate which might wish it were different is Warner Communications, which owns *Mad* after a series of corporate mergers that began in 1960 when Gaines's accountant told him no individual could pay income taxes on the kind of money *Mad* was making even then. "Warner leaves us alone because we're very successful and I'm very cantankerous," said Gaines, a 51-year-old multimillionaire. "We could make millions merchandising, but we don't want to rip off our kids and their parents. Warner's would love it, but I always chase away the smart boys by telling them to fire me. There are obvious advantages to being a maniac when you deal with corporate types."

The insides of the magazine are predictable and unpredictable. There is a potpourri of linear slapstick, sight gags on the pie-in-the-face level, and features like "The Lighter Side of Crime in the Streets," and parody and satire that my son sometimes needs help to memorize. ("Venus Envy," a women's lib satire, was a little beyond him.) If the magazine is changing, Feldstein says, it is a trend away from "Ha! Ha!" and toward a more knowing "Oh, boy!"

The most regular features (and I think the best) are television, movie, and magazine satires: "Gall in the Family Fare" . . . "The Heartburn Kid" . . . "Passionate Gun Love—the magazine for the devoted gun worshipper."

In "Gall in the Family Fare," by a moonlighting television writer named Larry Siegel, Starchie Bunker, "America's Beloved Bigot," gets a visit from his "old World War II buddy," who turns out to be Adolf Hitler. Next come two official types who want to see "Dolf"—they look like F.B.I. but it turns out they're CBS offering Hitler his own series with his own "adorable TV family . . . like a dumb wife, two moronic children and a pet wolf!"

In "The Heartburn Kid," the honeymooning not-so-nice Jewish boy from the Bronx meets his dream WASP girl on the beach and . . .

"Look, Kooly, I realize I have a wife! But I'll leave her for you! I'll get a divorce!"

"Benny, you don't understand! I come from a God-fearing, religious home! We believe in certain rock-bound principles . . . among which is the sanctity of Marriage and the Family Unit! Divorce is wrong . . . and cruel . . . and unthinkable! It's just NOT the American Way!"

"Then how do you feel about fooling around with a married man?"

"Now, THAT'S the American Way!"

In "Gun Love," featuring articles like "Tracking the Wily English Sparrow Through Brush and Blind," there is an editorial, "Opening Shots!", attacking gun registration legislation:

"You take away guns and people will find other things to kill with . . . like sticks and rocks, and ax-handles, and axes! . . . Every citizen has the right to bear arms. It was written into the Constitution by our forefathers in the 1700's. Take away the people's guns, you Washington Finks, and who's going to stop the Redcoats! . . . Why DO those Washington Pinkos want us to register our guns? . . . They want to hand us pens, and forms to fill out. And then they want to *embarrass* us! Because they know that many gun-owners can't write!"

And it goes on and on: in a "Near Future" strip, a fisherman chops a hole in the garbage to drop his line in the Hudson River; there are pot-shots at Joe Namath, Kung Fu, Bell Telephone, millionaires, waiters, parents, children . . . and everything. In "Boredom-12" one of the cops tries to save a suicide on a window ledge with this dialogue:

"Why would a nice guy like you want to kill yourself?"

"What's there to live for? Work is hard! Pay is low! Taxes are high! Politicians are crooked! Morality is crumbling! God is dead! And the world is about to explode in an Atomic War!"

"Is there room on that ledge for me? Move over and we'll jump together!"

Some of the best shots, of course, are at Richard M. Nixon—each week, two of the magazine's 100,000 subscribers cancel in rage at attacks on the White House—and some of them have been eerily prescient. In December, 1971, pre-Watergate, *Mad*'s back cover was a likeness of Nixon in the classic three monkeys pose with the inscription, "See No Evil . . . Hear No Evil . . . Well, Two Out of Three Ain't Bad!"

What does it all mean to me, to Jeff and his thirteen-year-old sister, Cindie, an occasional *Mad* reader, to you, to your kids? "It means . . . it isn't boring, that's what it means . . . like, you know, like the stuff you write," said my son the wiseass in the only usable quotes in a two-hour interview. It means good—to some extent, the kid can spot the sham piling up all around him. *Mad* is true; at least it tells a lot of truth that he doesn't hear from Nixon, Exxon, CBS, Miss Piper . . . and from me.

"The one thing we do know around here is that we have a tremendous responsibility to those kids, there might be 10 million of them if five see each magazine," said Gaines, with Feldstein nodding in agreement. "We hope we're not telling them anything except to think for themselves and not believe everything they read and hear on television or from politicians."

Have you ever thought that you might be turning them into hopeless little cynics?

"Maybe. I hope not. But we all need some cynicism. It's easier to get it from us than being smacked in the head 30 times before you know what the world is like. . . . We're fair, we knock every-body, regardless of race, color, or creed."

One parent I talked with, a 46-year-old editor with a twelve-year-old daughter, thought that discovering *Mad* might have been one of the best things that could have happened to her. "I think it made her secure in being skeptical," he said. "The questions about basic premises were already there. She was already aware that some-one out there was always trying to manipulate her. One reaction to that would be to withdraw and she would have been inclined to do that, but *Mad* makes it easier to counter . . . it really strengthens a young ego. On one level, she couldn't handle people, other kids, who were nasty, but *Mad* provides a range of come-backs. Kids quote them, they use them. In fact, *Mad* is a comeback at the whole world. . . . It's really a shortcut to a kind of sanity-preserving sophistication. . . . It does for them what the Marx Brothers, even the Three Stooges, did for my generation. It points up the difference between reality and appearance; it's that simple."

*Mad*men get a little antsy over that kind of philosophical or psychoanalytical crap. "Gee, the Marx Brothers," said Feldstein, "I mean that's going pretty far out. . . . No one, I mean no one here would compare us to . . . (his voice dropped) . . . the Marx Brothers are special, greatness . . . I don't know."

They're real people—Gaines dressed like a newsstand guy, Feldstein more Seventh Avenue with shiny clothes and a gold ID bracelet with a diamond chip, Jerry De Fuccio from my old neighborhood in Jersey City—they're still in touch, like the old editors I used to know at *The Daily News* who really watched television, really read and were interested in the stuff they put in the paper in those days. The *Mad*men are on Madison Avenue—they moved up from Lafayette Street a few years ago when Gaines became convinced there was a Phantom Thief in the old building—but they're not with it, and they weren't fooled for a minute by Woodstock, Rap Brown or Richard Nixon. When you look back, their viewpoint of the passing parade has often been clearer than *Time*'s or *Newsweek*'s.

When you look closely, *Mad* also turns out to be a magazine of old-fashioned morality. A couple of years ago, Vernard Eller, a professor of religion at LaVerne College in California, did a little treatise arguing that *Mad* was doing more to propagate the Ten Commandments than the churches of California.

"*Mad* magazine shows at least something of the same understanding of freedom that the Ten Commandments do," Dr. Eller wrote.

"Their magazine is dedicated to helping kids become free and stay free . . . the negativity of (the Commandments) wording is indeed the invitation for man freely to find whatever style of life suits him—as long as he avoids these few pitfalls that would destroy his freedom altogether. . . . The difference is that the Ten Commandments, upon seeing these, warn against them, while *Mad* makes fun of them."

A little too pompous for *Mad,* and it leaves out the magazine's eleventh commandment—"Thou Shalt Not Commit Hypocrisy"— but the good doctor's going in the right direction, even if Gaines and Feldstein felt compelled to write a brief introduction to his book that said:

"Criticism we can take; praise from his kind could kill us . . . We reject the insinuation that anything we print is moral, theological, nutritious or good for you in any way, shape, or form. We live in the midst of a corrupt society and intend to keep on making the best of it."

Plight of the American Language

Jean Stafford

Jean Stafford is a novelist, essayist, and short story writer whose *Collected Stories* won the Pulitzer Prize in 1970. "The official language of the United States is now cant," she says here: ". . . Radio, television, the press, and all those other agencies that are dedicated to lulling and hoodwinking the public into talking falderal have so gummed up our language with solecisms and mongoloid bastards ("Vietnamize," "bodifier," "commonality") and knock-kneed metaphors and gibberish that a new kind of censorship should be in order. . . ."

In the April 1806 issue of *The Monthly Anthology and Boston Review,* republished by Nancy Hale in 1963 in her anthology *New England Discovery,* there appeared an article entitled "A New Language Proposed" by William Smith Shaw, which read in part:

> Since the liberation of our countrymen from the tuition of a cruel stepdame, who fondly hoped that in the decrepitude of age she should be nourished and sustained by our labour and love, our citizens, while engaged in lawful commerce, have been exposed to violence and impressment. The licensed buccaneers and royal robbers of the ocean have divorced our citizens from their friends and families and compelled them to exert, in the service of a king, every muscle not palsied by fear of the thong and scourge. Remonstrance only admonishes them of their power of inflicting still greater injuries, and the specious plea of justification is that *similarity of language prevents discrimination between Englishmen and Americans.* It is now proposed to strike at the root of the evil and to construct a language entirely novel. [The ingredients of Shaw's concoction will consist of indigenous Indian, Negro, and Irish dialects.] When this language shall have become . . . universal in our country, we shall be in a world by ourselves, and will surround our territory by an impregnable wall of brass, and all sit down, each in his whirligig chair, and philosophize.

In 1806 Shaw was writing with his adder's tongue in his cheek. Today he would be persuaded that his proposition has been adopted, that the roots of our language have been infused with a bane more deadly than the nightshade. He would be gloomy. Besides the neologisms that are splashed all over the body of the

American language like the daubings of a chimpanzee turned loose with finger paints, the poor thing has had its parts of speech broken to smithereens: Setting the fractures and dislocations has been undertaken by tinkers with tin ears they have fashioned for themselves out of old applesauce cans; and now verbs are used as nouns and nouns are used as verbs ("This course is structured for students interested in the overall construct of existentialism," says the college catalogue) ; and upon its stooped and aching back it carries an astounding burden of lumber piled on by the sociologists and the psychologists and the sociopsychologists and the psychosociologists, the Pentagon, the admen, and, lately, the alleged robbers and bug planters of Watergate. The prognosis for the ailing language is not good. I predict that it will not die in my lifetime, but I fear that it will be assailed by countless cerebral accidents and massive strokes and gross insults to the brain and finally will no longer be able to sit up in bed and take nourishment by mouth.

Perhaps I am wrong, and it may already be in the terminal ward, soon to kick the bucket. Several years ago a citizen as concerned as I am about the grave condition of our dear old friend sent me an article that he had ripped untidily out of the late *Look* magazine. He had found the magazine abandoned on the seat of an airplane that he had boarded in Philadelphia for New York; during the two-and-a-half hours the plane circled La Guardia Airport before giving up and going back to Philadelphia to land and not to rise again, he read and reread the inflammatory propaganda, mesmerized like a nightingale being stared down by a cobra. The author, William Hedgepeth, billed by *Look* as a "pursuer and lover of the sun," advocates not euthanasia for the invalid but the amputation of all movable parts and, if breath stubbornly persists, burial alive. He begins with a panegyric to Janis Joplin, who was at the time ululating to a fare-thee-well throughout the land. "No pukey, careful-metered lines sung here . . . ('Ahhee WOOGPleaghhuh woo,' she erupts.) But everybody gets the point. The point is how she feels, and they are eager to pick up, share it with her, feel it with her. People don't speak this way to them anywhere else—not even at home." (Not even at home? The poor old folks on the yonder side of thirty, nodding in their rocking chairs in shawls and carpet slippers, haven't even caught on to McLuhan yet.) Hedgepeth continues:

> No one lays it on the line; no one translates deep-felt gut feelings into language and says it like they sense it. . . . Our language, in its present shape, just can't handle it; and people—particularly young people—are

becoming aware of this flaw in their tongue. . . . As a
vehicle for the huge input of new ideas and information, straight English is inadequate. And because, at
present, it's untrained to operate in this dimension,
people are feeling around elsewhere for ways to express
the new reality in words (or in wails, grunts, growls,
shrieks, or sounds no one's yet labeled) . . . . There'll be
no need to cling to formal grammar to convey meanings.
Speech doesn't have to be linear; it can come out as a
compressed overlay of facts and sensations and moods
and ideas and images. *Words can cramp your style.*
[Italics mine.]

This bring up the question of whether we have perhaps reached
a point in evolution beyond which there is no return; or can we
still go back to that peaceful valley in the province of the Rhine,
the Neanderthal, and—as we fashion our crude instruments from
unrecycled waste—rap in grunts, tell it like it is in whinnies and
baas, and, growling, mate to bring forth a race of such simon-pure
idealism and untrammeled honesty that it will be able in a trice
to demolish everything the Western world has been about for the
last 5000 years? Will we then have achieved the golden age of what
Mr. Hedgepeth calls "interpersonal communication"? He does
not, I think, hope for such a paradise in the immediate future,
because, he says, "Until we all become telepathic, we can't hope
to grasp more than a hazy fraction of what's in another's head; but
meanwhile we have to clear our existing channels of communication
of all the subterfuge and conflict-laden verbosity that stand between
us and what we could be."

In this last article of his faith, I am with him 100 percent, and
I think we might begin by giving the heave ho to his expressions
"existing channels of communication" and "conflict-laden verbosity," which have to me less meaning by far than the heehaws
given voice to by the donkeys in the pasture across the road
from me.

Radio, television, the press, and all those other agencies that are
dedicated to lulling and hoodwinking the public into talking
falderal have so gummed up our language with solecisms and
mongoloid bastards ("Vietnamize," "bodifier," "commonality")
and knock-kneed metaphors (in *The New York Times Book Review* on September 2, 1973, I read in the review of a new novel
that one of the characters was "haloed with clout"; my only comment is "Faugh!") and gibberish that a new kind of censorship
should be in order; the board should be made up only of persons
demonstrably literate, precise, immune to the viruses of jargon

and whimsey, and severe in their quarantine of carriers of the aforesaid.

At the same time that we have relaxed the prohibition of obscenities in the press and on the air and in the movies, we have clamped down on straightforward speech, and euphemisms teem; they do so with such a thunderous racket that it is next to impossible to tell what anybody is talking about. Once when I was listening to a detective describing on television the defusing of a bomb in the $2 million TWA ransom plot in 1970, I thought how bewildered I would have been if I had not tuned in at the beginning but had only picked up, ". . . we continued to render the suspected object inert." The fuzz are ever so keen on genteel pidgin: "The intoxicated individual exited the vehicle." You know full well that if the *drunk man who got out of the car* said, "*Exited* is not a transitive verb; it must be followed by a preposition," the arresting officer would relinquish his white gloves and, saying, "Up yours, mother," would clap on the handcuffs. As liars are called "pathological" and on these grounds are excused because they are "sick" and are treated with a lenity that would not be accorded plain garden-variety liars, so sinners and boors and bores are said to suffer from an inability to "relate." *Relate,* except when used in the sense of "to recount," requires the preposition *to* just as *exit* must be accompanied by *from.* My friend Laurence Lafore, the historian (it was he, by the way, who was on that plane from Philadelphia and found Mr. Hedgepeth's hymn of praise to Anthropoidese), puts the matter thus in a pamphlet of rules he gives all his students: "To say, 'He does not relate,' is not more sensible than to say, 'He does not.'" These sad sacks who can't relate are often further described as having "nothing going for them." What should be going for them? Should an agency supply them with tops and windup toys and free tickets to a carrousel? There's one thing that's going for just about everybody, whether he relates or not, and that is television, which spreads new plagues with the speed of light.

The writers of advertising copy, while they may be exemplary husbands and fathers and citizens, are blackguards by trade, and the one who thought up "Winston tastes good like a cigarette should" ought to be put into stocks for a month and be fed mutton soup through a tube. And so treated should be his colleague who, with odious smirks, compounded the crime with the sadistic follow-up, "What do you want, good grammar or good taste?" We are now mercifully spared this disgrace on television, since the tobacco companies can no longer hawk their poison on the air; but the damage has been done. Let us examine the willful coquetry of this illogic: If we assume that the pranksters have sufficient vocabulary to get them through a simple intelligence test, they know that *taste* has two meanings, and they are, therefore, with galloping whimsey, inventing an ambiguity out of whole cloth (except that it is not whole but is as leaky as Swiss cheese). *Taste* in the sense of "flavor," an attribute of a physical thing, cannot be offered as an alternative to *taste* in its meaning of discernment or critical judgment or the appreciation of fitness. The two cannot be equated any more than, say, birdsong and geology. It is a lousy, stupid joke. And a dangerous one: Toddlers, who have not yet learned to smoke but have begun to learn to talk, can and do pick up most insalubrious, most deleterious habits from the mischievous rascals of the airwaves. One summer day—*after* the ban—there stole upon my ear a chorus of lilting children's voices, and, going to the window, I beheld a band of little girls on their way to Brownie camp. Their marching song was "Winston Tastes Good," and then came the defiant battle cry, "What do you want, good grammar or good taste?" What *I* wanted was to go out and tan the backsides of the whole troop, wash out their mouths with brown soap, and have their teenaged leader cashiered from her command.

Countless useful, onetime-respectable words have been so defaced and debased and deformed that those of us who look upon ourselves as the custodians of the mother tongue find our vocabularies diminished. We hesitate to use a word lest it be misconstrued in the incorrect but faddish sense. One functional word I miss is *irrelevant*. *Irrelevance* has come to denote the condition of "not being with it" or "not making the scene," of not being involved in a cause, whether it is the legalization of marijuana, the right to substitute the peace symbol for the stars in Old Glory, the renunciation of celibacy by the clergy, the decapitation of all policemen and all members of the standing army, or the movement to unman sexists.

Lately the word *ethnic* has taken a fearful trouncing and for all practical purposes has, I'm afraid, been kayoed for keeps. I was invited once to an "ethnic" dinner party. The eight guests were American-born Caucasians: One was a Jew, one was of German descent, one of Hungarian, one of Norwegian, the other four of Scotch-Irish-English. Our first course was sashimi, a Japanese dish of raw pickled fish; the entrée was couscous, the staple of Tunisia; our salad was Maste khiar, a Pakistani concoction of cucumbers and yoghurt (I found it rather nasty); and for dessert we had gingered kumquats. The whisky beforehand was from Tennessee, and the wines were French. In the original sense of the word,

our menu (save for the vinous and spiritous matters) was indeed
ethnic, but we were not an ethnic gathering. Nor would we have
been if we had consisted of a Puerto Rican, a non-naturalized im-
migrant Pole, a black from Mississippi, a Copt, an Israeli, a
Sardinian newly arrived from Cagliari, a Ukrainian, and a Pres-
byterian patchouli oil merchant from the Seychelles. For, when
the word first came into English in 1470 (my authority is the OED),
it meant, "Pertaining to nations not Christian or Jewish; heathen,
pagan." If our dinner party had been held any time between
that date and 1851, we would have been securely within the ethnic
pale. After 1851 the word took on a larger meaning and one
closer to its root; it came to be synonymous with *ethnological,* the
adjective deriving from "ethnology, the science which treats of
races and people, their relations, their distinctive characteristics,
etc." The etymon is *ethnos,* which means simply *nation* and is
to be distinguished from the largest social order, *demos.*

In 1972, therefore, our group was, according to the new meaning,
no more and no less ethnic than if we had been a Bengali, a
Berber, a Hopi, an aboriginal Australian of the Gurindji tribe, a
practitioner of voodoo from Port-au-Prince, a Shintoist from
southern California, and a Gabonese pygmy with a pantheon made
up of animal, vegetable, and mineral deities. By the same token,
our menu was no more and no less ethnic than if it had begun
with pâté de foie gras and gone on to haggis and turnips, followed
by a Mexican avocado salad and topped off with baklava. (We'd
all have been so sick we wouldn't have given a hang about our
ancestry.)

In the present heyday of linguistic buffoonery, the word has been
spirited far away from its source, and it is used so broadly and
so loosely that it has little meaning left. I once read in an article
about Betty Friedan in *The New York Times* that as a girl growing
up in the Middle West ". . . she was intelligent and a Jew. Her
friends overlooked her appearance and brains, but when it came
time for the pubescent savagery of sorority pledging at Peoria High
School, *ethnics* [italics mine] could not be forgotten." The lexico-
graphers of *Webster's New International* (the second edition; I
do not countenance the third), of the OED, and of *The American
Heritage Dictionary* do not list the noun *ethnics,* and I do not
know what it means. (I can guess, but I don't choose to.) In
the next sentence, though, I got a clue when I read that, not having
been asked to join a sorority, "the outcast . . . vowed. . . ." Am I
to take it that to be ethnic is to be an outcast and that *ethnics*
are the stigmata by which the pariah is recognized? Are they akin
to genes? Or are they *imponderabilia, je ne sais quoi,* like sex

appeal or mother wit? The term, as Ms. Friedan's apologist uses it, seems to be one of opprobrium among the rednecks of Illinois.

Elsewhere, however, it emanates glamour, and on another page of the same edition of the *Times,* I read, *"Ethnic* is the word for fashion's here and now. It started with the young and their reaction against mass production, which left them craving individuality. . . . If you enjoy zipping around the city, shopping for the real, hand-made thing—and in many spots speaking in a foreign tongue. . . ." So, then, are ethnics interchangeable with exotica? With handmade articles? How lucky is that hypothetical miss breathlessly flitting from East Side to West Side and all around the town, buying an evzone jacket here and a jellaba there, a Peruvian cartridge belt in a super little shop reeking of llama curds and whey, a pair of Masai ear stretchers and a nose torment to match, a Chinese laundry yoke, and a great big Lithuanian coat made of sheet metal and reindeer hide and buttoned with genuine cobblestones. From ghetto to ghetto she trips, this bonny lass, in her high-principled craving for individuality and the real ethnic thing; and remember that in many spots she will, if the *Times* has its way, be speaking in a foreign tongue. Undaunted, we presume, by Arabic and Latvian, and managing, in pidgin Kurdish, to bargin for a pair of papush with tinkly bells on the ethnic twinkle-toes. Flipping a few pages further through the *Times,* that good, gray comic book, I found that Gimbel's, catering to "the sportive lifestyle" (don't get me started on *lifestyle*; I'm rabid enough as it is) was offering "Folkloric Wool Jacquard Ponchos." I suspect that *folkloric* is the vernacular for *ethnic.* I would like to point out, Mr. Up-to-the-Minute Gimbel, that M. Joseph Marie Jacquard was an astute businessman who did not fool around with any old-timey folkloric whimwhams: By 1812, 11,000 of the looms he invented were in use in *factories,* and I've little doubt that the industry must now show a tidy annual profit.

Although the terminal letter of the word is, so far, still *c,* I cannot help feeling that in time it will be replaced with *k,* and then *ethnik* will have something in common with *beatnik* and *nudnik.* The fact is that everybody on earth is ethnic, just as everybody is *foreign* except within the limits of his own territorial imperative.

Other words have been kidnaped, so to speak, from their rightful dwelling places, and the ransom asked for the return to their homes is too high ever to be paid. Such a word is *charisma.* I am not sure, but I believe it became fashionable during the Kennedy administration, and at the start it was used more or less correctly to describe one of the President's assets, which was—and I quote again from the OED—"a rare quality or power attributed to those persons who have demonstrated an exceptional ability for leadership and for securing the devotion of large numbers of people." Unfortunately the admen and the gossip columnists got their grubby hands on the word, and now it is used by furriers to tout autumn-haze mink jackets and by perfumers (by the way, there is a perfume on the market said to be made of "strawberry musk"; since when does a strawberry have a glandular sac beneath the skin of the abdomen of the male that excretes *musk?*), and by the press agents of Hollywood starlets. It has come to be vaguely synonymous with *charming,* and it has acquired a worldly aura. It derives, in fact, from the Greek word meaning "grace," and when it was used anciently by theologians, it meant "a gift of God." What a beautiful word! How rare and subtle an essence it defines, and, therefore, how carefully and seldom it should be used!

We are scarcely a nation now at all; we are, rather, a conglomeration of very nearly countless incoherent splinter groups. It seems to me that, paradoxically, it is our very conformity of speech and passing passions that have exploded the integer to which the founding fathers pledged their lives, their fortunes, and their sacred honor. And it seems to me, further, that this conformity has come about—a great part of it at any rate—through the reliance on platitudinous invectives, lifeless abstractions, and generalizations. News now travels instantly, and so does the language in which it is couched: Let someone of importance in Washington misuse *hopefully,* and before the hour is out, a cesspool repairman in Waukegan is saying to a customer, "Hopefully the pipe ain't broke too bad," and a hostess in Newport is saying, "Hopefully the sun will shine on the day of my *fête champêtre,*" and college professors in Massachusetts and wheat farmers in Wyoming and editorial writers in Virginia are all eagerly saying and writing down this nice, shiny, new boo-boo. Within a week the unwholesome gobbet has been assimilated into the language and has settled permanently.

If everyone is to have a radio or a television set and is to be subliminally infused with the homogeneous palaver of the announcers and commentators and your friendly Chase Manhattan banker and the purveyors of mouthwash, eyewash, and hogwash, what is going to become of regional speech? Who will carry on the rich oral traditions of New England and the South and the West? I reckon that convicts and children, who have the most time on their hands, will go on contriving slang and jokes, and, God willing, the wellspring will not be polluted and will not go dry, and hillbillies and pickpockets and able-bodied seamen and timbercruisers and southern politicians will go on sweetening the pot.

But the official language of the United States is now cant. As I said at the beginning, the condition of the *real* language is critical. Many of the neoplasms are malign and may be inoperable (e.g., *escalate, Vietnamize, input*), and about all we can do is pray. Some bird in the Watergate hearings, testifying to his true-blue, snow-white innocence of any knowledge of the "fruits of the bug," said, "Myself and two other individuals proceeded to the aforementioned location on Route XYZ, and Mr. Bandersnatch telephonically indicated to me that his answer to Mr. Jabberwock's inquiry was negative."

If H. W. Fowler, whose *Modern English Usage* is the most dazzling record of a temper tantrum ever written, were alive today, he would die.

How We Debase the English Language

Melvin Maddocks

In response to Jean Stafford's essay, Melvin Maddocks, columnist for the *Christian Science Monitor,* argues against her presentation: ". . . it's a bit sad that language-evangelism has to be delivered as a sermon rather than conducted as a conversation." Paired thus, directly adjacent to each other, the Stafford-Maddocks articles are designed to provoke the reader to weigh these two viewpoints. But the reader is also encouraged to speculate if Maddocks would apply his critique to *other* articles within this book.

Talk about Watergate to some people, and they'll shake their heads in sorrow and give you a lecture on the decline and fall of the English language.

Can the republic survive an adverb like "telephonically" at this point in time? That's their question, and they may be right. At least the Bible appears to be on their side.

For the final word on the confusion of life and the confusion of language there is the Tower of Babel (Gen. 11). "The whole earth," it will be remembered, "was of one language, and of one speech."

But the descendants of Noah had become arrogant, self-exalting: "Go to, let us build us a city and a tower, whose top may reach unto heaven." And the Lord said: "Go to, let us go down, and there confound their language, that they may not understand one another's speech. So the Lord scattered them abroad from thence upon the face of all the earth."

To people who talk or read or write with a degree of pleasure in words, this exile has always seemed a tragedy second only to the exile from Eden.

George Orwell, a great brooder about language, made "Newspeak"—semantics of lying—one of the major aspects of damnation in *1984.*

In an image that could have come out of Dante, the English critic Cyril Connolly spoke of the "pollution" of the "river" of language before the pollution of actual rivers became a popular crisis.

Now here is Jean Stafford, an excellent fiction writer whose "Collected Stories" won a Pulitzer in 1970, continuing the Jeremiads in "Plight of the American Language" in the *Saturday Review/ World*.

Is America a "divided nation"? Let other people worry in terms of politics. Miss Stafford worries in terms of language: "We are scarcely a nation now at all; we are, rather, a conglomeration of very nearly countless incoherent splinter groups." In a word, Babel.

It may not be an exaggeration to call the Staffords and the Orwells evangelists. They know of no sin more horrific than the debauching of language, and they fulminate against it in the Sunday style of Cotton Mather. Miss Stafford's Seven Deadlies read rather like this:

1. "Knock-kneed metaphors," like "haloed with clout"—a *New York Times* disaster which left Miss Stafford speechless except for a "faugh!"

2. Ghastly new words, like "commonality" and "bodifier"—the "daubings of a chimpanzee turned loose with finger paints."

3. "Parts of speech broken to smithereens." For instance, verbs used as nouns tooled into verbs, like "Vietnamize."

4. Obscenities. No examples necessary.

5. Euphemisms. Why euphemisms should flourish at the same time—virtually in the same breath—as obscenities is a contradiction Miss Stafford cannot explain. Who can? Yet four-letter words coexist weirdly with circumlocutions like: "We continued to render the suspected object inert." Translation: "We defused the bomb."

6. Incorrect grammar. Miss Stafford cannot resist adding to the punishment already laid on the author of "Winston tastes good like . . ." Her sentence, in fact, is straight out of Mather: Let the culprit "be put into stocks for a month."

7. The distortion of a noble word, stretched "so broadly and so loosely that it has little meaning left." A proper wailing goes up over the vulgarization of "charisma," originally meaning "gift of God"—a divine favoring.

For every sin Miss Stafford, like most language-evangelists, has a matching sinner. They are called radio, television, the press, admen, the Pentagon, dictionary editor, and jargon-laden academicians. The kindest names she can find for them are "linguistic buffoons" and "tinkers with tin ears."

It is a fine, soul-thrilling experience to hear Miss Stafford call down

fire-and-brimstone on the worms who keep misusing "hopefully."
How her eyes must blaze when she says: "The official language of
the United States is now cant."

Still, it's a bit sad that language-evangelism has to be delivered as
a sermon rather than conducted as a conversation. The awful
truth is that nobody's prose is perfect. Connolly didn't find Orwell's style all that distinguished, and Miss Stafford's colloquial-
isms ("sad sacks," "boo-boo," and "kayoed for keeps") seem below
her best form.

Back to school with everybody!

Semantics, Attitudes, and the Training of Teachers

Howard F. Livingston

Livingston is concerned that educational journals "are filled with controversies over which is the best grammar while the semantic implications of the My Lai massacre, abortion legislation" and a host of other issues are totally ignored. He identifies causes for this neglect and suggests ways to improve the quantity and quality of teacher training in semantics. The author teaches at Pace University in New York; this article was read as a paper at the Conference on English Education in Des Moines in April 1970.

Probably the best way to begin this paper on Semantics, Attitudes, and the Training of Teachers is to begin with a definition of semantics. This pays homage to the amenities of rhetoric and at the same time offers one the opportunity to illustrate two semantic principles:

The first is to correct myself—I am not going to present you with *the* definition of semantics. I can't; in fact, nobody can. To quote Irving Lee: "Words don't mean; people mean." All I can do is tell you what I mean when I use the term semantics and assure you that most people in the field will agree. The second principle concerns itself with the process of defining. It was Bertrand Russell, I believe, who reminded us that a definition is a verbal stratagem that enables the definer to do what he wants to do anyway. The process of defining is a process of exclusion as well as inclusion. Now, what do I mean by the term "semantics"?

To me, semantics concerns itself with the analysis of language operations as language operations relate to human behavior. Semantics concerns itself with the multi-relationships that exist between symbols (primarily language), their referents (that for which those symbols stand—reality), and the effect of those symbols on those who use them (people). Semantics tries to make clear the processes by which human beings formulate situations into words and react to these linguistic situations. To me, the popular definition—"semantics is the study of meaning"—is somewhat misleading and inadequate and leads to that idiotic apothegm—"Oh, it's just a question of semantics," implying one, the speaker and listener really are in agreement; and two, the study of meaning is an exercise in nit-picking. Yes, semantics is the science of meaning, but its efficacy is best derived from the How, When, and Why of meaning as well as the What.

Writing in the *English Journal* (November, 1969), Professor
Charles Weingartner defines semantics as the study of language
operations in real human contexts, with emphasis on the human
consequences of these operations. His definition places the processes of meaning-making at the center of language study. Unfortunately, semantics is not at the center of language study; its presence in the curriculum of English is barely discernible. And when
it is taught, it is usually treated like an arcane system of principles
and techniques, totally unrelated to human beings in language
situations. Yet the rationale for the inclusion of semantics in the
study of English begins with the aims and purposes of education
in general. Education in a democracy has the fundamental responsibility to educate free, independent minds, capable of exercising
judgments and distinguishing truth from half-truth. In an age
where the mass media, the government, and the business community swamp us with so much verbal garbage, separating the real from
the unreal and the meaningful from the meretricious becomes a
matter of national survival.

> Generals, clergymen, advertisers, and the rulers of to-
> talitarian states all have good reasons for disliking the
> idea of universal education in the rational use of lan-
> guage. To the military, clerical, propagandist, and au-
> thoritarian mind such training in language seems pro-
> foundly subversive. To those who think that liberty is
> a good thing . . . a thorough education in the nature
> of language, in its uses and abuses, seems indispensable.

Despite our articulated aims as educators, and despite our aims as
English educators (I assume most of us agree with Prof. J. N.
Hook's "Classic Statements on Teacher Preparation," *English
Journal*, April, 1963, that the good—not superior, mind you—the
good high school English teacher should have a detailed understanding of how language functions, including knowledge of the
principles of semantics), despite this, the lack of attention given
to semantics—the human meaning-making processes—in the teaching of English and in the training of teachers of English seems, to
quote Prof. Weingartner, "nothing less than incredible."

What accounts for this condition in English education? What are
the prevailing attitudes towards language study, towards the study
of meaning, towards semantics?

Language study in the English classroom has been—and still is, by
and large—equated with the study of grammar. The study of language *is* the study of grammar. Whether teachers in the English
classroom have their students diagram sentences in the traditional
mode, or construct trees in the transformational mode, or chop
sentences into their immediate constituents in the structural mode,
these activities seem to satisfy our responsibility for language study.

Human beings in language situations, i.e., meaning-making, i.e., semantics is on the periphery of language study. Our journals are filled with controversies over which is the best grammar while the semantic implications of the My Lai massacre, abortion legislation, combat pay in Cambodia, and what Vice-President Spiro Agnew really means are totally ignored. Our students are demanding an education that is relevant; the N.Y. State Board of Regents has asked the school systems to develop relevant curricula, and we, in the name of language study, continue to fill the English classrooms with diagrams, trees, or structures, depending upon which linguistic church we belong to. Only now, we don't call these activities grammar; we call them linguistics. What astute semanticists we really are! Why not teach our students how to perform such feats of verbal legerdemain? Incidentally, recent studies still haven't shown any correlation between knowledge of grammar and the ability to write or read.

So much for attitudes towards language study. What are the prevailing attitudes towards language and meaning? Towards semantics? It seems to me that the problem here is one of naiveté. Everyone is quite sure that he knows what he means. Why not? Haven't English teachers taught generations of students to regard the dictionary as the arbiter of meaning thereby implying that the meaning of words once ascertained are fixed forever? (Incidentally, as a teacher, have you ever contradicted the dictionary? Should you? Can you?) Moreover, it seems that today it is not really necessary to understand what the other fellow means. In this age of Aquarius it will suffice to sense what he means. After all didn't George Wallace, Hubert Humphrey, and Richard Nixon all come out for "law and order" and "peace with honor"? As communicators, making, sending, and receiving meaning, we hold a naive assumption about language and the communication process: we expect to be understood—how much more realistic if we expected to be misunderstood. Possibly, the following diagram of a communications situation [see next page] can illustrate the difficulties communicators must contend with in transmission of meaning.

An awareness of the complexity of this communication reality might change some naive attitudes about meaning and understanding, and lead some, perhaps, to recognize the validity of semantics in the English classroom and in teacher training.

Another attitude that might account somewhat for the absence of semantics in the English curriculum is the cult-like behavior of some general semanticists who, in their apotheosis of Alfred Korzybski, tend to neglect the contributions of other scholars interested in the same linguistic phenomenon. Be that as it may, it would be foolish for English educators to throw out the baby with the bath water. S. I. Hayakawa, Wendell Johnson, and Anatol Rappaport have much to offer in the study of language, thought, and behavior.

Model of a Communication Situation

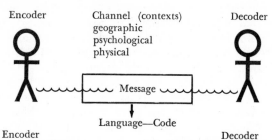

Encoder	Decoder
1. Seen (physiological filters)	1. Heard (physiological filters)
2. Perceived (psychological filters)	2. Conceived (psychological filters)
3. Evaluated (past experiences, attitudes, biases)	3. Evaluated (past experiences, attitudes, etc.)
4. Encoded (sub-verbal language)	
5. Encoded (verbalized—2, 3, 4 occur simultaneously)	

These then are the prevailing attitudes one encounters when seeking the inclusion of semantics in the English syllabus: one, grammar, albeit sterile, firmly entrenched and representing the totality of language study; two, a disdain for the science of meaning, based on an unhappy combination of ignorance, naiveté, and insecurity. It is this insecurity that leads me to a discussion of semantics and teacher training.

As I see it, the problem in teacher training is twofold—quantity and quality. First, thousands upon thousands of English teachers haven't the foggiest notion about the nature and operation of language simply because certification requirements ignore language and meaning. A cursory examination of course requirements shows that more English education departments *require* the history of the English language than *offer* a course in semantics.

Do we really believe the great vowel shift is more important than the awareness of physical and geographic context in the analysis of Spiro Agnew's Montgomery, Alabama speech? Do we really believe that Grimm's law is more relevant than an understanding of the semantic implications of the My Lai massacre?

To me, it is a matter of great concern and frustration: concern, because we are ignoring the study of meaning in the training of teachers; and frustration, because I don't know what to do about it.

While quantity is the more critical problem in semantics and teacher training, quality is another and by no means an unrelated problem. There are about 200 courses in Language and Meaning given on the undergraduate and graduate levels in this country. In too many of them, unfortunately, semantics is studied as an end in itself. While this is no doubt warranted in terms of scholarly inquiry, it leaves much to be desired in terms of teacher training. Too many teachers and teachers-to-be leave such courses with a list of principles that they may or may not understand (depending on whether you insist upon an operational definition of "understand"), and too many of them are unable to apply these linguistic insights to the language situations of everyday life. They may know I. A. Richard's first canon of symbolism and his symbol, referent, reference triangle, but they ignore his injunction that insists that language is always produced by human beings for human purposes to share human meanings. What seems to be needed is a course in applied semantics. Such a course might explore the semantic implications of the following or similar current issues:

1. Abortion Legislation— (What is "life"?)
2. My Lai Massacre— (Relate to language)
3. Israeli Problem over Question: What-Who is a Jew?— (Moses, Jesus, Marx, Einstein, Sammy Davis, Jr., Father G. Baum, S.J.)
4. Agnew's Montgomery Speech— (Geographic context as a determinant of meaning)
5. Machine Translation— (A 16-million dollar failure)
6. Science, Language, and the Brain—Language (metaphors and reality)

One can uncover a multitude of similar exercises for such a course based on real language situations and involving meaning-making.

Let me close by quoting Ashley Montagu, the noted cultural anthropologist, who shares my concern:

> The way we talk about ourselves and our institutions, the way in which we use long established "respectable" terms, leads us to make unrealistic and destructive evaluations of ourselves, of others, of the man-made world, and of the world of nature. It is seldom understood that the world we perceive is the world we see through words, that the world of experience is the world of arbitrarily conferred meanings. Each of us has learned to see the world not as it is, but through the distorting glass of our words. It is through words that we are made human, and it is through words that we are dehumanized.

Let Them Eat Wonderbread

Peter Klappert

"Poetry and the other verbal arts, can, in fact, act as a corrective for political abuses," says poet Peter Klappert of Harvard University. Discussing the relationships between poets and politicians, Klappert observes that professional politicians seem to rely more and more on the imprecise use of language. This is not a matter of negligence and ineptitude, he points out, it is a matter of calculation and skill.

Politics has become our new national sport, complete with major and minor leagues, league standings, coaches, managers, and pinch hitters. Poetry, on the other hand, can hardly be called a popular art. In spite of the basic differences, a close relationship exists between the two professions. Poetry and the other verbal arts can, in fact, act as a corrective for political abuses.

I will want to come back to this point, but first I want to suggest a few ways in which the two fields stand opposed to each other.

Politicians are pragmatists. They deal with specific events in the outer world, with this harvest or that economic crisis, this war or the next war. Their concerns tend to be short-term and topical—as we know all too well—and, although we *want* them to deal with specifics, from past experience we *expect* them to talk in generalities. More astonishingly, we expect politicians to distort facts, misrepresent their true intentions and beliefs, and, in short, lie to us. In the last few years political language has become so imprecise that we are left with what Robert Penn Warren calls "imaginary solutions to imaginary problems of imaginary people."

Poets, on the other hand, are idealists, or Edenists—or, as someone has put it, disillusioned Edenists. They are notoriously impractical, since "poetry makes nothing happen." Like politicians, poets deal in specifics, but they do so in order to shed light on the human condition in general. That is, whereas the politician is expected to use generalities to talk about specific events, poets use specific events to discover and express larger truths. Poetry talks about the inner man in the outer world and, doing so, helps us to see what is—what might be.

Does this argument begin to sound rigged? Well, I'm a poet. And poets, like all creative writers, are also, in a sense, liars: They frequently present fictional situations as if they were real. The characters and events in a novel may not be based on anything that actually happened, and similarly the details in a poem may be "made up." None of this really makes much difference, in art, as long as the novel or poem tells us something true—something that "rings true"—about human experience. The truth in poetry is not factual truth but a truth of being and feeling. Carrying the point further, I would say it does not matter how good a poet is technically: If he is not honest in his poems, he is nothing.

The poet Ezra Pound made some terrible mistakes during World War II, but no one, I think, has accused him of deliberately misrepresenting his beliefs. I would like to quote from his essay "The Serious Artist," written in 1913:

> Bad art is inaccurate art. It is art that makes false reports. If a scientist falsifies a report either deliberately or through negligence we consider him as either a criminal or a bad scientist according to the enormity of his offense, and he is punished or despised accordingly. . . .

> If an artist falsifies his report as to the nature of man, as to his own nature, as to the nature of his ideal of the perfect, as to the nature of his ideal of this, that or the other, of god, if god exists, of the life force, of the nature of good and evil, if good and evil exist, of the force with which he believes or disbelieves this, that or the other, of the degree in which he suffers or is made glad; if the artist falsifies his reports on these matters or on any other matter in order that he may conform to the taste of his time, to the proprieties of a sovereign, to the conveniences of a preconceived code of ethics, then that artist lies. If he lies out of deliberate will to lie, if he lies out of carelessness, out of laziness, out of cowardice, out of any sort of negligence whatsoever, he nevertheless lies and he should be punished or despised in proportion to the seriousness of his offense.

This is pretty strong stuff, and I realize that it may even sound self-righteous. I am *not* suggesting we apply these standards to politicians—or, for that matter, that politicians speak in poetry. I *am* suggesting that we need to demand more honesty, and specifically more honesty of language, from the people who purport to represent us.

There is a distinction to be made here between what we want and what we expect. We *want* and *expect* a poet to be honest; if he is not honest, he is a bad poet. We *want* a politician to be honest, but we do not expect him to be; as a matter of fact, a "good" politician is a "successful" politician, and success in politics seems to depend increasingly on the ability to deceive.

This brings us to the relationship between truth and precision of language and to the way in which poetry can act as a check on politics.

One of the things that distinguishes poetry from other kinds of discourse is that poetry uses all the resources of language—denotation and connotation, word sound, rhythm, multiple meaning, etymology—the whole shebang. Of all the verbal arts poetry is most often credited with keeping language fresh, accurate, energized. In a very real sense the test of a poet's sincerity is the commitment he has to his medium: words. Words are not simply a means; they are in themselves—in their heft, feel, plunge, resonance, shape, aerodynamics—part of the end.

In politics, however, words are simply a means to an end, and it appears that the end frequently justifies any means whatsoever. For this reason political satire is almost always satire of language. To take a recent example, Philip Roth's *Our Gang* was prompted by Richard Nixon's statement that he could not square abortion with his "personal belief in the sanctity of human life—including the life of the yet unborn." Nixon made that statement the same day he announced he would "review" the conviction of Lieutenant Calley. Roth's satire, in turn, is written entirely in the form of speeches, transcripts, interviews, and news broadcasts—all of which are double-talk.

We have not yet reached 1984; that is, we have not yet reached a state of "doublethink." Nevertheless, George Orwell's warnings are relevant today. In 1946, in his essay "Politics and the English Language," Orwell observed:

> One ought to recognize that the present political chaos
> is connected with the decay of language, and that one
> can probably bring about some improvement by starting
> at the verbal end. . . . Political language—and with
> variations this is true of all political parties, from Con-
> servatives to Anarchists—is designed to make lies sound
> truthful and murder respectable, and to give an ap-
> pearance of solidity to pure wind.

I do not think we have made any improvement since 1946, and a recent University of Connecticut study, in which a consensus of 400 people found politicians less "truthful" than TV repairmen (but more truthful than used-car salesmen), suggests that I am not alone in this belief.

The striking exception for some has been George McGovern. Surely his campaign, with its emphasis on candor, has been made possible by a widespread distrust of all office seekers. Ironically, a kind of double standard has resulted: Commentators are quick to criticize McGovern's apparent wafflings while they ignore the studied vagueness of the "pros." Consequently, one of McGovern's strengths in the primaries, his willingness to explain the issues, has been turned to his own disadvantage. This double standard was already operating in the Humphrey-McGovern debates when, as Mary McCarthy has noted:

> McGovern's modest efforts to formulate clear positions on a few issues were joyously seized on by Humphrey in the spirit of a political blackmailer who has in his hands statements tending to compromise his opponent with large blocs of voters. Humphrey's strategy was not to argue the validity of those positions but simply to challenge McGovern with the fact of having embraced them.

Only a few months later we find McGovern charged with having altered his positions over the years as if modifying a stand is, in itself, hypocritical.

At the same time, long-term McGovernites fear their candidate will stop trying to educate the public on the issues and will retreat to "moderate" (i.e., undefined) programs and slick, speech-writers' formulas. As I write, the evidence is not yet in. McGovern's notorious "one thousand per cent" and his contradictory statements on Pierre Salinger's trip to Paris suggest—to me, at least—a disturbing tendency to confuse candor with the strong, immediate response to reporters. They do not suggest willful deceit, and they do not compare with Lyndon Johnson's calculated misrepresentations in 1964 or Richard Nixon's "secret plan" for ending the war, in 1968. On the other hand, for all his directness, McGovern has never been a colorful speaker, and the slogan making in his recent speeches sounds unlike the man I heard debate Sen. Jacob Javits in the mid-Sixties.

McGovernites may find themselves disappointed by their candidate, but they would be naïve to be both disappointed and surprised. Professional politics, as it is euphemistically called, seems to rely more and more on the imprecise use of language. This is not a matter of negligence and ineptitude; it is a matter of calculation and skill. The advertising geniuses, who play a central role in our system, know all the tricks of language a poet knows, as do the various ghost writers and press secretaries. No one has suggested they are producing art, except perhaps the debased art Ezra Pound describes, though they are certainly producing a debased democracy. Moreover, the various media multiply the problem—whether through objective reporting, economic necessity, or willing complicity. And yet, when Spiro Agnew criticizes the media, he does so for all the wrong reasons.

I cannot believe that my claims are controversial, but let me make an attempt to document them. There are, of course, all the old propaganda techniques: name calling, glittering generalities, transfers, testimonials, card stacking, plain-folks syrup, and the bandwagon approaches (now called "gathering momentum"). The most popular technique seems to be "generalization," the indiscriminate use of words that mean little or nothing and that can stand for almost anything (words and phrases like "concern," "circumstance," "vital interest," "real meaning," "epoch-making," "historic," "unforgettable," "age-old," "inevitable," "realistic," "patriotic," "democratic," "socialist," "Communist," "fascist," "self-determination," "freedom," and "justice"). The meanings of these words must be determined by context, but their contexts are generally designed to keep them meaningless.

Politicians are afraid of the phrase or image that is too vivid: It's likely to backfire. Curtis LeMay no doubt thought he was using a figure of speech when he talked about bombing North Vietnam "back into the Stone Age." But he inadvertently touched some deep American guilt, and most of us took him quite literally. In general, however, politicians have been successful in refining away expressions that might disturb a squeamish voter. Vietnam alone provides a whole dictionary of such refinements, many of which have been pointed out by George W. Ashworth in the *Christian Science Monitor* and Frances FitzGerald in *The New Yorker:*

> *Hamburger Hill* became *Hill 937*
>
> *maximum pressure* became *protective reaction*
>
> *free-fire* zones became *pre-cleared fire-zones*
>
> *naval ambushes* became *water-borne guard posts*
>
> *bombing* became *armed reconnaissance*
>
> *search-and-destroy operations* became first *search-and-clear missions*, later *reconnaissance in force*.

Have you heard of *napalm* lately? No, but you may have heard of *selective ordnance*—though, how napalm is "selective" I do not know.

The CIA does not *murder;* it *terminates with extreme prejudice.* The *Communists* destroy *houses* while the Allies destroy *structures.*

Communists live in *infested areas,* which must be *sanitized* by *relocating* the *noncombatants* in *strategic hamlets.*

Given such terminology, one can only wonder in what sense Richard Nixon claims he is "ending the war." Or what Secretary of War—excuse me, I mean Secretary of *Defense*—Laird means by "astonishingly" and "successful" when he asserts that "Vietnamization has been astonishingly successful." "Vietnamization," by the way, was a word outlawed by President Thieu because it suggested that "this war has been directed by the Americans and is just turned over to the Vietnamese people's care."

I could continue listing examples, from all areas of political discourse, for many pages. But if I do, we will not have room for the "lift of spirit" that, I've been told, is what "this nation needs above all." Furthermore, I would probably be giving "aid and comfort to the enemy," and—if you found yourself "in agreement" with me—we could all be charged with "conspiracy."

How, then, can the verbal arts act as a check on political abuses? And, particularly, how can poetry, which I've admitted is not a popular art, counteract such a massive degeneration of language? Certainly poetry is not about to rival the primaries on the Nielson Ratings. For the past fifteen to twenty years, however, poetry *has* been enjoying a small boom. Increased college education, the use of some media techniques, and the general availability of publishing equipment have played their parts. More importantly, however, poetry itself has become more accessible and more topical.

Contemporary poetry is too explosively diverse for easy generalization, but perhaps a few trends can be noted here. For one thing, poetry has lost its fear of social commitment. Under the tyranny of the New Criticism, which extended from the Thirties well into the Fifties, the poem was seen as a self-contained, coherent verbal object, essentially detachable from the biography of the writer and his historical situation. For all its virtues, the New Criticism turned poetry away from its possible landscapes toward an increasingly timid corner. The change from what Philip Levine calls "Those twitch-nosed/academic pants-pisser poets/of the 50's" came in many ways and from many quarters.

It came from the San Francisco poets and the hysterical energies released by Allen Ginsberg's *Howl* and from the Black Mountain poets with their interests in perception and qualities of voice. These movements brought new interest to the work of William Carlos Williams, who had long sought the peculiarly American (as opposed to British) language and speech rhythms to deal with plain American things. At almost the same time the well-respected but "academic" Robert Lowell helped inaugurate "confessional" poetry by publishing *Life Studies.* Other poets began the reinvention of surrealism, or started mining foreign literatures. All of which, fed into and fed by the turmoil of the Sixties, has led to a great poetry upheaval. The often bitter fruit of this new ground has been wide experimentation, an unprecedented interest in poetries previously ignored—the unique visions of women, blacks, American Indians, people in prison—and a voluminous poetry of social commitment.

"A good cause is no excuse for a bad poem" is a truism—and a cliché with which many poets are no longer content. In the 1960s such poets as Robert Bly, Galway Kinnell, and Denise Levertov organized "Read-ins for Peace"; these, and Walter Lowenfels's anthology *Where Is Vietnam: American Poets Respond,* demonstrated how entirely possible it is to write a *good* poem on a good cause. This is not to say that all or even the best writers are poets of social conscience but only that our conscience is one of the "real" things poetry puts us in touch with. "The disease of our time," Robert Penn Warren has written, "is the sense of being cut off from reality. Man feels that a screen has descended between him and nature, between him and other men, between him and the self." The sheer number of people reading and writing poetry suggests a profound desire to "get back in touch."

There are good arguments that this quantitative increase has caused a qualitative decrease. The title of this article was suggested by the observation, in the same week, by Alfred Harbage and Alan Pryce-Jones, two critics writing on opposite sides of the Atlantic, that American writing is becoming like American bread—porous, tasteless, and mass-distributed. I agree with these men that we are swamped in mediocre verbiage. Moreover, highly emotional issues are especially likely to put across poems that, at a few months' or years' distance, seem thoroughly second-rate. But there *is* also a quantity of first-rate writing around, writing that fulfills the goals I cited earlier.

I would like to end with two such poems. One deals directly with the pity of war, for, as Wilfred Owen wrote, "The Poetry is in the pity." The other deals satirically with the last administration's vocabulary. Both can be set against specific remarks by politicians.

Randall Jarrell's poem "The Truth" came back to me as I listened to Richard Nixon's May 28 speech to the Russian people. He spoke at length about Tanya Savichev, a heroine who is to Russians what Anne Frank is to Americans:

> Yesterday I laid a wreath at the cemetery which com-
> memorates the brave people who died during the siege
> of Leningrad. . . . At the cemetery I saw the picture of
> a twelve-year-old girl. She was a beautiful child. Her
> name was Tanya. The pages of her diary tell the terrible
> story of war. . . . [Nixon paraphrased the diary.] Let
> us do all we can to ensure that no other children will
> have to endure what Tanya did and that your children
> and ours and all the children of the world can live
> their full lives together in friendship and peace.

One need hardly point out the crude sentimentality or belabor the
hypocrisy of such a statement. Granted, there was much killing in
the world that day that was not Mr. Nixon's fault; but, as he spoke,
his air force was making new orphans. As a Russian woman re-
marked, "Even my children said, 'If he's talking about peace, why
doesn't he say something about Vietnam?' " Moreover, Nixon, who
has said, I'm told, "Politics is poetry," carefully avoided any description of what Tanya actually endured.

The Truth

When I was four my father went to Scotland.
They *said* he went to Scotland.

When I woke up I think I thought that I was dreaming—
I was so little then that I thought dreams
Are in the room with you, like the cinema.
That's why you don't dream when it's still light—
They pull the shades down when it is, so you can sleep.
I thought that then, but that's not right.
Really it's in your head.

And it was light then—light at *night*.
I heard Stalky bark outside.
But really it was Mother crying—
She coughed so hard she cried.
She kept shaking Sister,
She shook her and shook her.
I thought Sister had had her nightmare.
But he wasn't barking, he had died.
There was dirt all over Sister.
It was all streaks, like mud. I cried.
She didn't, but she was older.

                                    I thought she didn't
Because she was older, I thought Stalky had just gone.
I got *everything* wrong.
I didn't get one single thing right.
It seems to me that I'd have thought
It didn't happen, like a dream,
Except that it was light. At night.

They burnt our house down, they burnt down **London**.
Next day my mother cried all day, and after that
She said to me when she would come to see me:
"Your father has gone away to Scotland.
He will be back after the war."

The war then was different from the war now.
The war now is *nothing*.

I used to live in London till they burnt it.
What was it like? It was just like here.
No, that's the truth.
My mother would come here, some, but she would cry.
She said to Miss Elise, "He's not himself";
She said, "Don't you love me any more at all?"
I was *myself*.
Finally she wouldn't come at all.
She never said one thing my father said, or Sister.
Sometimes she did,
Sometimes she was the same, but that was when I dreamed it.
I could tell I was dreaming, she was just the same.

That Christmas she bought me a toy dog.

I asked her what was its name, and when she didn't know
I asked her over, and when she didn't know
I said, "You're not my mother, you're not my mother.
She *hasn't* gone to Scotland, she is dead!"
And she said, "Yes, he's dead, he's dead!"
And cried and cried; she *was* my mother,
She put her arms around me and we cried.

Jarrell's poem is spoken by an English child about five years after
he has lost most of his family in World War II. With few changes
it might be spoken by a Vietnamese. The boy in the poem is fairly
confused about what has happened, and he thinks war is the permanent condition of mankind, but he is more in touch with "the
truth" than many of our officials are.

The second poem is by George Starbuck and is called "Dear Fellow
Teacher." It is a funny, angry poem, at a remote pole from Jar-
rell's "The Truth." The poem is a response to a statement by
Lyndon Johnson cited in the first line.

Dear Fellow Teacher

I must confess I'm tired of these demonstrations.
Surely there must be better demonstrations
against brute force than brute force demonstrations.
Come now and let us reason together like
the Old Man says. What kind of a demonstration
is this from academically trained minds?
Is a stalled freight our cogent demonstration?
Is a blocked highway where some unwashed mob
panics at a mere word like "napalm" our
idea of perspicacious demonstration?
Would Aristotle, master of demonstration,
have dignified with the proud name "demonstration"
this massing of dumb bodies under flags?
Would Euclid have admired such demonstration?

What are we after with these demonstrations?
Accommodation? Compromise? Then let
that spirit permeate our demonstrations.
Was it not Secretary Rusk who said
We have already made our demonstration
of readiness to negotiate unquote?
What could be more amenable than that?
And had we not in fact for five whole days
called off, forsworn, and utterly regrouped
(for that is how we made said demonstration)
our prior and like-minded demonstration
of readiness to negotiate unquote?
Were we discouraged? Did we not resume
what McNamara calls our demonstration

that we shall not be bluffed or made to yield
until, in Bundy's words, some demonstration
of comparable etcetera unquote?
Lyndon, I'm sick and tired of demonstrations.
There is a demon in these demonstrations.
I'm fed up with the mere word "demonstration."
Furthermore, I accept your demonstration
that this or that or any demonstration's

about as much use as a plugged piastre.
Like alibis, like sides of beef on spits,
like children in thatch villages of huts,
if you don't watch them they get overdone.
That's the damn thing about these demonstrations.
Let's everybody go out and stop one.

Unlike politicians, poets are not obliged to offer "solutions," although poets deal with much more than just esthetic problems.
Poems do not offer programs, they offer insights; they do not alter
events, they are events. In the highest sense I think poetry strives
to engage the whole being, and when the whole being is so alerted,
it will not settle for dehumanized jargon and rhetorical puffery.

Speaking only for myself, I confess a strong inclination to disbe-
lieve all solutions, since they are usually offered by people who
have, at best, a poor understanding of the problems. Our understanding can be no better than our language. 1 am not suggesting
that we read poetry in order to choose the next President but simply that we need more of poetry's vision and precision in our political life. We need to cut through the word-paint and, as a poet
has said, "get down where our obsessions are." Because the only
political problems are human problems. . . .

*And finally, my friends and fellow Americans, let me say this. I
know that none of you are nervous snobs or effete Nellies; and you
know that the protagonists, the pretentious polyps, the prestigious
prestidigitators, the Princetonians, the prefects, the polyandrous
platypuses, and the Patagonians have been cutting into the very
muscle and fibrous tumors of our defense mechanisms. Therefore,
remember the spirt of Vienna, the spirit of Glassboro, the spirit of
Moscow, the Spirit of St. Louis, the spirit of Seventy-Six, and the
spirit of Christmas Past. Ask not what you can do to your country,
but what your country is doing to you. What this nation needs
above all is a lift of the spirit, the lift of a driving dream, and a
good mouthwash.*

Symbols, Language, and Violence

Rollo May

Noted author and psychologist May (*Love and Will*, among other books) contemplates the role of symbols, which he feels should serve as a bridge to communication between people. However, May admits that unfortunately "the deep suspicion of symbols, and the impoverishment of ourselves and our relationships which is both cause and result, is rampant in our times." As an example of the insights that symbol analysis provides, May shows how one can interpret Vietnam as a symbol of Asia, whose qualities of mediation and subjectivity threaten traditional American values. May was a featured speaker at the 1974 NCTE convention in New Orleans.

Violence and authentic communication are mutually exclusive. Put simply, you cannot talk with someone as long as he is your enemy, and if you can talk with him he ceases to be your enemy. The process is reciprocal. This is why when we are violent toward another we cannot communicate; rage, say, or a hurt pride demands immediate revenge. The capacity to talk is then automatically blocked by neurological mechanisms that release adrenalin and shift the energy to the muscles in primitive preparation for fighting. If we are middle class, we may rapidly pace back and forth until we can control our violence enough to put it into words; if we are proletarian, we simply hit out.

It is in the throwing of bridges to one another that symbols are so important. We can see the reasons for this when we consider that symbols make language possible. Language arises from an underlying web of readiness for understanding, an empathetic tie between people, a capacity to identify with each other. This potentiality for understanding is much more than mere words. It implies a state of we-ness, a bond that potentially unites people, the prototype for which is the fact of gestation in the mother's womb and of birth. If there had been no womb in which we first grew as embryos, language would not be possible; and if there had been no birth, language would not be necessary. The individual is both bound to others and independent from them at the same time. Symbols serve as a bridge over that chasm between human beings to establish the bond again. When the bond between human beings is destroyed—i.e., when the possibilities for communication break down—aggression and violence occur.

The Distrust of Words

The deep suspicion of symbols, and the impoverishment of ourselves and our relationships which is both cause and result, is rampant in our times. We experience the despair of being unable to communicate to others what we feel and what we think, and the even greater despair of being unable to distinguish for ourselves what we feel and we are. Underlying this is the loss of the symbols and myths upon which personal identity and language are based.

The breakdown is shown in the students' protest against "words, words, words" they must listen to, in their sickness of heart at hearing the same things mouthed over and over again, and in their readiness to accuse faculty and others of "word garbage" or "verbal masturbation." This is generally seen as a criticism of the lecture method. But what they really are—or ought to be—talking about is a particular *kind* of lecture which does not communicate "being" from one person to another. We must admit that all too often this has been a characteristic of academic life and makes the student protest against irrelevant education more relevant.

The shelves of our college libraries are weighed down with books that were written because other books were written because still other books were previously written—the meat of the meal getting thinner and thinner until the books seem to have nothing to do with the excitement of truth but only with status and prestige. And in the academic world, these last two values can be powerful indeed. No wonder the young poets are disillusioned with talk and hold, as they did in the San Francisco love-in, that the best poem is a "blank sheet of paper."

At such a time, in our alienation and isolation, we long for a simple, direct expression of our feelings to another, a direct relation to our being, looking into the eyes of the other to see and experience him, or standing quietly beside him. We yearn for a direct expression of his and our moods and emotions with no barriers. We seek a kind of innocence which is as old as human evolution but comes to us as something new, the innocence of children in paradise again. We long for expression of intimacy through our bodies, to short-cut the time intimacy usually takes; we want to speak through our bodies, to leap immediately into identification with the other, even though we know it is only partial—in short, to bypass the whole symbols-verbal-language "hang-up." Alas, this is an illusion! Direct communication is given only to the saints and mystics. We exist "after the fall."

As an illustration of the disintegration of language, I report a short section from a TV news report coming half a dozen days after the invasion of Laos, while the invasion was as yet unannounced in this country. Secretary Laird had come out of a meeting with the Armed Services Committee and was accosted by the usual group of reporters.

Reporters: Sir, it is rumored on all sides that we have been making plans to invade Laos. Is this true?

Secretary Laird: I have just come from a meeting of the Armed Services Committee, and I wish to say our discussion of the draft was valuable and harmonious.

Reporters, protesting: That's not the question, Sir. Also: *Isvestia* has already reported the invasion.

Laird, smiling: You know *Isvestia* does not write the truth.

Reporters ask the first question over again.

Laird: I will do whatever is necessary to protect the lives of our boys in the fighting field. No more comment.

He walks away.

Now no one could say that Secretary Laird speaks any untruth: obviously, everything he says is factual. The only point is that his language denies the whole structure of communication. There is no relation in his answers to the question asked. In one extreme and persistent form, this is called schizophrenia; but in our day it simply is called politics.

We forget at our peril that man is a symbol-making creature. And if the symbols (or myths, which are a pattern of symbols) seem arid and dry and dead, they are to be mourned rather than denied. Loss of symbolism should be seen for what it is, a way-station on the path to despair.

Words and Symbols

Symbol comes ultimately from the Greek *sym-ballein*, which means to draw together. The antonym of symbolic is diabolic. This word comes from *dia-ballein*, meaning to tear apart. In this sense we live in a diabolic age, an age torn apart, an age which does not have the symbols to cast light upon meanings and values.

The importance of language in an evolving culture is that it consists of *symbolic forms* through which we can reveal ourselves, and through which others stand revealed to us. If there are no such forms, one is like a man who finds himself in a dream wandering in a foreign country where he can understand nothing of what is being said around him nor feel anything from the person next to him; and his isolation is great indeed.

During the week end of the moon landing two summers ago, a TV reporter interviewed members of the crowd milling around Central Park just after the landing. In answer to his question of what they were waiting for, a common response was, "To see the extravehicular activity."

Now this phrase gives one pause. I pondered it a while. Its main word is six syllables and highly technical; it tells, like many technical phrases, what the astronauts are *not* going to do (the activity being *extra*vehicular) rather than what they are going to do. The word "activity" may mean any act under the sun—swimming, flying, crawling, diving, etc. There is no poetry in the sentence, no meaning which is not technical, nothing personal. One finally discovers the polysyllabic phrase means "to walk on the moon." But that is a poetic phrase: no word of over one syllable—coming straight out of one's own life (from the age of one in which he learned to walk)—a phrase associated with all the romance of the moon. It is actually more truthful than its scientific parallel in the sense that it reveals not an abstraction but an act that is done by human beings like you and me. The more technical we become without a parallel development in personal communication, the more alienated we also become. The more, then, *communication* becomes *communiqués.*

The breakdown of communication is a spiritual breakdown in that words get their communicative power from the fact that they participate in symbols. Through drawing meanings together into a Gestalt, a symbol has a numinous quality which points toward a reality greater than itself. The symbol gives the word its power to carry across to you some meaning from the emotions of the other. The breakdown of the symbol is thus a spiritual tragedy. The symbol always implies more than it states; it is essentially connotative rather than denotative. Thus words, in so far as they are symbolic, point to more than they can specifically say; what counts is the afterglow, the meaning rippling out like wavelets when a stone is dropped in a lake. It is a Gestalt like that which the poet uses. A form emerges out of the very speaking of words—which is why people tend to become more poetic when they report something under stress.

An Example of a Symbol: Vietnam

The Vietnamese war, an example surely of gross violence, cannot be understood without reference to the *symbols* that underlie it.

These symbols have to be found in a dimension below all the published reports. Vietnam is a *symptom* of the fissure in our civilization; and symptoms often are expressions of symbols. The violence and aggression in America would not have been avoided, nor even greatly lessened if the war had not occurred, but it *did* occur. And it must be for some good reason.

The causes and purposes of the war have been characterized by a murkiness. We have been going through a strange series of actions like a man caught in quicksand. When we can't say what happened or why, when we are caught in continuous dilemmas, when we feel that we are men walking in a nightmare, doing things today because we did certain things yesterday because of things we did the day before—when these things occur, we do well to look for some symbolic meaning.

The language uses about the Vietnamese is "gooks," "little yellow devils," and other words indicating that they are not fully human, cannot speak like human beings or reason, as was said by Lieutenant Calley in his trial. Included in the body count are "buffaloes, pigs, cows," implying that they and the people are in the same category. Thus the war of extermination can proceed without the customary prohibition against killing. The people are treated like savages, and the same goal of genocide is in effect as with the Indians.

The pieces of the jigsaw puzzle begin to fall into place enough to suggest a hypothesis. Vietnam is the symbol of a *religious* war, a holy war against the infidel. In a religious war the conflict cannot be compromised but drags on and on until it becomes a way of life. Like the wars of the Reformation, it is not fought for markets or acquisition of land but for spiritual reasons—which makes it so hard to stop, and so much like the wars of extermination that the Spaniards fought against the Moors. "When (wars) are fought for the minds and hearts of men," as Thurman Arnold writes, "when it is a struggle between the Catholic and the Protestant churches, or between Communism and Capitalism," neither side can afford to compromise on any issue.

Vietnam is a holy war in that it is a struggle for men's minds and spirits. The "unbelievers" are only partly unbelievers in Christianity—that issue has become merely nominal. The unbelievers rather represent those who do not have faith in things believed essential for the survival of America. Strictly speaking, it is *not* a war against Vietnam—that little country only has the great misfortune of being the battlefield. It is an ideological war against what threatens the West, namely Asia.

So we must now ask, What does Asia mean in America? What is the symbolism of Asia among contemporary Westerners?

Asia is *meditation*. The critical influence of the Hindu and the Buddhist religions on the campuses of Harvard and Yale and Berkeley is not to be bypassed as mere whim. The gurus and their "transcendental meditation" are taken very seriously because they minister to a deep hunger in us which is not assuaged by modern technology.

Asia is *subjectivity*. The Eastern subjectivity is the polar opposite to American objectivity in academic and industrial life. This constitutes a deep and lasting threat to American habits of behaviorism, and the kinds of philosophy which have largely been a kibbitzing on science.

Asia is *empathy*. Even in making a business decision in Japan, I am told, the problem is discussed until the chairman makes the remark, "We have come to such and such a conclusion." There is no vote, no conscious agreement, no formal consensus. There is only the chairman's *empathetic* sensing of the direction of the discussion, a method that seems to be more effective than many American ways of running a board meeting.

Asia is an attitude of *reverence for nature*. Nature is accepted as part of life. This is in radical contrast to the American attitude that nature is here for our exploitation. ("God said unto them, Have dominion over the fish of the sea, and over the fowl of the air, and over every living thing that moveth upon the earth.")

The conclusion this points toward is: the war in Vietnam is a war against the qualities which psychologically and spiritually threaten traditional American life. I speak in terms of qualities unconsciously assumed and believed in, rather than a set of external creeds. These qualities *would* genuinely threaten the competitive materialism of America, the worship of success, our individualism which isolates man from man, our false values in the size of our house and the expense of our motor cars. In this sense the war takes on a curious and macabre logic.

But we must press further. Are these qualities Asia stands for—meditation, subjectivity, empathy, reverence for nature—not actually the direction in which America herself has to move? Do we not fight our own *selves* in fighting the war in Vietnam? Are these not the qualities we need as a corrective to our Western biases of four centuries, and would they not come as balm? Do we not therefore fight what is unconscious in ourselves and our own body politic?

Clearly we fight our own hippies when we fight Asia. Multitudes of young people, following the Asian model, have taken a compassionate attitude toward nature, which they believe is important in the overcoming of pollution. Thousands of them dress like Asians, with gowns, saris and long hair. Their life in monastic communes, their interest in flowers, their failure to realize "time is money" and their unconcern with time itself, their getting pleasure from the moment—all these are more Asiatic than Western.

It is a lot easier to conduct a war half way around the globe—difficult as that is—than to fight our own hippies, our own young people, our own American gurus and yogis. The latter war would be unthinkable—even with Secretary Laird's logic. But we can fight it by sending the very youth who would be the threat in this country to stand against the forces far around the world which actually threaten our own establishment, not only on the nearest corner where there is a school and a church but also in our own homes and in the deepest dogmas of our own hearts.

Seeing the Vietnamese war as a symbol gives us, finally, one source of hope. It is to be remembered that converts, from St. Paul on the Damascus road to the alcoholic lying in the Bowery, fight hardest against the new truth just before they become converted to it. This is always the way the daemonic works in an individual: it is his own self—albeit denied and projected—which he fights. And the closer he gets to it, the harder he fights. Until relatively recently, when the outcry became too great for the President not to hear, the United States fought harder the more she became mired in the quicksands of Vietnam.

The qualities of Asia are potentially positive and good values for America. But they would and do cause radical changes in our politics and daily life. In this sense it is a conflict between the new world and the old, the old world now having become spiritually the "new world" for Western civilization. These are the symbols, which, I propose, are being born in contemporary America.

The liberal arts are concerned with the symbolic interpretation of man through the ages and at present. Symbols are in the basic sense its scene. I believe that the liberal arts are thus essential not only to man's imagination but to his survival as a human being. I regard liberal arts as crucial to our preservation of men and women, not as ants or bees but as creatures who can choose values—that is, creatures with consciousness and with an awareness of their history.

126

The Road to Radicalism: A Semantic Aberration

E. W. Cardaci

"The Road to Radicalism" first appeared in *ETC.* in September, 1971. Because of its clarity and concreteness, the author was invited to revise and update the article for this collection; unable to do so, because of current workload, E. W. Cardaci offers this fruitful advice to the editor, and to the readers: "If you want the article$_{1971}$, it's yours; perhaps it can serve as a historically dated example of a point you want to make. But, 'student'$_{1974}$ is not 'student'$_{1971}$, is not the highly visible social problem referred to in the article. Whereas 'student'$_{1974}$ may be considered apathetic, self-centered, cynical, and/or alienated, 'student'$_{1974}$ does not seem to be succumbing to radical chic, the Communist Manifesto, the Weathermen, trashing, and bombing. Times change. In short, simple updating can't be done. A whole new semantic analysis is needed for 'student'$_{1974}$." Hopefully, other teachers will take the hint and do their own analysis of "student"$_{1974}$ or "student"$_{1975}$, etc.

I'd like you to think about Johnny for a moment—not the celebrated Johnny who can't read—the other one who has a comfortably high IQ, does well in school, and reads all manner of materials quite nicely. You never hear any worries about this child during his public school years. He's the culturally advantaged child. He pleases everybody, earns good grades, makes a high SAT score, and is accepted into a good university. What's more, he doesn't seem likely to fail there either.

Then, quite suddenly, Johnny goes socially berserk. He's anti-capitalism and procommunism. He's anti-American and pro-Chinese. He won't talk to anybody over thirty, but everybody over thirty is analyzing him from the point of view of the observer's particular discipline. Now, Johnny may be suffering from a bad case of adolescent rebellion. He may be cracking under culture shock or future shock, urban overcrowding, the competitive rat race, or permissive parents in his past, but I contend that his biggest problem is, frequently, a semantic aberration. After all, high IQ can almost be defined as an ability to work in verbal abstractions, and the value-profile of a student tends to be highest in the theoretical area.

Let's approach this look at Johnny in terms of a semantic case history. His disillusionment with democracy as a utopian ideal might have grown something like this: If today he is a nineteen-year-old flaming revolutionary, we can assume he was born in 1951. At the tender age of nine, he listened to John F. Kennedy's inaugural address, learned something of the black's struggle for equality, and tried to understand. When he was twelve, he had grasped the fact in history class that one of the triumphs of democracy was the peaceful change of office even between opposing parties, but that year he suffered the shock of presidential assassination.

When he was thirteen, he was learning in school that the United States is a representative democracy. The representative, he learned, was to vote the will of his constituency so that all laws would represent the majority will. He may have wondered, then, why the representatives in the 1964 campaign always made speeches and never listened to their constituents. He may have wondered why the things the representatives said were so ambiguous, but his real attention was soon diverted to the clear and evident issue of Vietnam. Mr. Johnson vowed to contain the war, and Mr. Goldwater vowed to enlarge it. The voters gave Mr. Johnson's pledge their landslide approval. Then President Johnson enlarged the war, and Johnny went back to see what he had missed in the definition of representative democracy.

That same year, Johnny was learning the Amendments to the Constitution. He memorized Amendment XV: "The right of citizens of the United States to vote shall not be denied or abridged by the United States or by any State on account of race, color, or previous condition of servitude." It seemed like learning nonsense syllables to him, for the TV showed him congressional debates over the elimination of the poll tax, and the blacks were decrying the blatant methods for preventing Negro voting in the southern states. True, abolition of the poll tax was accomplished by Amendment XXIV adopted that year, but can we blame Johnny for wondering if it would have any greater practical effect than his memorized Amendment XV, adopted in 1870?

He shelved the problem, then, feeling he was just too young to understand, but he watched the struggle of the blacks as they demanded equality, and he wondered about that while he memorized such abstractions as the Bill of Rights and the Civil War Acts, all of which told him the blacks already had equality. Then, one day his father drove him through the slums.

In 1968, he was hard at work learning the Gettysburg Address for a high school speech contest, when Robert Kennedy was shot in another campaign for a "peaceful change of office." And when he read poll after poll showing 80 percent of the people were in favor of strict gun control laws, but saw those laws defeated in Congress, he was understandably puzzled at the meaning of "government of the people, for the people, and by the people . . ."

By this time, the relationship between the verbal abstractions he was learning in school and their concrete, three-dimensional referents in the world about him was showing understandable strain. By the age of seventeen, he was developing a streak of cynicism. Poor Johnny. The last straw was learning that political speeches are intentionally vague, because people read meaning into ambiguities to match their own beliefs. It's a cheap way to earn votes. He snickered when his civics teacher told him the voter's obligation was to vote on the issues, and he offered to lend that teacher a copy of *The Selling of the President 1968*.

Now a nineteen-year-old college sophomore with experience, he has already tried to exercise his "right of peaceable assembly" and been turned back because he didn't possess a parade permit. He was not surprised when a "busted" friend was released on bail. He knows Amendment VIII to the Constitution states that "excessive bail shall not be required . . . ," but neither was he surprised to learn, thirty days later, that the poor blacks who were demonstrating with his friend were languishing in jail, though not indicted, because *they* had found the same bail excessive.

At this point, either the verbal abstraction or the concrete reality had to be abandoned. For the sake of his sanity, he decided that democracy was suspect. He threw away the "map" and took a very critical look at the "territory."

Now let's trace the same course, briefly, in terms of capitalism: Long ago, the spirit of Christmas tangled with hard-sell commercialism on Johnny's Saturday-morning cartoons. The spirit of Christmas lost, and Johnny was duly punished by the frustration of going to bed on Christmas night with two beautiful broken toys—one that didn't work as advertised, and one that he found he didn't really want. He wondered a bit about Santa's inept elves, but he didn't doubt American know-how . . . yet.

Somewhat later, he fell in love with a well-advertised, banana-seated, sissy-barred, low-slung bike, only to find that he always ran out of breath trying to keep up with his less-fortunate friend on an old beat-up conventional racer.

Still loyal to American industry, he battled his mother over where nutrition came from, supporting his arguments with material from commercials and package labels in favor of sugar-coated corn puffs, white bread, and high-energy chocolate. The fifth-grade health book, however, agreed with his mother, and for the first time he looked askance at capitalism, advertising, and TV.

He began to wonder why business supported the puritan ethic of hard work in such a way that the reward always seemed to be the right to consume in a status-seeking race.

When he discovered girls, he forgot about abstract versus concrete capitalism for a while, but there it was again. His class in sex education was assuring him that love must be a warm, human relationship based on mutual trust, while the advertising industry kept showing him the trappings and deceits required for catching a girl—or worse, the methods she must use to lure him.

Is it any wonder, then, that by the time he reached advanced adolescence, he took abstractions about "American ingenuity and technical superiority" with a grain of salt? He had seen his mother weep with exasperation over many a concrete example of planned obsolescence.

No corporate image of saintly community action could very well stand up against the concrete realities of Earth Day. He saw the foam, silt, and filth in the river he toured. He carted nonreturnable bottles and cans to the dump from the local parks. He breathed the smog from smoke stacks and exhausts. Abstract slogans didn't stand a chance. Cynicism began to come easy.

He back-slid only once. Lured by that great American temptress, the automobile, he allowed himself to be seduced. Ignoring Ralph Nader, he bought a car, but now he's afraid to drive it because it has the light-weight control arm that could snap at any time, and he doesn't have the $120 or more to have it replaced.

To make his life story short, he is now nineteen, and whenever someone extols the abstract glories of a free market, he quotes *Chemical and Engineering News:* "the margin of superiority in a consumer item seldom lies in the product's technical superiority but in its mode of distribution or brand name." (*Consumer Reports,* November 1970, p. 630.) Again, where the verbal abstractions met concrete reality, the verbal abstractions broke down, and Johnny assumes that the capitalistic ideal is something of a fraud.

So far, Johnny has the same problem the rest of us have. Our three-dimensional reality is a long way from our verbal abstract ideal. But remember, Johnny has been living in the public school system where the only meaning the word *communism* is allowed to have is a connotation of total negation. He doesn't know what it is, but he knows that the same people who had him memorizing democratic abstractions assured him that communism is evil. Those people are now suspect, and as the credibility of the source decreases, the believability of the opposition message increases.

Furthermore, nobody in the public school system has taught him general semantics, because it's too threatening. To quote Postman and Weingartner, "Educational systems are largely designed to enjoin citizens, within varying but harmless limits of objectivity, to accept the verbal maps drawn by political leaders. When educational processes do not do this, they usually become suspect. . . . Semantics on all grade levels below college is still what might be called a fugitive enterprise." Johnny has been well protected from his best defense.

Growing up, he felt his senses were extended by the television tube. Concrete reality was his. Couldn't he see the slums, the pollution, the drug investigations, the political battle? And with considerable wisdom, he chose reality over words. But that television camera was barred from China, was banned from Cuba, and never had the freedom to record reality in Russia.

Then how can we possibly be surprised at Johnny's reaction when he suddenly meets the *Communist Manifesto,* or one of its disciples? With no semantics to guide him, Johnny, quite predictably, climbs aboard a typical two-valued orientation, reasoning something like this: Democracy is suspect and capitalism is short-sighted, self-centered, and probably corrupt. I am against capitalism. Marx is against capitalism. I must be for Marx. Then he compares his oh-so-fallible real world with the rosy verbal communist utopia, and a radical is born. From here on, it's all dissonance-reduction.

No one has ever told him that you can't make a rational comparison between a reality and an abstraction. We could, therefore, cure him quickly by taking him on a tour of the communist nations and teaching a course in comparative reality, point by point. He would soon discover that Mao's China is farther short of the communist abstract ideal than America is of the democratic ideal. He would soon see that communist industry in Russia pollutes quite as effectively as capitalist industry in the United States. He would find, in short, that fallibility and corruptibility are human, not just democratic, traits.

It would, however, be cheaper and easier if he had had semantics in school. Then he would know that while we can compare Russian reality with American reality or the *Communist Manifesto* with the Federalist Papers, we can't mix them up. Basically, that's the semantic aberration he's suffering from, and that, in my estimation, is why Johnny doesn't roll up his sleeves and put his talents to work solving some of the very real problems that America is currently suffering. That's why Johnny, the radical, throws bombs.

Politics and the American Language

Justus George Lawler

Lawler thinks about the unthinkable, bringing up a subject which most of us would rather not think or talk about. Of the many, many articles about military misuse of language, most writers have concentrated on the horrifying examples which can be drawn from the Vietnam war. Lawler, instead, reminds us of total catastrophe—thermonuclear war—and discusses the language manipulation involved. In a provocative, poetic essay, Lawler claims that "the rhetoric of the strategists was born not only of the marriage of Madison Avenue and the Pentagon," but also of the priests and poets. Lawler is editor-in-chief of Continnum Books and teaches at Xavier College in Chicago.

It is now a little more than a decade since Herman Kahn published under the disarmingly insouciant title, *Thermonuclear War: Three Lectures and Several Suggestions.** As most people will remember, the book was a kind of apocalyptic *summa demonica* in which all the gadgetry of advanced technology, all the sophistication of computerized devisals, all the chill detachment of the finest *espirit géometrique* were marshalled to prove that even after a major thermonuclear exchange the ensuing death and destruction would be *quite* tolerable: a judgment Kahn reaffirmed a year later in *Thinking about the Unthinkable* with the observation that "people can and do rise to the occasion." Notwithstanding the fact that "rising to the occasion" was a counsel out of Kipling which could have no bearing whatever on a tragedy of such magnitude as to make the periodic panics that swept a plague-infested Europe appear as trivial historical aberrations—notwithstanding this fact, the judgment was embraced eagerly by both the military and their lay advisors, of whom Edward Teller was perhaps representative enough. Writing in 1962, Dr. Teller opined:

> Everything we have, in other words, could be produced by our present industrial complex in only about three years. . . . Even if our industrial plants were totally destroyed in an all-out attack, properly fed and equipped survivors living in austerity and working with complete dedication could rebuild our industrial plant to its pre-attack productive capacity within five years. (*The Legacy of Hiroshima*, p. 255)

* For a more detailed treatment and complete bibliographical references, see my *Nuclear War: The Ethic, The Rhetoric, The Reality* (Westminster, Maryland: 1965).

Ten years ago Dr. Kahn sometimes appeared to differ from his subsequent cinematic caricature, Dr. Strangelove, by not much more
than the only slightly disconcerting fact that Kahn never actually
took his doctorate. But now, a decade or so later, Herman Kahn
seems to have undergone a benign transmogrification, and where
he once defended the "icy rationality" of the games theorists (with
a non sequitur which itself betrayed considerable emotional bias)
by demanding: "Would you prefer a warm human error? Do you
feel better with a nice emotional mistake?"—where this was the secure self-complacency of a decade ago, we more recently find him
asserting:

> We know a great deal about weapons effects, but
> most of this is laboratory and test knowledge. The fact
> that popular expectations of nuclear war tend to be
> apocalyptic may demonstrate an intuitive wisdom—at
> least with respect to the psychological reactions to be
> expected, if not the physical results. As such, these
> intuitions may be more valid than methodologically
> more scientific but humanly less imaginative analyses.
> . . . (Annals of the American Academy of Political and
> Social Science, November, 1970)

The volte-face has been dramatic, a public metanoia all the more
incomprehensible since even ten years ago the efforts of Kahn and
his colleagues to cut the throat of intuition had been severely crit-
icized, and this not merely by practitioners of the "soft" disciplines,
humanists, sociologists, psychologists, etc. It was not a political
scientist, with an understandable rancor at the invasion of his field
by assorted physicists and mathematicians, who wrote: "In fact the
abstract theory of games is a branch of pure mathematics almost
wholly irrelevant to decision making": these were the words of a
Nobel Laureate in physics, P. M. S. Blackett, in his Studies of War,
also published in 1962. The models and scenarios of the gamesters
at Rand and Hudson had to be checked, according to Blackett,
"against the conclusions reached in a more intuitive manner."

Though Kahn's prose is still as wordy as ever (the Annals essay
runs close to 20,000 words), and the thinking almost as wooden
("problems of nuclear war" is a "field" he has "practically left . . .
and there are few younger people entering the profession"), the
conversion from raisons d'état to raisons du coeur is a very real
phenomenon. It may be due to a score of causes, separate or con-
verging, which I leave to others to analyze. However, what I want
to proffer seriously as at least one important factor worthy of examination is the universal chastening of rhetorical modes over the
past decade, a visible purifying of the dialect of the scribe, so that
it is simply no longer patient of the stuffed and baggy argot prev-

alent in almost all strategic studies of the sixties—and now, happily, evident only in the mintage of the Pentagon. A decade ago, Kahn's cant ran like this:

> I design buttons and I work very hard at designing buttons, both day and night. I got a group of people working about eighty hours a week nowadays designing buttons, and they are all very dedicated, they all think they are doing very good things. I don't think they are evil. I think they are, you know, an extraordinarily good group of people. (*Unintended War*, p. 56)

Kahn's current patter is considerably less glamourless—the old troper is dead, and dead for reasons which transcend in significance his demise, and therefore invite the attention of us all.

If there is no concept there can be no spoken word. So at least the old manuals of grammar and logic indicated, and for what follows I think we can rely on those traditional notions of language and thought. (Though one can hardly broach the subject without observing that the one student of language who has done the most constructive non-traditional linguistic theory has also been the most vigorous critic of the delusive "realism" Rand and its epigoni stood for: Noam Chomsky.) Assuming the manuals to be correct, how then could one ever have discussed the utterly non-conceptualizable subject of possible total thermonuclear extinction? Or to adapt Kahn's favored oxymoron, how could one talk about the unthinkable? How could one, for example, sanely talk—as Richard Fryklund putatively did in his *100 Million Lives*—about a "thinking man's way of devastating"?

In fact, it was a question that did not much vex the professional deployers of weaponry; they simply evaded it entirely. The incineration of all life was never really faced; what was faced were the academic problems of the algebra of death, the abstract problems of adjusting, equating, and manipulating the wellbred symbols of annihilation. The minters of nuclear newspeak whitewashed the sepulchers with the same jingling slogans ("peace is our profession"), the same crypto-sexuality (SM 72 Goose, Hermes and Nike, GAM 63), the same fudgey endorsings, philosophic, patriotic, theological (Plato, Minuteman, Apollo) as had their mentors, the account execs of the agencies.

At this distance in time, one can only muse over what afflatus stirred the creative spirit of what bard at the think-tanks on the occasion of the publication of *Soviet Military Strategy* to coin the countertactic to a "bigger bang for a buck" with "more rubble for a ruble." And one wonders what grave Rand laureate first let the nation snuggle up with mass murder in the lyric flight of a few "lobbed" "nukes." The rhetoric had matured from that earlier period when the umbilicus of the first atomic "baby" was severed from the womb of the "Enola Gay." The growing adolescent at the initial hydrogen test series was named "Mike"; and two years later the "fallout" from "Bravo" (now a sturdy youth) settled on a Japanese fishing boat and achieved the first "bonus kill"—the results of the subsequent official investigation appeared under the title "Project Sunshine." Now, with mortal syntax rampant, the nation hailed the blithe spirit of its first "birds," and purple riot ran through the macabre currency factories as the Pentagon Parnassians launched successively such nukenames as Davy Crockett, Oriole, Navaho, Houndog, etc. As the "hardware" rolled from the assembly lines, more elaborate "buttons" were needed; as the buttons increased, more nuclear "consoles" were developed; as the consoles multiplied, more countries wanted to join the "club."

No doubt, in part, the most sacred familial and traditional names were invoked to preserve the nation's sanity, to preserve its ability to live with itself and its evil in the face of this most perverse spawn of cancerous technology. No doubt, in part, the motive was also to domesticate the monstrosities, to acculturate them and make them merely another element in the ordinary furniture of the mind, in order that endlessly proliferating "generations" of new weaponry could be fabricated without restraint. No doubt; but only *in part*. For even more (and paradoxically), while the motive was to reduce the devices to the status of ordinary objects, it was equally to "distance" them, to exoticize them and thus engender a kind of aesthetic attitude towards them—an attitude which characterizes what the French Situationists call the "société du spectacle."

By so translating the new weapons into remote objects of contemplative enjoyment, the arms psychosis displayed itself, on the part of its purveyor-panderers as exhibitionistic, and on the part of its consumer-victims, as voyeuristic. By definition, the voyeur is a bystander who is totally disengaged, who has no personal bond with the object, and for whom the object has no value or meaning in itself; it is a completely detached, neutral instrument of the spectator's narcissism. The object is kept, as it were, at arm's length, and impinges on the observer only to the degree that it feeds his self-enclosed, involute fantasies—fantasies which, in turn, generate a mood of overweening power in which all residual sense of the object as an independent reality becomes utterly eclipsed.

Now, it is the contention here that it is precisely this breaking of the aesthetic distance, this rediscovery of the emotional bond, which

has wrought the conversion of the icy rationalists to the world of
intuition. The voyeur supinely gazes in endless mental ipsation
at a "spectacle" which has been so distanced that only its surfaces
are manifest—and with surfaces one doesn't relate. The intuiting
man, who has broken through the screen of the superficies, of the
glamorous labels, is implicated in the object, relates to it, and in
the radical sense of the word, knows it "intimately." It is no longer
a static, utterly predictable entity; rather it shares in the changing,
fluctuating mind ("like Gieseking playing Scarlatti") of its observer—and this reciprocity of subject and object creates a continuous spiral of ever new, ever more unpredictable, ever more
compounded relations. All of this I would take to be reflected in
the tentativeness, the unassertiveness, of a statement from trans-
mogrified Kahn, in a Hudson Institute tract of 1971:

> However, even one hundred missiles can probably do
> a great deal of damage even against a country with a
> very large defense system, or at least there will be enough
> uncertainty in physics, in engineering, in tactics, in
> weapons effects and in failure mechanisms, so that no
> one would lightly test the performance of the system.
> (*Why ABM?*, p. 67)

Note, too, in passing, that we now talk simply about "ABM," an
abridged, reasonably scientific ascription (and only inveterate
voyeurs should employ Mr. Nixon's *nom* "safeguard"—also, and
hardly surprising, a brandname soap).

But the rhetoric of the strategists was born not only of the marriage
of Madison Avenue and the Pentagon (a case of love among the
runes, if ever there was one) ; it was equally the whelp of priests
(of a sort) and poets (of a sort) —so putting to an uneasy end the
perennial conflict between the members of these two rival craft
unions. Thus it would seem, at least as evidenced by the language
employed, that we have been witnessing both psychological de-
mentia and religious aberration. This new rhetoric was modelled
not only on the pattern of a poem, but on that of a sacred poem.
It not only employed such metaphoric modes as personification and
euphemism, but relied heavily on tag lines and rythmic repetitions.
Perhaps an even better figure than the sacred poem would be the
rimed catechism of the New England Puritans in which strophe
after strophe demanded the congruent antistrophe; in which, to
take a couple of random examples, the very muttering of the maging
phrases, "ninety miles off our coast," or "winding down the war,"
would automatically elicit a collective "Amen" to Castro and the
Viet Cong. Like grand inquisitors of the great society (and its
less-great and less-social successor regime) the nuclear clerisy used

this *Rituale* to exorcise the community's fears and to instruct it in the ways of true faith.

For it was a matter of faith we were dealing with, and not of sight. *Fides ex auditu.* This kind of faith came by hearing the ministrant at the liturgy of nuclear strategy repeat over and over again, to pluck another example out of the randomness of history, the hypnotic incantation: "In your heart you know he's right." The primacy of heart over head is the kind of primacy one can accept only in the context of religious cult.

One of the articles in the *credo,* of which this chanting in unison was the sacramental sign, was that only the ordained dispensers of the mystery were to be trusted. Only they had been empowered in the Shekinah of the War Room to gaze upon the nuclear "presence" unblinkingly, and to communicate with the powers of the air. It was this anointing by thrice-great SAC which endowed one strategic prelate, Dr. James E. Dougherty (a "professional" Foreign Policy Specialist), with the knowledge that "the pacifist is invariably an amateur *(read,* "gentile") in the field of strategic analysis *(read,* "cabala"). A similar sense of segregation from the profane informed most observations on nuclear theosophy over the past decade, so that the deacons of deterrence had no hesitation whatever about invoking in their own favor a higher wisdom than was reachable by unordained folk, and in arguing on grounds that simply transcended the comprehension of the laity. *Sic,* Dr. Bernard Brodie of Rand: "In many important instances there is far more relevant knowledge available to us than non-specialists are in a position to understand." In all religions it is never a matter of greater insight or intelligence that differentiates the elect from the reprobate: it is a question only of "position"; of grace. Things just look different from within the sanctuary than from in front of the fane.

Not only did the high priests attest most virtuously to the miraculous power of their words, so that by their mere affirmation things were as they said, but they also bore public witness to the depths of their own faith. And one cannot read without feeling the compunction of the unwashed those martyrial memoirs, conveniently leaked to the press (or perhaps merely wafted to the media by angelic powers), about the long nights, the darkling vigils, of Mr. Johnson when, tormented by infidel pacifists, he sleeplessly reaffirmed the righteousness of his ways. The true priest has ever been sustained by his sense of mission; like the sainted *idiota* he holds to his predestined course undeviatingly, while all about him, the wayward, the uncommitted, the backsliders are wavering—*but* also sleepless. And what doth this priest deliver unto his people when, puffy-eyed, he emerges at dawn? He says, naturally (or rather, super-naturally), "Believe on me." "Though your sins be scarlet, I shall make them white as snow" (*sicut Nixon*).

For the true believer it is never a matter of opinion or insight that distinguishes the heretic from him; again, it is a matter of divine faith. As the gnome goes: Radiclibs are Comsymps. Anathema. In strictest definition, "a credibility gap" is overcome only by a "leap of faith." Ultimately the unbelievers were not guilty of ill-will, bad judgment, or illogic, but only of a lack of that knowledge which was realized in the *koinonia* of the faithful, that knowledge which passeth the understanding of heresiarchs Fulbright and Gore (both later skewered at the grand national *auto da fé*), Church and Mc-Govern. How were they, benighted by sin, to know that the lan-guage of true religion, like that of true poetry, is the language of paradox? "We are ending the war" by "expanding the war." "Surely, surely," this was no ordinary mortal discoursing. Indeed it wasn't. The lightly lipped phrases, like the secret language of druidic priests, were merely talismanic ejaculations to cleanse the soul while bewitching the mind. It was that stammering of the un-speakable (or unthinkable), which at best took the form of glos-solalia, known as "speaking in tongues"—in forked tongues the stiffnecked heretics would say.

Well, come the new epoch (and welcome), and the great god Pan is dead, buried on a remnant of his once vast domain (the Pan-handle?). What kills the great religions? Where is Osiris, Dagon, Quetzalcoatl (*pace*, D.H.L.)? Down the tides of history; washed away by intolerable social conflagration, the last inundation of the Nile, the "thrice-battering" by Israel, the Pepsicoatl of conquista-dores—*and* the horror of a Vietnam.

The new language is aborning, midwifed by new poets and priests (indeed by a poet-priest, Berrigan), a language which may recall the great vaticinator, Yeats' "the element of strength in poetic lan-guage is common idiom," or the prefaces of Wordsworth ("nature's priest"), or Herbert's (a true poet-priest) "Riddle who list, for me, and pull for Prime."

America's Need to Know

Norman Cousins

Norman Cousins, editor of *Saturday Review/World*, has long been recognized for broad vision, internationalism, and world-consciousness. In this article, he begins with the sad litany of recent political lies in America; noteworthy here is that he stresses not merely the words, but the deeds—the referrents *out there:* "the things we did that we had to deny." Yet despite the dangers and problems, the abuse of power, words, and weapons, he concludes with an affirmation of hope, a call to idealism, a vision of the necessity of truth and the intelligent rule of law in the world. This article was adapted from a talk Cousins gave at a Magazine Publishers Association symposium in New York in 1973.

The subject before this symposium is "America's Need to Know." Need to know what? Obviously, the need to know the truth. Truth may be an esoteric language, as Carl Van Doren once suggested, but it is the only language that the U.S. government is authorized by its people to speak. Americans need not be grateful for being told the truth by their government; this is their natural right and expectation.

In recent years, however, a strange new notion has gained ground. It is the idea that government has options with respect to the truth. A possible beginning date for this departure is 1947, when the government was authorized by Congress to practice secret violence, deceit, and subversion as essential parts of the conduct of U.S. foreign policy.

The underlying theory was that we were living in a hard, predatory, cloak-and-dagger world and that the only way to deal with a potential totalitarian enemy was to imitate him.

We may live in a world of plot and counterplot, but we also live in a world of cause and effect. Whatever the cause for the decision to legitimize and regularize deceit abroad, the inevitable effect was the practice of deceit at home. Examples are not difficult to find.

When it was revealed that the United States was secretly involved in an attempted coup against the government in Laos in 1959, we couldn't compartmentalize our denials. We couldn't tell the outside world that we had nothing to do with it and not expect the American people to be deceived along with everyone else.

Another example was the Gulf of Tonkin Resolution in 1964, which provided the legal basis for enlarged military operations in Indochina. It turned out that the administration had lied to Congress and the country about the episode in an attempt to obtain the authorizing resolution. Again, in 1966, the government announced a pause in the bombing of North Vietnam in order to probe for Hanoi's willingness to undertake negotiations. The bombing was resumed a month later with the announcement by the President that the efforts to arrange negotiations were unavailing. It was later learned that the probes had in fact turned up a positive response. Still another example: Late in 1971 the President declared that no military operations had been conducted against Cambodia. Pentagon officials testified to the same effect before a Congressional committee. It was later established that more than 3000 bombing operations had been carried out against Cambodia.

The main danger in all these and other episodes is represented not just by the break with truth but by the things we *did* that we had to deny. If truth is to mean anything, it must be a total process, including policies and actions of government that require neither concealment nor later denials or apologies.

Another prime liability of authorized lying in foreign policy is that it makes for bad habits. It makes officeholders casual about the practices of deception. In a world in which it is difficult to know where foreign policy ends and national policy begins, it is all too easy to transpose bad habits from one to the other. Not that it is all right to lie if the practice is confined to foreigners. The main point is that we went off the track the moment we went into the international business of deceit. From that point it was only a short and convenient step to use deceit and underhanded tactics in the general affairs of government at home.

It is all too easy to assume that all we have to do to correct these ominous failings is to identify rascals and throw them out. The cleansing process is essential, of course, but at some point soon it will be necessary to go beyond names and faces and to get at the structural flaws that have developed in government in recent years, flaws that will have to be repaired if an open society is to be preserved.

Truth in government will not assert itself. It has to be institutionalized. Truth needs a form of its own that transcends the men who happen to be in charge of the machinery of government at any given moment. This is what is meant by a government of laws rather than of men. This is what the main design produced by the Philadelphia Constitutional Convention of 1787–89 was all about. But this design has been slipping away from us in recent years. We have permitted exceptions from principle in the operation of

our society, exceptions that should not be accommodated or metab-
olized. We have made it possible for men in government to become bigger than the laws they have sworn to uphold.

The problem, to repeat, is not met just by changing men. The
problem can be met only by restoring and bolstering the basic principles of the society. There should be a test at the earliest possible
moment, for example, of the constitutionality of any government
agency that can spend large sums without public accounting, or
that can make decisions vitally affecting the foreign policy of this
nation without constitutional sanction, or that can engage in subversion abroad.

Former Attorney General Nicholas B. Katzenbach, writing in the
current issue of *Foreign Affairs,* proposes that only intelligence-
gathering activities be maintained. "Specifically," he declares,
"there should be no secret subsidies of police or counter-insurgency
forces, no efforts to influence elections, no secret money subsidies."

Mr. Katzenbach's proposal seems incontestable. Nothing is more
basic in American history than the need to respect the principle
of self-determination for all peoples. It is no accident that the
Declaration of Independence begins with a reference to a "decent
respect for the opinions of mankind." This doesn't mean that all
that is required of us is to acknowledge the existence of other
peoples. What it means is that the rights of other people, including
the right to truth from us, are no less inviolate than our own. For
our society was dedicated to the proposition that it is a human
enterprise before it is a national enterprise.

It will be said that we live in a chaotic and insecure world, that
our style in the international arena is dictated by others, and that
we have no choice but to play the game according to the way
others play it.

Yet it is precisely because we have to take the world as it is that it
becomes necessary to rise above the game if we wish to make our
mark. We cannot expect to succeed in the world political arena by
being more volatile than anyone else in the game of combustible
anarchy. We will succeed only as we represent a rallying center
in the world for a less hazardous and more sensible future for all
people than is now apparent. We are apt to command a wider audience by talking about the possibilities for human progress than
about shadowy balance-of-power or balance-of-terror strategies.

The proper model for America in its world position today is
not Prince Metternich but Thomas Jefferson. And if we are looking for philosophical guidelines, we will find that James Madison

and William James have far more to say to us than Niccolo Machiavelli.

Certainly let us take the world as it is. It is a world of anarchy, a world in which each nation regards its national security or national advantage as being its primary and frequently its solitary concern. But the sum total of all these individual national concerns is a volatile spew. There is not a government in the world that doesn't require traffic lights at the busy intersections of its metropolitan centers; yet the absurd notion persists that separate absolute national sovereignties can go their own way without mammoth collisions.

Everyone understands what happens when the machinery of law in a small community suddenly breaks down, but there is no comparable awareness of the dangers that confront every member of the human species because of the absence of law enforceable on nations. Heads of government unfailingly and unceasingly denounce lawlessness within their own countries; yet they totally resist the development of responsible law among themselves.

The essential truth, therefore, is that no rational process now exists for assuring the basic safety of the human species. We stumble into the future day-to-day, dependent for our survival more on the hope that our margin for error may not have been completely exhausted than on a working design for a peaceful world.

It is not reasonable or logical to assume that the national statesmen will lead the way in the taming of nations or in the rebuilding of the United Nations into a governed world. Do not expect, Alexander Hamilton wrote, nations to take the initiative in developing restraints upon themselves.

Governments are not built to perceive large truths. Only people can perceive great truths. Governments specialize in small and intermediate truths. They have to be instructed by their people in great truths. And the particular truth in which they need instruction today is that new means for meeting the largest problems on earth have to be created. Individual nations can unleash wars but are incapable individually of preventing them.

A single government cannot by itself keep the oceans from becoming a global sewer or the sky a poisonous canopy. Nor can a single government eliminate the need for the weapons that cost the world's people 250 billion dollars a year with resultant impoverishment.

But an individual government can work with the large truth that our earth has to be governed. It can identify causes of world anarchy. It can come forward with a great design for safeguarding our small planet. It can recognize that we are dealing no longer with narrow concerns but with the safety of the human habitat.

The American people are paying a fearsome price today for the dominant condition of lawlessness among nations. This condition works back on the conditions of life inside the United States. It dominates the national budget. It is the prime cause of the inflation and the severe strain on our economy. It diverts energy, attention, and resources from our main needs. It subtracts from the quality of life. It makes a caricature of our ideals. It creates a mood and a context in which it is all too easy for the national security to be confused with the security of political parties or their leaders. It gives a President more personal options than it was originally intended he should have; nor is it healthy for the American people that he should have such options.

The big challenge, therefore, is to create a situation in which truth can live a less unnatural and precarious existence than at present, and in which the right to know doesn't depend on special dispensations. We do this best by making the achievement of world law the central and open objective of our foreign policy.

Any nation that comes forward with such a design can expect to be rebuffed. But there is a distinction between rebuff and defeat. There is no defeat for the American people when they tie themselves to the great idea that human intelligence is equal to human needs. Beyond the clamor of clashing ideologies and the preening and jostling of sovereign tribes, there is a safer and more responsible world waiting to be created.

3

A Call to Action . . . and Some Responses

. . . an eloquent exhortation for action . . . followed by speeches concerned with language abuse delivered by leaders of academic and scholarly organizations . . .

The Rhetoric of Peace

Robert F. Drinan

Congressman Drinan of Massachusetts, a Jesuit priest, was formerly the Dean of the Law School at Boston College. A leader in the anti-war protest movement, Father Drinan has never been known for his timidity: he was the first congressman to introduce a motion for the impeachment of President Nixon, and, as a member of the House Judiciary Committee, helped draft the articles of impeachment. But even congressmen get cowed by the myths and stereotypes of the "English teacher." Drinan delivered this speech at the 1972 Boston meeting of the Conference on College Composition and Communication and began by noting: "I approach you today with fear and caution. I feel that if only I had a copy of Strunk and White's little masterpiece *The Elements of Style* clutched to my bosom, I would be immune to any criticism by the distinguished English teachers from all over the country who are here today. As a refugee from the academic community, I am particularly sensitive to the importance of your role. You are the trustees of the English language. . . ."

Language is not merely the way we express our foreign policy; language *is* our foreign policy. In Washington some of your students and the students of your predecessors exhibit no respect whatever for the honest use of language. Their language is dishonest because it expresses untruths but also, and more insidiously, because it masks the truth in jargon and non-statements so inscrutable as to confute the most able translator or cryptographer.

I do not impute to your profession responsibility for the false statements, the lies, which are uttered in Washington. Even an English professor's accountability stops short of that hideous prospect. However, in the matter of officially-proclaimed marshmallow prose—language which is really non-language—it does seem to me that you have some professional responsibility.

The American Medical Association wins no awards for enlightened self-goverance or a well-defined sense of the public interest. However, if a substantial number of government-employed physicians were to perform open-heart surgery under unsanitary conditions, I have no doubt that the A.M.A. would protest. Today, whole departments of the Federal government, and most notoriously the Departments of State and Defense, are systematically ravaging the English language; and the trustees of the language, or at least most of them, have not protested.

This anti-social misuse of language has not been totally ignored. Russell Baker, in the *New York Times* of December 1, 1971, expressed his outrage at the abuse of language: "The Pentagon," said Baker,

> has abandoned bombing as an instrument of war because it is considered bad taste. Instead of bombing it is now equipped to use such new techniques as the thermonuclear exchange, the limited air strike confined with surgical precision to strictly military targets and the protective reaction.
>
> Each of these, admittedly, involves the placing of exploding bombs on or near the property and persons of foreign states with which our Government may be experiencing poor relationships. Still, bombing is such an ugly act that the United States Government can no longer be associated with it. This is why we had to use the protective reaction last week.

Mario Pei, one of our most distinguished students of the misuse of language, has also noted the trend toward non-language. Dr. Pei has given us a new coinage for obfuscation by government: he calls this form of non-language "true weasel words," and he states, in an article titled "The American Language in the Early '70's," "The four prime areas for weasel words are, as usual, the military, government, politics, and commercial advertising." Pei's insight is precise: "The real military contribution to language," he says,

> comes from the higher echelons. Here we find not only those reprehensible and often deplored terms, *kill ratio* and *body count* (they have been in use for some years, yet none of our dictionaries records them) but also *green backing*, used to describe the hiring of mercenary troops or the financing of such responsive governments as those of South Vietnam and Cambodia, likewise unreported by any dictionary. . . . *Protective reaction* is Pentagonese for such operations as Cambodia and Laos, and displays the usual euphemistic quality of the language of the generals. . . . The finest sample is perhaps the one coined by the Air Force to replace the word *demonstration,* previously used for an accounting review of a contract, to which General Teubner had objected on the ground that *demonstration* had become a dirty word in other connections. He suggested *audit review* as a replacement, which would have been reasonable enough; but the staff writers gave him more than he had bargained for: *Data Accounting Flow Assessment,* with a suitable abbreviation, DAFA.

More than twenty-five years ago, George Orwell observed trenchantly that "political speech and writing are largely the defense of the indefensible . . . political language has to consist largely of euphemism, question-begging and cloudy vagueness." It is my duty to report to you that the objects of Orwell's observation are at this moment comfortably ensconced in the State and Defense Departments and, ironically or predictably, they are the very individuals who in so many other respects are bringing us closer to the Orwellian vision of a sterile 1984.

Even the incoherent among us have observed the non-writing on the wall. As Jerry Rubin announces in *Do It,* "a dying culture destroys everything it touches . . . and language is one of the first things to go." "Language *prevents* communication," Rubin concludes.

The proposition that language prevents communication appears utterly absurd until we examine some language which has oozed out of the Defense Department recently.

It would be difficult to identify a subject on which lucid language is more necessary than the subject of our international military policy. Surely, the Secretary of Defense should be in a position to clearly state, in plain language, our international strategic objectives. Here is a central paragraph from the address of the Secretary of Defense on this subject—in a key section of his defense budget request statement to the House Appropriations Committee on March 4, 1971. This paragraph, I should say at the outset, is part of an exposition under the non-title, "A Strategy of Realistic Deterrence." I quote Mr. Laird:

> It is not realistic or efficient to expect each country to develop an independent self-defense capability against all levels of non-Chinese and non-Soviet attack. The drain on allied manpower and on their economies would inhibit the achievement of economic growth, and therefore, the political stability which is essential to military security. At the same time, deep historical, social and political inhibitions to immediate and effective regional mutual security arrangements in some areas must be recognized. Thus, a careful balance must be achieved between independent capabilities and collective arrangements. One of the most important means available to the U.S. to stimulate and to help aid in the development of these capabilities and arrangements is the provision of appropriate security assistance to our allies.

I have read that paragraph five times, and I am confident that it is devoid of meaning. The Secretary of Defense is making sounds, but he is also mute. Did language prevent communication here?

Perhaps the Secretary would have better communicated the Administration's intentions by dancing or showing animated cartoons.

Non-language phrases like the one employed by the Central Intelligence Agency to order a political assassination—"termination with prejudice"—are not humorous, at least not in any conventional sense. The phrase "black humor" does not begin to convey the ghastliness of such homicidal euphemisms. In fact, the Defense Department jargon is not funny, because it is really a kind of psychologically impenetrable barrier, a barrier which keeps the people out and the insulated administrators in.

I submit that the systematic use of such opaque terms as "protective reaction," and the hollow sentences of the war planners, do far more to hide the decision-making process of the Defense Department from the people—and from Congress—than any secrecy-classification rules.

I submit that if every utterance of the Defense Department were made in an ancient language not understood by anyone, we would know very little less about the real military policies and intentions of our government than we now know.

I submit that the use of empty words by the Defense Department is not the accidental by-product of a metastasized bureaucracy; rather, it is an essential part of a pervasive scheme to keep Defense Department decision-making a secret—unknown and unknowable by any potential critics. Let me add that the residents of the Pentagon have much reason to fear public exposure, as the Pentagon Papers, the Anderson Papers and much other evidence indicate.

The title of this talk contains the word "rhetoric." The first definition Webster's assigns to it is "the art of speaking or writing effectively." Anyone who examines the use of language by the Defense Department will have to admit that their language has been effective. The President proposes to spend 78 billion dollars for war-related purposes in fiscal 1973, and even the most conscientious objectors in Congress and elsewhere find insuperable the task of figuring out where and for what purpose that sum would be spent.

Along with other members of a congressional group called Members of Congress for Peace Through Law, I have examined in detail several military spending items, including, for example, the question of how many United States troops should be stationed in Europe.

I have discovered that not only are the words used by the Defense Department on these subjects inscrutable or unavailable for my review, but that even the statistics, the financial analyses, are designed in such a way that no one who does not possess the Pentagon code book or computer program can understand them. Of course, I should add that the incidence of secrecy of Defense Department data is directly proportional to the degree of its relevance.

Fortunately, the rhetoric of unlanguage is susceptible to attack. The attack is founded on an appeal to vanity, not an appeal to the public interest: even the Defense Department does not relish being accused of incoherence. Each of us, to be effective in his own rhetoric, must make that accusation. We must proclaim not only that the emperor is naked, but that he is engaged in unspeakable acts. If enough of us make that claim clearly enough and repeatedly enough, our efforts will have results.

We have already had some small but important results. When I and several of my colleagues in the House of Representatives forced the issue of the clandestine non-language of the CIA last year, there somehow resulted the creation of a CIA Subcommittee of the House Armed Services Committee, a subcommittee headed by a very responsible congressman, Lucien Nedzi of Michigan.

When the Navy Department recently presented me with repeated non-language statements on the status of a problem confronting a constituent of mine, I arranged for high Navy officials to visit my office and discuss the matter in clear sentences. On other occasions, in the context of military appropriations and foreign assistance bills, members of Congress have sought with at least partial success coherent statements from the Defense Department.

The influence of the English profession in re-establishing comprehensible language as the medium of a democratic society could be enormous. The close textual analysis of critical government documents by you and your students would be a first step in affirming the value of clarity and the value of honestly used language.

I propose that you consider as the textual basis of an English course three documents which reflect the issues I have discussed. They are, first, *United States Foreign Policy, 1971, A Report of the Secretary of State* (Dept. of State Publication 8634, March 1972, U.S. Government Printing Office) ; second, *National Security Strategy of Realistic Deterrence, Secretary of Defense Melvin Laird's Annual Defense Department Report, Fiscal Year 1973* (U.S. Government Printing Office, February 15, 1972) ; and, third, *The Pentagon Papers As Published by The New York Times* (Bantam Books, 1971). Six months of intensive study of these materials would teach any student more about government and the uses and abuses of language than years of civics and political science courses. Six months of such study would inevitably result in a new rhetoric by student and teacher alike, the rhetoric of peace.

The rhetoric of peace is the effective use of language by individuals whose motives and understanding differ from the motives and understanding of this Administration. The rhetoric of peace is founded on Paul Tillich's judgment that "The passion for truth is crushed beneath the weight of undisputed authority."

We can and will clearly, calmly, and vigorously persuade the American people that they are the real power in this country. When more of us come to the inevitable conclusion that we are entitled to more accountability from those who collect our money, spend it, and in the process place our lives and civilization in peril— then we shall have spoken effectively. Ladies and Gentlemen, I urge you to reaffirm your trusteeship of the English language.

General Semantics: Where Is It Now?

S. I. Hayakawa

At the NCTE convention in Minneapolis in November 1972, Hayakawa assessed the success and failure of the General Semantics movement, a movement in which Hayakawa was an important leader—as author of *Language in Thought and Action* and longtime editor of *ETC*. The following essay is the transcript (slightly edited) of that speech. In this retrospective analysis, Hayakawa contemplates the failure of General Semantics to achieve its idealistic goals, but also observes that the movement has had continued endurance and success in stimulating individuals to a greater sensitivity to language.

One thing that we might talk about as regards success and failure in communication is *our success or failure in communicating semantic ideas* to the entire community as we had hoped to do. There are certain successes and failures that give us pause. It's 50 years since the publication of Ogden and Richards's *The Meaning of Meaning*. It's 40 years since *Science & Sanity* of Alfred Korzybski. It's 34 years since Stuart Chase's *The Tyranny of Words*. And—I shudder to think about this—but it's 34 years since the publication in mimeograph form of the experimental edition of my own *Language in Action*. It's 26 years since Wendell Johnson's *People in Quandaries*; it's 31 years since Irving Lee's *Language Habits in Human Affairs*. These are all works that you're familiar with. These are all pioneering works in semantics.

I remember that period in the 1930s and the early 1940s—how we were all caught up in a kind of a messianic zeal. We were about to save the world. Except that we got plunged into World War II shortly afterwards, and that wasn't much help. But we were captivated by the concept of "The Manhood of Humanity" formulated by Alfred Korzybski in 1921: that mankind was going through its childhood and adolescence and wouldn't become mature until it understood itself better. And so we thought maybe we were on the threshold of the manhood of humanity.

I remember very, very vividly the Denver conference on General Semantics in the summer of 1941, just a few months before Pearl Harbor, when the theme of the conference throughout was our great excitement at the idea of having found some kind of intellectual method by means of which some of the tragedies of the world could be averted. But, since those days, we've had wars ever since. Nothing but war, if not a hot war, a cold war. And so, I speak to you now, four or five wars later, with a certain sense of discouragement that our messianic zeal just didn't pay off, didn't carry through what we had hoped to do.

The world on the whole is unaffected by General Semantics. Neither the Protestant nor Catholic Irish seem to know very much about it, and nor do the Israelis nor the Arabs. Where we continue to be divided and hate each other and when things break out into violence, we try to say over and over again: there is a failure of communication on the part of the speaker or hearer or both, that language may also be at fault, and so on. But, people pay no attention, they go on shooting each other. And so there's no evidence of semantic sophistication having penetrated into the Department of Defense, or the state legislature of California, or New Jersey, or New Mexico, or not even Minnesota, perhaps. And people keep saying the same old foolish things, and acting on them. It's kind of discouraging, after putting 30 or more years of your life into this.

You have all contemplated the fact that we live in an age of an "information explosion." But one of the things that gave birth to semantics is the fact that we are also in the middle of a *misinformation* explosion. With the proliferation of mass communications, with the development of radio, especially, a generation ago, we found ourselves surrounded by hawkers and pitchmen, hard and soft sells, persuaders hidden and overt. We are bombarded daily by millions of words by print and electronic media. We have to develop some kind of critical method by means of which we decide whom and what to believe.

Do you recall in the 1930s—some of you will recall, and some of you weren't born—the Institute for Propaganda Analysis that was founded in Columbia University in 1936? In 1936 also, Sinclair Lewis published his novel *It Can't Happen Here,* in which he pictures the success of a radio demagogue developing a fascist state in the United States. In 1938 was *The Tyranny of Words;* in 1939 was my prepublication edition of *Language in Action.* In 1938 I attended the first Korzybski seminar.

We all knew then that the misinformation explosion was a danger to the world. Why? Well, because Hitler had succeeded in persuading millions to share his crazy views and it was a danger to the whole world, a danger from which we recovered only at the cost of millions of lives—what a tragic cost! But Hitler got there by radio. He got into every German living room. And do you remember that appalling sense, some of you who are old enough to remember, that appalling sense of tragedy when Hitler's armies walked into Austria, and the Austrians collapsed without firing a shot, because they had been softened up by radio propaganda? And if that's the power of radio, then where are we? And this was the response: this is why Sinclair Lewis responded by his *It Can't Happen Here;* this is why there was an Institute for Propaganda Analysis; this is why the semantics movement was developed.

How is propaganda evaluated? It cannot always be evaluated by scientific method, since propagandistic statements are rarely capable of proof. But propaganda can be approached with a scientific attitude. And some kind of discipline in the orientation of science is necessary to inculcate a critical attitude towards words, our own as well as others, so that our lives may be governed by that skepticism and that respect for fact that characterizes the rational and civilized mind. And that's what we saw in General Semantics at the time, and that's the reason for our enormous enthusiasm for the subject. And I'm sure many of you as teachers shared in that excitement, not only at that time, and many of you who are younger, have shared in it again. Over and over again semantics has come to us as a kind of revelation.

But in spite of all that we did in semantics, we are living in a time when rationality has suddenly gone out of fashion. In the world of hip literary intellectuals there are cults of mysticism, fads for such things as *I Ching,* an ancient Chinese system of fortune-telling. People tell each other's fortunes and decide their fates by shuffling Tarot cards or by consulting astrologists. On the political Left there flourishes, or flourished until recently, a cult of violence, like the Weathermen, devoid of any serious intellectual or social analysis, yet capable of producing followers cross-eyed with mindless fanaticism. Never has rationality been so badly needed as in a period when intellectuals themselves are spearheading the drive towards anti-intellectualism. I mention only two names, let's say Theodore Roszak and Charles Reich. We read them like crazy in English departments. Many people regard them as the wave of the future, but they are specifically and unashamedly trying to be anti-intellectual and anti-critical.

So, on top of all of this, one important change that has taken place since the 1930s is the fact that we've had burst upon us, especially from the end of the 1940s onwards, the whole phenomenon of television. And what have we, in semantics, done to sharpen additionally our critical powers, to take care of that enormous instrument for penetrating our minds, our lives, our imaginations, with picture, with song, with color, with attractive things to eat and buy? What's television going to do to this society?

There has been, I'm afraid, no comparable development in semantic theory to take into account the age of television. Marshall McLuhan has made some very astute and fascinating observations on the subject, but the problem with Marshall McLuhan, of course, is that he is unsystematic, and he prides himself on that fact. He's provocative, but he doesn't follow through with an intellectual method that we can apply.

I remember early in the 1960s starting to lecture (the 1960s was kind of late, but I did begin to lecture on the impact of television) on the unforeseen consequences of television. In 1959 I remember addressing a Westinghouse broadcasting conference at Stanford on the impact of television on society. In the 1960s I gave a paper before the American Psychological Association on the subject of television under the title "Who's Bringing Up Your Children?" You hear of parents thoughtlessly leaving their kids in front of the TV set day after day, hour after hour. The television set is bringing them up. Not grandmother, not uncles and aunts, not father and mother, but the television set. And what are we producing as a result of bringing children up in that way? I try to raise these questions. I don't think these questions have been raised often enough.

Some of the insights that we need about television have come from outside the area of semantics—from outside the semantic discipline itself. I'm not altogether happy that we were not in there—all of us who are teachers and students of semantics. You will recall that the founder of General Semantics, the late Alfred Korzybski, used to say that everything we experience is a result of a process of abstraction and selection. We see what we are looking for and, more importantly, we do not see what we are not looking for. These principles apply just as much to the newspaper or television reporter as they do to the average citizen.

You will recall a recent book by Edith Efron, *The News Twisters*. As she writes (and this is a wonderful summary of the process of abstraction), the events selected for coverage by television are a matter of choice; the facts isolated are a matter of choice; the participants involved are a matter of choice; the authorities and experts cited are a matter of choice; and even this is not where selectivity stops. It continues throughout the period in which the reporter sits down at his typewriter. He selects a vocabulary; he selects connotations, implications, associations, dramatic structure, organization. Emotional, intellectual, moral, and political stresses—all these are a matter of choice.

As Edith Efron has said—do you remember she analyzed closely the news broadcasts of the seven weeks prior to the 1968 election—she found an enormous pro-Democratic bias. She herself happens to be a Democrat in politics. But she says that the news coverage is not fair. It's abundantly clear that reporters, whether journalists or TV newscasters, have no more sophistication about the perceptual process that Korzybski wrote about than the average typesetter or cameraman.

Furthermore, as Ms. Efron's study demonstrates, *what* is to be reported and *how* it is to be interpreted are determined on all three great networks—ABC, CBS, and NBC—by the same kind of people—as Mr. Agnew has pointed out too—people who have snobbish disdain for Lyndon B. Johnson's Texas accent and culture, people who also have a snobbish disdain for Richard M. Nixon's middle-American style and George Wallace's Southern-style conservatism.

In the coverage of the Democratic National Convention of '68, which resulted in a disastrous confrontation between anti-establishment youth and the police, television reporters were extraordinarily sensitive to the harassment of the young by the police. But they were not at all sensitive to the harassment of the police by the young demonstrators. Most of us still haven't heard about that, although that was a very important part of the scene. Well, Ms. Efron does not accuse anyone of lying, but she does accuse them, not only of selective perception, but also of selective use of language to protect the Left and to discredit the Right. Here's a nice example: George Wallace's opponents before that election threw fruit; they threw tin cans and rocks at him. But television reporters described them as *demonstrators* and *hecklers*. Now it's one thing to heckle verbally, but it's another thing to throw a rock. But they did not make the distinction, they just called them *hecklers*. As Ms. Efron writes, in seven weeks not one reporter expressed the view or quoted anyone as expressing the view that this outbreak of physical attacks on Wallace was *an assault;* it was illegal; it was morally wrong. What emerges from editorial opinion is the clear-cut implication that violence from the Left, never named as such, is legitimate if directed at the racist Right. As Ms. Efron continues, it need hardly be said that however one may condemn Mr. Wallace's Rightism or racism, he's entitled to the full protection of the law, just as much, let's say, as a Communist Black Panther arrested for threatening to murder President Nixon. And it is a curious fact that this cardinal principle of

American ethics and law totally vanished from the minds of net-work reporters during the Wallace campaign.

Let me try to restate the question: After 30 or more years of teach-ing and studying semantics, where are we? In one sense, in the public sense, we aren't anywhere. It doesn't seem to affect public policy or decisions to make war, or whatever. There's another place where we are nowhere. At this point semantics is not even fashion-able. That is, no discussion of it appears in the hip literary journals like *New York Review of Books,* or *Partisan Review,* or *Commentary,* or *Public Interest*—these are the real exciting intel-lectual vanguard. They never discuss semantics; they apparently never talk about Korzybski. They may talk about Kierkegaard, they may talk about Teilhard de Chardin, they may talk about Jean Genet, but they don't talk about Korzybski anymore.

So where are we? Well, you and I, as teachers, know where we are. You must have had the experience, as I have had over and over again, of having your former students come back to you and say, "The course you gave me in semantics was a turning point in my life." And I've been teaching long enough now, so that people 40 and 50 years old occasionally write me letters and tell me exactly this!—that reading one of my books, or studying one of my books in a class taught by one of you in this room perhaps, was a turning point in their lives.

Just the night before last, I lectured in El Camino College in Torrance, California, which is a part of Los Angeles, and I can't tell you how moved I was when six different people out of that audience came up with the 1941 edition of *Language in Action* and asked me to autograph them. Somehow semantics penetrates inside one's deepest evaluations and means something in the long run. So we are hitting *individuals,* even if we haven't hit the culture as a whole, or as I said earlier, the Defense Department.

I ask these people, when I encounter them, "Where did you study semantics?" and they give me all sorts of wonderful answers: at Los Angeles City College, at Chicago Teachers College, at Trenton State University in Trenton, New Jersey, at Westchester High School, at Temple University, at Florida Southern, at the Univer-sity of Missouri Department of Journalism, where the study of semantics has been compulsory for a long time. It is taught by teachers of speech, of English, of communication arts, and so on. This is where semantics is hitting, and it's *still* hitting people in a very important way, even if it's not fashionable, as I say, in the prestigious literary circles.

Perhaps, ultimately where it does belong is with the people: you study semantics in high school, you study it in freshman English, you study it in Introductory Speech, and ten years later you have forgotten how you got to be so smart. And so you quote the books you read more recently and it doesn't occur to you to go back to quote Irving Lee's *Language Habits in Human Affairs,* which stuck in your minds. Maybe that's exactly where it belongs—at that stage of late adolescence in high school or college—when young men and women are arriving at their intellectual maturity and they find an intellectually critical method that liberates their minds from the dogmas and shibboleths of the family or church or the neighborhood in which they were born, which suddenly liberates their minds so they begin to listen to television more critically, to listen to radio programs more critically, to read more critically, and listen to your lectures more critically . . . and to mine.

Maybe that's exactly where it belongs—in the teaching profession, in the transition from adolescence to adulthood. And this is why I felt it very important to come and join you today. I think that people in an organization such as the National Council of Teachers of English are the real forefront in semantics. You've got to keep it going. You hit them exactly at the right time when they need it. And insofar as you do this, I think that there continues to be a great future for semantics, and will continue to be, as I say, from late high school years to early college years. There you will make an impact. And your students will write to you 30 years later and say *"thank you, very much."*

Learning from Watergate

Frank McCulloch and Morton Malkofsky

In this editorial from *Learning* (September 1973), the editors perceptively link authoritarianism in the classroom, lip service to the "open" classroom, and the current political scandal: "Watergate and the machinations and maneuvers that preceded it were ugly, not so much for what they revealed to us about our leaders but for what they told us about ourselves."

In the fall of 1973, 15 months after it first surfaced, four months after it began to dominate television screens and headlines, what does Watergate mean to America as a nation, to all of us as citizens of that nation?

A good deal less to many of us, it now seems clear, than what some more assertive political science professors, journalists and members of Congress might have hoped. But that is understandable. Events in Washington, even when they involve the nation's mighty, take place at a great physical and emotional distance from most of us, and what doesn't directly and immediately affect our daily lives holds our attention briefly, if at all.

So it was marvelously easy, as Watergate ground on into the summer, to turn away, to profess boredom, to dismiss the conduct of the principals as a natural and even forgivable part of the dirty game of politics, to put it all down in the final analysis as a particularly persistent, strident and unpleasant squabble between two groups of whom most of us are not very fond anyway—politicians and journalists.

It was that. But it was also, and far more importantly, a process by which an ugly growth on the body politic was exposed. That growth's tissues were our own boredom, our inclination to write the whole thing off as an aberration, the unsavory actions of an unprincipled few, over whom we had no control and for whom we held no responsibility. How easy it became to draw a neat and comforting dividing line between "us" and "them"—and how certainly tumors thrive in such a climate of benign neglect. For no civilization survives for long without strong and carefully tended social and moral fibers. When social consciousness and social conscience begin to decay, the fibers rot with them. The surest sign that rot is present is not that persons in position of trust have betrayed it, but that their followers turn away with a yawn. As all too many of us put it, ho-ho-ho-hum.

What, in the same fall of 1973, does Watergate mean to American education?

The question requires a stepping back in time, from the days Watergate began to dominate the headlines, to a point from which it can be seen that what preceded Watergate was of deeper significance than the event itself. For the cliché is accurate: Watergate was only the tip of the iceberg. Beneath the surface was a carefully planned and skillfully orchestrated campaign by the executive branch of the United States government to grab power—a pattern of political behavior chillingly familiar in other lands but which Americans either failed or were unwilling to recognize in their own country. It was the closest this nation has ever come to a coup d' état, not, in this case, by those out of power, but by those in power, in order to consolidate, hold and increase that power.

Not in America, we all shout. It can never happen here. Watergate helped prove that.

But did it? The truth is that the drive toward concentration of power in the White House was not unique. The educational community should, in fact, recognize the scenario rather clearly. To be sure, the cast of characters in education's drama is not as star-studded, the dialogue is less sensational, and the action seldom takes place front and center on the national stage.

But the critical substance of the issue—the domination, ideological and otherwise, of one over many—is the same. It may, as a matter of fact, have been in a more advanced stage of development in the schools of America than it was in Washington, circa 1972–73.

It is true that by that time education had already undergone its own Watergate disclosures. The Silbermans, the Kozols, the Kohls and the Herndons had already spotlighted how authoritarians take over a classroom. The day of the omnipotent teacher and regimented children was therefore presumably past. But was it? Is it? The fact remains that a classroom teacher, armed with certificates from state and university, is routinely handed an operational structure that has a potential for tyranny at least as great as any in the dreams of the most power-hungry despot. What the teacher's constituency lacks in size, it makes up in innocence and receptivity. Moreover, teachers, unlike politicians, have no need to barter for power; it is bequeathed.

Open and *free* have become education catchwords in recent years.

When they first gained currency, they presumably stood for freedom of both spirit and intellect. In that sense, they were shorthand for a teacher's commitment to relinquish power, to resist the temptation of imposing ideas and set ways of learning and thinking. With implementation, the words came to mean what those who used them chose them to mean. Classrooms called "open" were all too often little more than furniture showcases. Rows of bolted desks were replaced by rugs, cushions and high-rise work areas. The assumption was that if a classroom *looked* open, it was open. Freedom of thought and learning were confused with freedom of movement. Few teachers, however, took seriously the commitment to surrender real power. Kids were and are expected to reach a given set of objectives at a given time along a given route. Free to get up and walk about the room? Certainly. Free to think and plan and learn for themselves? Now that's another matter.

The stakes for all of us in this are extremely high. For the events that preceded Watergate did not take place in a vacuum. Their existence and acceptance depended upon a passive or unseeing or bored citizenry. But any parent, any caretaker of the young, knows that passivity and blind acceptance of truth from on high and ennui are not natural in a healthy toddler. Self-assertion, resistance to arbitrary commands and a maddening inclination to ask "why?" are. They characterize the preschooler. They characterize the kindergartner.

Then, subtly, comes the change. And why not? Success in school, after all, is measured largely by the degree to which the student accepts the notion of one power seat, one commanding voice, one predetermined response to a predetermined question. If that is the path to success, why fight it—in school or out?

Watergate and the machinations and maneuvers that preceded it were ugly, not so much for what they revealed to us about our leaders but for what they told us about ourselves. It is time now to get on with the treatment of those tumors.

Lest, the next time around, we will not be so lucky as to have a Watergate.

Watergate and Education: Three NEA Statements

Old stereotypes of teachers and teachers' organizations must yield to current realities. The National Education Association stands as one example: the nation's largest organization of teachers, NEA made strong public statements early in the Watergate affair.

The events involving the Watergate affair and its related scandals affect us in a professional sense in a great many ways: our students are affected; we ourselves are affected; and, our government is being profoundly affected, and changed, right before our eyes. This is the stuff of which government, history, public affairs, social institutions, sociology, psychology, political science, law—the stuff of which nearly all the subjects we teach are made. This *is* the world for which we are trying to prepare our students. To ignore the very substance we are trying to teach is, in my opinion, so far beyond the basic tenets of the teaching profession as to be untenable.

Catherine Barrett, 1973 President
National Education Association

The National Education Association urges Congress to investigate—immediately, completely, and thoroughly—the activities of President Nixon and his Administration. Every effort must be made to determine the possible need to impeach the President, or to determine that the President's name be cleared. . . .

The above resolution was passed by the NEA Board of Directors at its November, 1973 meeting in Washington. The Board also passed a motion supporting NEA 1974 President Helen Wise's recent statements on Watergate. In a letter to President Nixon dated October 24, 1973, Dr. Wise said:

The nation's 2.2 million teachers share in the ground swell of public outrage registered by millions of Americans in the Administration's handling of the Watergate scandals. . . .

Truth Is a Linguistic Question

Dwight Bolinger

"Truth is the most fundamental of all questions of appropriateness in language." Thus Dwight Bolinger of Harvard University summarizes his Presidential Address to the Linguistic Society of America in December 1972. "Communication presupposes non-concealment between interlocutors, which logically excludes all forms of deception, not merely propositional lies. The lie, broadly conceived, is therefore a proper object of study for linguists, and a necessary one at a time when lying is cultivated as an art." "As members of society," Bolinger continues, "we have an obligation to contribute our skills in this as much as in other ways. Happily, a number of linguists have begun to respond by investigating the lies implicit in presuppositions, deletions, indirections, and loaded and jargonesque elements in the lexicon." Emphasizing that lies "embrace the hidden and unconscious, as well as the barefaced and deliberate," Bolinger itemizes some of the common techniques of the subtle lie, concluding that "Public officials hide behind the images that Madison Avenue creates for them, and lies hide behind the face of truth."

The drift of this paper can be summed up in an expression that first saw the light of day in 1942. For almost three years, from 1937 to 1939, American volunteers had been part of the army that fought against Hitler and Mussolini in Spain. After the vortex of Hitlerism had finally sucked us in, one would have expected those trained and seasoned young soldiers to be admired for their foresight and sought out for their experience. But nothing of the sort happened. In one of those perverse labelings that propagandists are so good at, they were passed over as 'premature antifascists'. To have admitted their foresight would have been to admit our own lack of it.

Every generation has to rediscover love. So, I suppose, every generation must rediscover jargon. Here is a 1972 definition by L. E. Sissman: 'all of these debased and isolable forms of the mother tongue that attempt to paper over an unpalatable truth and/or to advance the career of the speaker (or the issue, cause or product he is agent for) by a kind of verbal sleight of hand, a one-upmanship of which the reader or listener is victim.' Stepping back to 1955 we hear James Thurber calling for a psychosemanticist, or for anybody, who could treat us for what he called 'the havoc wrought by verbal artillery on the fortress of reason', by a language 'full of sound and fury, dignifying nothing'. Going back another quarter century to my own college days, there was Sir Arthur Quiller-Couch with his essay 'On jargon' (1916). Running the film in reverse a good 200 years more, Sir Ernest Gowers 1948 quotes an admonition 'delivered to the Supervisor of Pontefract by the Secretary to the Commissioners of Excise'. It reads: 'The Commissioners on perusal of your diary observe that you make use of many affected phrases and incongruous words, such as "illegal procedure," "harmony," etc., all of which you use in a sense that the words do not bear. I am ordered to acquaint you that if you hereafter continue that affected and schoolboy way of writing, and to murder the language in such a manner, you will be discharged as a fool.' It would be a simple matter to round out the history with quotations from Erasmus and Thucydides.

All very interesting, you may admit, but what does it have to do with us? There was a time when it would have been hard to believe that any linguist could admit that it had anything to do at all. Those of us who trekked across the semantic desert of the forties and fifties could hardly have been blamed for feeling that life had lost all meaning, except perhaps differential meaning. Not that there were no respectable scholars interested in how meaning can be abused in language. In 1941 there was a group calling itself the Institute for Propaganda Analysis, numbering among its officers Clyde Beals, W. H. Kilpatrick, and Charles Beard, along with other notables. (I insert at this point, as a sign of the times, the fact that after thirty years of suspended animation the Propaganda Analysis group began to show signs of life again this fall, and was calling on linguists for coöperation. But the original group had no linguists in it.) Of course there existed at about the same time a flourishing school of General Semanticists, very much involved in such questions. Yet I don't need to remind any of the veterans in LSA how these lower-class people were looked down upon. Leonard Bloomfield regarded their leader, Alfred Korzybski, as a kind of soothsayer, and Korzybski's own jargonesque prose did little to dispel that impression. In any case, linguistic engineering (to use a bit of jargon from our own side) was totally absorbed in establishment activities such as army specialized training, literacy programs, and language policy in emerging nations. This was where the money went and where the action was. The linguist up to very recently has been a more or less useful social sideliner, but not a social critic.

Happily, I think we can say that this aloofness has begun to thaw somewhat. In a sense we are repeating the two phases of the protest movement. First came civil rights. In our terms, this has meant studies of Black English and Harlem Spanish and so-called deficit language in general. Now we are approaching something akin to peace and welfare demonstrations in the form of demands on the 'white standard' for accountability. The National Council of Teachers of English is one step ahead of us. In November they set up a Committee on Public Doublespeak; one of its members, Wayne O'Neil, is also a member of LSA, so we may expect the gospel to be spread any day now. What makes me more certain of this is the fact that the Boston *Globe,* when it carried the account of the Committee on Public Doublespeak, identified Wayne as Rabbi Wayne O'Neil. Robert Hogan, Executive Secretary of NCTE, described the charge of the committee in these terms: 'The question is not just whether subjects and verbs agree, but whether statements and facts agree.'[1]

Though I suspect that a majority of linguists would still want to reject it, there is also the plea made recently (1972) by Congressman Robert F. Drinan. He was addressing himself to teachers of English, and he had this to say (279) : 'In the matter of officially proclaimed marshmallow prose, it does seem to me that you have some professional responsibility.' Whether we deny this or not, we are being pushed toward it by events both in our field and from outside. Take the grammar of the sentence. There aren't many big nuggets left in that gold mine. Right now the prospectors are swarming over presuppositions, higher sentences, and other things whose purpose or effect is exactly to make explicit what writers and speakers get away with in their self-serving prose. Context is in, both linguistic and social. And we have rediscovered the lexicon, including the morass of connotations, euphemisms, and general chicanery. The last refuge left for the weakhearted seems to be phonology. The rest of us are finding it more and more difficult to keep ourselves undefiled.

As for events outside the field, our government—the very government that is the greatest abuser of language—finds itself caught in the embarrassing necessity of enforcing honesty in order to collect its taxes. Only so much money can be squeezed out of a family budget; so, in true gangster fashion, the small-time operators are being liquidated. There are the dealers who for years levied usurious rates of interest and were allowed to get away with it by the neat semantic trick of labeling them 'carrying charges'; also the local rent gougers, and the minor medicine men with their pill-promoting prodigies and their end-product, the drug culture. Government hits back by giving us truth in lending, truth in labeling, and truth in advertising. These are narrow gains. If we want the truth that government requires of its own business partners—e.g., which insurers give value for their premiums or which automotive manufacturers build safe transmissions—we still have to go to court to get it. All the same, there is a danger for those bent on concealment. A taste of truth is like a taste of blood. The subject should never have been brought up at all. Now that it has, truth is in the headlines, pushed there by the two-way struggle between governors and governed, each bent on finding out about the other—the governors to sniff out our private feelings, which could pose a threat to our control; the governed to know the decisions that affect them, but of which they may not be the beneficiaries. The medium of all this knowing is language, and linguists are in the line of fire.

If this widespread clamor for truth only embraced the way language is used, it might affect us less intimately. But it is also directed at the way language is. Here the target is not so much government as the whole of society. Julia Stanley 1972a shows us a lexicon replete with terms of barter referring to women, and few or no counterparts referring to men. Robin Lakoff in a similar study (1973) exposes the undertow of condescension and depreciation even in two such innocent-looking terms as *woman* and *lady*. Women are taught their place, along with other lesser breeds, by the implicit lies that language tells about them. Now you can argue that a term is not a proposition; therefore merely having the words does not constitute a lie about anybody. The words may be there, but it takes people to put them together, and so people may be liars but words are not. This argument has a familiar ring. We hear it every time Congress tries to pass legislation restricting the possession of guns. A loaded word is like a loaded gun, sometimes fired deliberately, but almost as often by accident. And even when you feel like firing one on purpose, it has to be in your possession first. Lots of casualties, some crippling ones, result from merely having weapons around.

I'm sure that many linguists will sympathize with these social concerns and agree that they should do something about them—but as citizens, not as linguists. How is truth to be defined so as to involve us professionally? Before I try to answer that, let me at least see if I can show that linguists who already accept some responsibility for language use can't consistently say that truth is irrelevant to linguistics. Here, adopting a suggestion made to me by Julia Stanley, I raise the question of appropriateness in language. Appropriateness is just as pertinent to content as it is to form. If linguists allow themselves a professional interest in how well a dialect or a code fits a place or situation, they cannot logically turn their backs on the fitness of language to facts. Let's hope that this comparison will satisfy at least some of the sociolinguists among us. It will not be quite so easy to convince those who feel that linguists who tangle themselves in anything having to do with messages and contexts thereby cease to be scientific. Still, we can snatch a reminder from what has been happening to us in the last decade or so. We are now fully involved with meaning, and from the meanings of the parts to the meaning of the whole is only one more step in the same direction.

The definition I propose for truth will not make it more precise, but it will establish the right connections. Consider how we use the verbs *inform* and *misinform*. They require either human subjects or message subjects. We say *He misinformed me with his letter* or *His letter misinformed me,* but not * *The clouds misinformed me about the coming rainstorm.* Truth is that quality of language by which we inform ourselves. This rules out the logician's analytic truth, which is no more than consistency within language. Literal truth it includes only partially, because literal truth—the kind one swears to tell on the witness stand—permits any amount of evasion. I think it also has to be distinguished from historical truth, because in language that informs there has to be an element of timeliness. We can say of truth what is said of justice: truth delayed is truth denied. But the most insidious of all concepts of truth is that of literalness. Advertising capitalizes on the legal protection that it affords. The California prune-growers tell us that prunes, pound for pound, offer several times more vitamins and minerals than fresh fruit; literally true. The oil industry advertises that no heat costs less than oil heat, which has to be true because no heat costs nothing at all. These cases of verbal thimblerigging depend on an old ethic that winks at the clever and laughs at the gullible. In simpler times they were part of our education; but in today's complex world everyone is an ignoramus about something—about diet, about the workings of our electronic whigmaleeries and arcane bureaucracies, about the flammability of fabrics, the potability of water, or the meaning of Form 1040A. The possibilities of deception have passed the bounds of tolerance. It is no longer innocent fun when the Barnums and Baileys hang up their sign reading 'This Way to the Egress'. The egress has lost her imaginary feathers and shivers out there in the cold with the rest and the best of us.

I have tailored my definition of truth to fit what speakers mean to have understood. Within a social setting, any other definition is a game. Appropriateness is not to be taken between facts and abstract sentences, but between facts and sentences plus their contexts—and contexts include intentions. Not because I can justify it if anyone wants to debate the point, but just to get this kind of truth as pure as I can distill it, I'll go a step farther and say that when two parties are in communication, anything that may be used which clogs the channel, and is not the result of accident, is a lie. I am trying to paint the lie as black as I can by not requiring that it be intentional. There are consciously intentional lies, of course, but there are also lies by habit, and people who believe their own propaganda and chiefs of state who surely harbor such a concept as that of a little lie being part of a larger truth, on the analogy of War is Peace or what you don't know won't hurt you. So I'd rather make falsehood embrace the hidden and unconscious, as well as the barefaced and deliberate. By contrast, truth would always be prompted by the active willingness to share what we know. There are some people for whom this willingness may be almost habitual. We still try to make it that way with our children, in the small society of the home.

Now I hope I am ready for the linguist who wants to maintain his scientific integrity. I quote from Robin Lakoff again (1972:907). She writes: 'In order to predict correctly the application of many rules, one must be able to refer to assumptions about the social context of an utterance, as well as to other implicit assumptions made by the participants in a discourse.' The ingredient of the social context that is relevant to truth is the disposition to share what we think or know, and it is reflected in our choice of words and often in our choice of grammar. The very existence of a large part of the lexicon depends on it, and it explains at least part of the survival value of some constructions.

Let me start with some examples from grammar. The easiest to document from current discussions are the ones that involve deletion, so my first example is the case of the missing performative. Parenthetically, if you prefer to believe that a performative is inserted when it is present rather than deleted when it is absent, it makes no difference, since nobody doubts that WHEN they are present, performative verbs are explanatory. Take the case where somebody in authority makes a pronouncement like *America is lagging behind Russia in arms production*. With no indication of the evidence, we have to take the claim on faith. But if the speaker says *I think that America is lagging,* or *My chief of staff informs me* or *I'll just bet America is lagging,* then there is a measure of honesty about how reliable the information is.

Compared with other omitted elements, the missing performative is the least of the deceptions. It is a mere peashooter in the liar's arsenal, because as long as a proposition is straightforward, whether it has an explicit performative or not, most people can muster

enough skepticism to ask for proof. It is when other less conspicuous things are deleted that dubious propositions are able to slip
past our guard. A number of these have been getting attention
of late, especially by Stanley, in studies of what she terms 'syntactic
exploitation' (e.g. 1972b).

My first example of these is the old story of the deleted agent of
the passive. This is the prime syntactic means for sophisticated
gossip. In place of *they say*, where a listener who is on his toes
will ask 'Who's *they?*', the speaker removes this temptation by putting the performative verb in the passive and keeping quiet about
they. In our culture this is a commonplace of newspaper headlines.
Shanks and Shaughnessey are having a dispute over a medical bill.
Shanks says that Shaughnessey sewed him up with a couple of
sponges and a scalpel still inside. Shaughnessey says that's a dirty
lie. Depending on how friendly the editor is with one or the other,
the headline comes out *Shaughnessey charged with malpractice* or
Shanks charged with slander. Either way, the reader is invited to
fill in the empty slot with more than one agent. The effect is to
magnify the guilt of one or the other party.

There are other instances of deleted agents that are more insidious.
Stanley (1972c:17) quotes a paragraph from Dostoevsky in which
eight passive constructions without agents succeed one another,
creating the impression 'of a faceless society in which the individual has no power, and all activities affecting citizens are carried
out by a nameless, impersonal "they" ' (1972c:19). To the extent
that such a view is accepted, the passive becomes a means of lying
on a large scale.

Another of Stanley's examples is the passive adjective. When we
use sentences like *In the 5th century the known world was limited
to Europe and small parts of Asia and Africa,* what do we mean
by *known world?* Known to whom? Since the phrase is a 'syntactic
island', it is not open to question, and we are able to get away with
ignoring three-fourths of the world's population. As Stanley puts
it, 'our attention is focused on the major predication' (1972b:11),
so that we can wonder about the accuracy of the geographical
claim, but not about who did the knowing. When Mutual of
Omaha proudly announces on its ecology-minded program 'Wild
kingdom' (31 December 1972) that *Man protects threatened animals,* it is able to give credit to the well-known human race without at the same time explicitly taking credit away.

Donald Smith 1972 adds a further case of an omitted element and
its exploitation, which he terms 'Experiencer deletion'. The most
typical sentences are those with the verb *seem*—which, as Smith

says (20), 'are favored in certain types of prose and speech such as by bureaucrats, educationalists or anybody who may wish, among other things, to disguise the sources of impressionistic assertions about the world'. One of Smith's examples is this (21), from *Beyond freedom and dignity* by B. F. Skinner: *The need for punishment seems to have the support of history.* Seems to whom? The lack of frankness on this score makes the claim irresponsible.

Not to overstate the case, we should recognize that some inept deletions are not due to attempts at concealment, but to having over-learned a rule of high school rhetoric: if you're a writer, make your references to yourself as few as possible. The passive with deleted agent is fine for this; it works out well in scientific writing where the emphasis is on processes, not on the people who carry them out. But some writers carry the prescription for self-effacement to the point of passivizing even a performative. So you get successions of more or less normal passives, capped by a sentence like *It is believed that these instructions will prove easy to follow.* This is a fair exchange of modesty for muddleheadedness.

We could go on with more examples from syntax, but it would be tedious because there are probably no two things that can be put together in a sentence that can't be used for some kind of fakery. Linguists make a great thing of the duality that developed between meaningless sub-units and meaningful higher units as defining human language; but long before that, there must have grown up a deadlier kind of duality whereby meanings were divorced from reality. As soon as signs were fully detached from things, it became possible for them to point at something non-existent or at the opposite of what they were supposed to point at. The practical joker who today turns the arrows from right to left on a one-way street surely had his caveman counterpart. This is not to say that bluffing and other forms of disingenuousness are unknown in the animal kingdom; but what distinguishes human mendacity is its capacity for elaboration. By the simple act of negation, any truth we utter can be turned into a falsehood. By merely changing the intonation, any doubt can be rendered a certainty.

But the power of the lie carries beyond the realm of elaboration into the realm of invention. We elaborate with syntax. We invent in the lexicon. I suspect that some syntactic lies are beyond our control. When a child is caught red-handed and says *I didn't do it,* it may be an instinctive reaction of self-defense. But the act of coining a new expression is conscious, and any lying there is deliberate. The very act of naming has consequences for our attitudes. Take a sentence like *He responded to her cry of distress:*

this uses a syntactic means that is at least neutral as regards sympathy. But in a sentence like *He responded to her distress cry*, you sense an incongruity. *Distress cry* adds something to the lexicon; it sets up a classification, and does it in a clinical way—for observation, not for pity or for hate. Karl Zimmer, in a recent study of nominal compounds (1971:14), finds that one necessary condition is that they be 'appropriately classificatory' for the speaker—i.e., represent a slice of reality and not a passing event. So by using them we can represent a happening as a thing. Now happenings can be prevented by attacking their causes or their causers, but things have a life of their own. They are independent of us; and if we fail to change them, it is because THEY are capable of resistance. The person who refers to migratory workers as wetbacks or weed-pullers excuses himself from responsibility for illegal entry and bad working conditions. That class of people simply exists.

The act of naming, plus some favorable or unfavorable overtone in the terms selected for it, is the favorite device of the propagandist and the ultimate refinement in the art of lying. Syntax you can penetrate. In a phrase such as *intelligible remark* or *acceptable excuse*, there's a submerged predication, all right; but it's at least represented by a detachable adjective, and if you think of it you can ask 'Intelligible to whom?' But the nominal compound is impervious: the predication is not only buried out of reach but out of sight.

This helplessness, I think, is what has focused the attention of political commentators on the lie of naming. Henry Steele Commager (1972:10) accuses the Nixon administration of replacing the Big Lie with great quantities of lies; but the interesting thing is that all the examples he identifies, as far as language is concerned, are nominal compounds. Here is the paragraph containing them (11): 'Corruption of language is a special form of deception which this Administration, through its Madison Avenue mercenaries, has brought to a high level of perfection. Bombing is "protective reaction", precision bombing is "surgical strikes", concentration camps are "pacification centers" or "refugee camps" . . . Bombs dropped outside the target area are "incontinent ordnance", and those dropped on one of your own villages are excused as "friendly fire"; a bombed house becomes automatically a "military structure" and a lowly sampan sunk on the waterfront a "waterborne logistic craft".' 'How sobering', he adds, 'that fifteen years before 1984 our own government should invent a doublethink as dishonest as that imagined by Orwell.' Congressman Drinan, after saying that 'Language is not merely the way we express our foreign policy; language IS our foreign policy' (279), goes on to add that

'The systematic use of such opaque terms as "protective reaction",
and the hollow sentences of the war planners, do far more to hide
the decision-making process from the people—and from Congress—
than any secrecy classification rules' (281). Charles Osgood
(1971:4) is equally impressed with the effectiveness of naming;
he mentions the title *Camelot* which 'conferred a romantic, even
chivalrous, tang to an ill-fated U.S. Army project designed to study
the causes of revolutions', and he says that 'to name an ABM system *Safeguard* certainly must make its possessors feel more secure.
A touch of nobility is added to raw power when intercontinental
ballistic missiles are named *Thor, Jupiter, Atlas, Zeus,* and *Polaris*—
although I miss the ultimate in semantic deception which would
be a missile named *Venus*.'

Again I should pull back an inch or two, so as not to make it appear that I think all the abuses of naming have an ulterior motive.
If the habit had not already been there, officialdom could never
have made capital of it. Out of its passion for supplying needs and
dealing with problems frontally, this society has bred a mania for
making everything tangible. It arrests every motion, solidifies every
event. The lowly clerk exhibits it when he lets you know that he
is *in receipt* of your message—nothing so ordinary as that he has
simply received it. The advertiser exhibits it when he offers you,
not a product that will make your battery last longer, but one that
will give you longer *battery life*. The bureaucrat merely follows
suit when, instead of talking about the side that has the most and
most powerful planes, he talks about the side that has *air superiority*.

The nominal compound at the service of bureaucracy is only the
wholesaling of those embodiments of prejudice that every speech
community allows to flourish in its vocabulary, terms in which
neutral semantic features are mingled with valuative ones. Most
likely everyone here has his own pet collection, from business, government, or daily life. My favorite is this quotation from *The
Sonoma County Realtor* of Santa Rosa, California: 'An alert real
estate salesman should learn how to express himself well and to
use psychology . . . Don't say "down payment"; say "initial investment". Don't ask for a "listing"; ask for an "authorization to sell".
Don't say "second mortgage"; say "perhaps we can find additional
financing". Don't use the word "contract"; have them sign a "proposal" or "offer" . . . Don't use the word "lot"; call it a "homesite".
Don't say "sign here"; say "write your name as you want it to appear on your deed".'[2] Here we see the unremitting struggle to
keep concepts free of their associations. A term such as *military
conscription* picks up unpleasant connotations along the way, and
is replaced with *draft*. *Draft* starts to pick them up in turn and is

replaced with *selective service*. Since a nation such as ours no longer wages war but only defends itself, it became necessary many years ago to change the name of the old War Department to the Department of Defense. In all these examples the exploiters of words are fighting to keep them free of certain semantic features. The other side of the coin is when they cling to features even though the actual conditions are absent, to use the word as a weapon. Calling a person a traitor is like throwing him in prison; both are symbolic acts. *Traitor* is a disgraceful name, prison is a disgraceful place. This works as long as people can be kept from their habit of re-interpreting in the light of the facts, and discovering perhaps that the whole prison concept is a fake. Either way you take it—whether fighting off semantic features from words, or trying, in the teeth of the evidence, to keep them—there is an accelerated rate of semantic change and greater confusion when we try to communicate, and to that extent we can speak of the corruption of language, for it is caused by deliberate and well-financed interference.[3]

I mentioned valuative features. The study of them is one that has gone on sporadically, but has never been central to our discipline. It would be timely to revive it now, especially in the context of paralinguistics, because there is an unmistakable tie with gesture. The more we learn about the concepts of attraction and repulsion, the better we see how pervasive they are in our ways of thinking and in most of our words. Within language, valuative features are transmitted from one part of the lexicon to another by hidden link-ups that doubtless reflect some basic fact about where and how the lexicon is stored in our brains. A few linguists were interested in this a decade or so ago and studied it under the rubric of phonesthemes, a certain type of sound symbolism. Let me give just one example. I was recently struck by the peculiar contrast in a pair of synonyms that, in any literal sense, ought to be about as close in meaning as any two words can get. The Merriam-Webster Third regards them as identical: *baseless* and *ground-less*. I was puzzled as to why *baseless* struck me as the stronger of the two; so I put the question to a seminar of three Harvard freshmen I was teaching, and one of them came up with the same explanation that had occurred to me: *baseless* echoes *base*. A baseless accusation, for instance, is one that is not only groundless, but also mean and unworthy. Language is a jungle of associations like this one, where a malevolent guide can lose any simple-minded wayfarer. For us to lead one another without leading one another astray requires a conscious act of will. Truth is not a highway. It is a trail hacked through snake-infested undergrowth.

One form of lying uses all the tricks so far described, but is distinguished from them by sheer quantity. I refer to what we might term obfuscation, more the province of the stylist than the linguist. A piece of obfuscatory prose may contain a message somewhere, but it is lost in the murk of rhetorical self-importance. Stanislav Andreski 1972 cites an example from Talcott Parsons:

> Instead of saying simply that a developed brain, acquired skills, and knowledge are needed for attaining human goals, Parsons writes: 'Skills constitute the manipulative techniques of human goal attainment and control in relation to the physical world, so far as artifacts for machines especially designed as tools do not yet supplement them. Truly human skills are guided by organized and codified KNOWLEDGE of both the things to be manipulated and the human capacities that are used to manipulate them. Such knowledge is an aspect of cultural level symbolic processes, and, like other aspects to be discussed presently, requires the capacities of the human central nervous system, particularly the brain. This organic system is clearly essential to all of the symbolic processes . . .'

Getting back to things of more direct concern to linguists, what if enough of them were to turn their attention to truth and falsehood for it really to make a difference? It is a risky business when scientists start developing tools that are capable of misuse. To bring to light the mechanisms of Machiavellianism may be to provide future Machiavellis with easy access. But I doubt we can teach today's Machiavellis much that they do not already know. This is one game where the con men have less to learn than their victims. Knowing how to lie—brazenly, delicately, urbanely, esoterically—is a question of survival for officials dedicated to fundamentally unpopular causes. For this we can partly blame our own eager acceptance of a cosmetic society. 'America', I once wrote (Bolinger 1962), 'is the first society to achieve a virtual taboo on the unpleasant.' Our advertising has convinced us of it, and our officials are afraid to say otherwise. Language is called upon to do the same thing as psychiatry—in Sissman's words, 'to paper over unpalatable truths'. The most pathetically pertinent example of psychiatric paper-over was aired recently on a Boston radio station. It seems that a psychiatric service has been set up to treat those abnormal people who are afraid of flying. It will not do for a traveling public to harbor any pathological fears about being trapped at thirty thousand feet with no place to go but down. Compare this attitude with that of the maritime regulations, according to which common carriers not only stock up with life preservers and lifeboats, but also conduct regular lifeboat drills among their passengers. Imagine the effect on travel if airline passengers were required to take part in parachute drills; and contrast that with the sweetly offhand voice of the stewardess giving perfunctory safety directions, trusting that her tone and her legs will distract you from her ominous words. This may not be dedication to the utmost in safety, but it is at least dedication to the utmost in playing down the need for it. Forget the parachutes and give us piano bars. When you have government, business, and camp-following psychiatrists teamed up in this fashion to make the normal in OVERT behavior seem abnormal, what can you expect with as pliant a medium as language?

Let's suppose that an aroused public were to begin paying as much attention to linguistic ecology as to environmental ecology. What might some of the reactions to this be—on the part of those who oppose truth—against which we should be forearmed? In business they are already visible as a reaction to the comparatively feeble jabs of the truth-in-this and truth-in-that campaigns (observe, please, that there is as yet no campaign for truth, period) . Another possible effect is the heightened reliance on war, especially the selling of war materials. War is popular, among other reasons, because it enables business to get along without customers. There are no finical housewives to complain that the plastic pellets in smart bombs are not penetrating deep enough. Another effect, of more direct concern to us, is the retreat from language. What I outlined in the first part of this talk was the retreat from PROPOSITIONAL language. Things are said, but said in such a way that even professional skeptics have trouble pinning them down. But after all that comes to light, then what? First there's the recourse of not making any claims yourself, but putting them as testimonials. Terence Langendoen 1970, in his critique of the Federal Trade Commission, points out (7-8) that 'all an advertiser needs to do to convert a misleading statement of fact into a misleading statement of opinion (which is hence exempt from sanctions) is to put it in the mouth of a celebrity or "average consumer".' Of late there has been a further refinement in testimonials, which consists in not making any outright claim, but staging a little dramatization. A pre-Columbian pedant announces that the world is flat, and this proceeds through a series of non-sequiturs to the conclusion that not all aspirins are the same. As a last resort, after the testimonial in its various forms direct and indirect, there remains the recourse of not using language at all, but merely making agreeable noises. We now leave the left hemisphere of the brain and move over to the right. In my personal count of radio and TV ads, I came up with about one in three that uses just language. The rest feature a mixture of language and music or other sound effects. With TV of course there are the dimensions of color and image. It tells us something about the importance of truth to language that the more you insist on truth, the farther those who care little for the truth retreat from language.

Truth is a linguistic question because communication is impossible without it. Unless social interaction is to break down, the lie must always be the exception. Robin Lakoff (1972:916) sets up five rules which she says 'define an appropriate conversational situation'. Here are the first three:

> Rule I. What is being communicated is true.
>
> Rule II. It is necessary to state what is being said: it is not known to other participants, or utterly obvious. Further everything necessary for the hearer to understand the communication is present.
>
> Rule III. Therefore, in the case of statements, the speaker assumes that the hearer will believe what he says (due to Rule I).

Government and business are making two arrogant assumptions. The first is that it is possible to have one-way monopolistic communication, with the public consuming official verbiage as it consumes the handouts from industry and welfare. The second is that Lakoff's rules are not important, only the illusion of them. Public officials hide behind the images that Madison Avenue creates for them, and lies hide behind the face of truth.

Linguists cannot excuse themselves from these uses of language, though they may find various ways of approaching them. Lloyd Anderson (1970:1) sees our field 're-opening itself to the study of rhetoric and literature, to communications and psychology, to continuous and fuzzy phenomena of the real world'—including, among its possible contributions, 'new rigorous principles of "false advertising" and "false communicating" for legal guidelines, for journalistic ethics, to support a new interpretive reporting distinct from propaganda'. It can't come too soon.

Notes

1. Boston *Globe,* 22 November 1972, p. 5.

2. Quoted in *Consumer reports,* October 1972, p. 626.

3. As far as advertising is concerned, no further examples are needed, for the mercenary bias is clear. As for government, to quote Drinan again (281), 'the use of empty words by the Defense Department is not the accidental by-product of a metastasized bureaucracy; rather, it is an essen-

tial part of a pervasive scheme to keep Defense Department decision-making a secret—unknown and unknowable by any potential critics.'

References

Anderson, Lloyd B. 1970. Journalism and linguistics: some mutual interests. Talk at student-faculty seminar, School of Journalism, University of North Carolina, Chapel Hill, October.

Andreski, Stanislav. 1972. Social sciences as sorcery. London: Andre Deutsch. (Cited in Time magazine, 25 September 1972, p. 67.)

Bolinger, Dwight. 1962. The tragedy must go on. American Liberal, November, p. 26.

Commager, Henry Steele. 1972. The defeat of America. New York Review of Books, 5 October, pp. 7–13.

Drinan, Robert F. 1972. The rhetoric of peace. College Composition and Communication 23.279–82.

Gowers, Sir Ernest. 1948. Plain words. London: His Majesty's Stationery Office. (Cited by Joseph Jones, American Speech 24:121, 1949.)

Lakoff, Robin, 1972. Language in context. Lg. 48.907–27.

————. 1973. Language and woman's place. Language in Society 2.45–80.

Langendoen, D. T. 1970. A study of the linguistic practices of the Federal Trade Commission. Paper read at LSA, 29 December.

Osgood, Charles E. 1971. Conservative words and radical sentences in the semantics of international politics. Social psychology and political behavior: problems and prospects, ed. by Gilbert Abcarian and J. W. Soule, 101–29. Columbus, Ohio: Charles E. Merrill.

Quiller-Couch, Sir Arthur. 1916. On the art of writing. Lectures delivered in the University of Cambridge, 1913–14, pp. 83–103. Cambridge: University Press.

Sissman, L. E. 1972. Plastic English. Atlantic Monthly, October, p. 32.

Smith, Donald. 1972. Experiencer deletion. MS.

Stanley, Julia. 1972a. The semantic features of the machismo ethic in English. Paper read at South Atlantic Modern Language Association.

————. 1972b. Syntactic exploitation: passive adjectives in English. Paper read at Southeastern Conference on Linguistics VII, 21 April.

————. 1972c. Passive motivation. MS.

Thurber, James. 1955. The psychosemanticist will see you now, Mr. Thurber. New Yorker, 28 May, pp. 28–31.

Zimmer, Karl E. 1971. Some general observations about nominal compounds. Working papers in language universals, Stanford University, 5.

Ethics in Public Discourse

Robert C. Jeffrey

This is the text of the Presidential Address Jeffrey delivered at the 1973 convention of the Speech Communication Association. Jeffrey criticizes the recent emphasis in research as behaviorally oriented, inhumane, and lacking in concern for ethical and moral values: "An integral part of a new rhetorical theory must be a renewed consideration of ethics in public discourse."

Many of you at regional or state conventions have heard me refer to several events and practices in our world today that threaten our ethical communication conduct. One of those practices is the employment, with tax monies, of an "Executive Flunky," if you will, as a mouthpiece for the President of the United States. Mr. Ziegler in the present administration holds this post. As communication strategists we have passively and uncritically accepted this practice, thereby harboring and condoning the institution of a Presidential Scapegoat, an institution that permits our highest elected officer to test public opinion in a quasi-official fashion. If reaction to the statements attributed to the President is negative the President can deny responsibility for the statement. With this simple mechanism of public statement by proxy we encourage both deliberately designed deception and abrogation of responsibility.

By permitting our highest elected officials and those they appoint to administrative posts to classify information as confidential, and by placing no constraints on those public servants, we deny the public information necessary for proper decision-making in the democratic process. Equally as reprehensible and deplorable is our national administration's malfeasant efforts to weaken the integrity of the press by deliberate design. At this convention last year, *New York Times'* writers Robert Semple and James Naughton concluded that the present administration has been so successful in undermining the credibility of the press that the public refused to acknowledge the Watergate saboteurs once exposed. That, of course, was prior to the Watergate Hearings. The word "coverup," however, has now become a household word and extends beyond the Watergate matter to areas perhaps yet to be discovered.

These practices are among many that lead inevitably to the conclusion that the American public refuses to demand an ethical responsibility from its leadership. It is a frightening prospect, and one that Richard Nixon viewed with alarm in 1970 when, recalling the bombing at the University of Wisconsin in that year, he said ". . . what corrodes a society even more deeply than violence itself is the acceptance of violence, the condoning of terror, excusing of inhuman acts in a misguided effort to accommodate the community standards to those of the violent few."

If we substitute the words "crime" or "irresponsibility" for the word "violence," we arrive at the basis for my remarks this afternoon.

The corrosive effect of the acceptance of deception has led to the cheapening of authority in America in recent years. Too many broken promises, too many empty words, too little real achievement of vital objectives, too many inept or insensitive or inexplicable decisions made by untouchable officials in unreachable institutions—all of these have undermined both the integrity of and our respect for the figures who lay claim to executive leadership and executive "privilege." This disintegration of administrative morality and accompanying public impertinence extend beyond the American Presidency to leadership in the universities, corporations, unions, and organized religion. Some of the practices of our profession have, in my opinion, contributed, however subtly, to this impalement of national morality.

First, the research emphasis in human communication has, for over a decade, been behaviorally oriented, accompanied by an abandonment in many academic programs of a healthy and balanced orientation with interest in humanistic and ethical aspects of communication. Historically, technological progress has always left in its wake agonizing political and social change, and even though earth's complexion has changed every minute since it first took off around the sun, what is so shockingly new about our changing world is that where it once changed imperceptively, it now convulses and heaves and shatters and reconstitutes itself before our very eyes. Reflecting this scientific upheaval is the behavioral and objective orientation in communication research in which the *human* as individual is often neglected and the *mass* as individual is subjected to experimentation and manipulation.

We have been "scientifically" aware, however, since the turn of the century that no objective reality exists, that every perception of objectivity, regardless of the sophistication and precision of our measuring instruments, in the final analysis, is determined by individual perceptivity and capability. It is amazing that since Planck's discovery of Quantum Theory in 1900 the "scientific" world has recognized the reciprocity between the scientist as individual and the world he seeks to control, and yet, we in Speech Communication are propagating as "new," "progressive," and "Innovative" a view of human behaviors strangely reminiscent of 19th century scientific thought.

Related to the emphasis on scientific investigation of communication behavior is a second practice contributing to the ethical and moral decline in our communicative society—an extreme concern with the development of images in leadership roles. As Daniel Boorstin so eloquently put it, "the making of illusions which flood our experiences has become the business of America." The sophistication of contemporary illusion *making* results from the subjugation of individual identity to group profile, inevitably leading to excesses in promoting products for human consumption and images for leadership roles. Encouraged by such falsified profiles of human behaviors, experimentation on changing human behavior on the basis of group norms rather than individual reasoning has become paramount. If, in persuasion, there were more concern for the integrity of the individual, there might be less need for truth in lending laws, truth in advertising laws and fairness in campaign practices legislation.

In speech criticism, our research and publications reflect a near obsession with tracing the development of images in political campaigns, resulting in an abrogation of our responsibility to students and the public. We no longer demand accuracy of statement, and too often train our students to be experts in the art of plotting the creation of deceptive practices rather than unmasking and indicting those practices. The loss of respect for the spoken word, an inevitable product of image making, has led former Attorney General John Mitchell, referring to the Nixon Administration, to assert, "You will be better advised to watch what we do instead of what we say." This statement led Richard Harris, in his book *Justice,* to remark that the statement was "the most astonishing admission of high level duplicity in government history."

A third practice of teachers and researchers in communication that has contributed to the lack of concern for ethical and moral responsibility on the part of American leadership is our growing preoccupation with the *superficial* dimensions of non-rational discourse, body rhetoric, the rhetoric of the streets, the rhetoric of numbers. Wayne Booth, recognizing both the rhetorical validity of such acts of persuasion and their inherent dangers, asserts: ". . . a case could be made for the claim that we live in the most rhetorical age of all time, if by rhetoric we mean whatever men do to change each other's minds without giving good reasons for change." Booth's extension of what constitutes rhetoric demands a return to an ethical consciousness.

An integral part of a new rhetorical theory must be a renewed consideration of ethics in public discourse. This consideration must of necessity revert to a discussion of Aristotle's determinants of a moral act. Father Lawrence Flynn succinctly describes the Aristotelian Determinants of a moral act in a 1957 article in the *Speech Teacher*. He reasons first that a moral act is dependent upon the establishment of a human act. He writes, "A truly human act proceeds from a rational agent who knows what he does and chooses freely to do it. The power to reason, which distinguishes men from brutes, underlies man's recognition of a means-to-end relationship. So, before we choose means-to-an-end we must know the end, the means, and the relation between them. To perform human acts we need knowledge and human choice. . . ."

To determine the goodness or badness of a human act, however, requires an analysis of the object, the act, the intent of the agent, and the circumstances surrounding the act. Consequently, in determining the ethics of a public statement, it is necessary to analyze what the speaker does, why he does it and the circumstances under which he does it. The measurement of effects of a public utterance may offer historical fact, but reveals nothing of the utterance's ethical structure. Even though the speaker's purpose or ultimate end is good, Aristotle would require that the rhetorical devices, techniques, methods, or fact pass the test of morality according to the three determinants. If the end sought by the speaker is good, the act of achieving that end is unethical if the speaker selects unethical means. Likewise, even though means to achieve an end are ethical or good, the end itself may be bad. Consequently, to judge the goodness or badness of a speech or other communicative act, all of the determinants must be satisfied. Deliberate falsification is morally faulty because it frustrates the natural purpose of speech in a democratic society which is to transmit judgments to auditors, and because it interferes with the auditor's judgment capabilities.

Since the human act, to be judged morally, must be deliberate and free, one might suppose that an unconscious misrepresentation or falsification that may result in a partial distortion or complete misrepresentation through ignorance would be excused. However, a speaker must assume the responsibility for his statements and, consequently, do all that is possible to remove his ignorance before making the statement. Ignorance cannot be claimed as an excuse unless it can also be shown that the speaker did what was within his power to remove that ignorance. Father Flynn would have us ask the question, "Did he use care proportionate to the importance and gravity of the situation?"

It has been and can be argued that the logical and emotional aspects of rhetoric are amoral, that they derive their morality from the good or bad intent of the speaker or agent. The use of logic in a particular discourse may be bad, but it is not morally bad unless the intent of the user is bad. The problem, then, is to determine the intent of the communicator or agent.

Often it is possible to determine the intent of the agent by the arguments assembled in the message. For instance, most rhetorical critics would consider Nixon's 1952 "Checkers Speech" logically unacceptable as a defense for misusing campaign funds. Few, however, have questioned the ethical base of the speech or the morality of the act. The general public response to the speech then, as now, lauded it as a monumental rhetorical effort. This kind of critical acceptance justifiably places the term rhetoric in dubious quarters.

Much to his credit, Barnet Baskerville wrote in his analysis of the vice-presidential speaking in the 1952 campaign that the "Nixon affair" served to unify a divided Republican party and elevated Richard Nixon to a prominence seldom enjoyed by a Vice-Presidential candidate. He also observed, "It seems to this observer that the phenomenal public reaction to the original charge, to the speech itself, and to subsequent counter charges, revealed an alarming preference to appearances rather than realities, a widespread preoccupation with legality rather than morality, and a subordination (by Democrats and Republicans alike) of ethical considerations to political expediency." The period of the early 1950's might well serve as the reference point for the beginning of the deterioration of responsible public discourse in the high levels of government. Hal Gulley wrote in *Today's Speech* in 1970, that ". . . America's public statement-making is less dependable, reliable, and candid than it was two decades ago; that we are witnessing a national drift toward irresponsibility toward public utterance. In some areas of our national life, we cannot now be certain that we believe what some people are saying." Gulley's report contained an alarming exposure of the cavalier attitude with which government officials view high level duplicity. He quoted former Assistant Secretary of Defense for Public Affairs, Arthur Sylvester, as saying "It is the government's inherent right to lie if necessary to save itself when faced with nuclear disaster; this is basic."

We as a nation in 1973 have been brought to the brink of moral and ethical deterioration in our government. No one in this audience need be reminded of the general and pervasive political debauchery associated with the amorphous term "Watergate." Testimony of men respected for their place in government has revealed the exalted place of the lie and of deceit. James Reston wrote in the *New York Times* "Future testimony from Messrs. Mitchell, Erlichman, Haldeman, and Dean may throw more light on who is lying and who is telling the truth. Meanwhile, it is probably better to follow Paul Porter's skeptical advice: 'I don't say these men are liars, . . . it's just that they have such respect for the truth that they use it sparingly'."

In this time of national despair and uncertainty, we should not neglect to celebrate the system of justice that has revealed the unethical conduct of some of our more respected leaders. Our system of justice may be slow in its process, but it offers assurance of ethical certainty in its results.

The real question, however, is not whether the guilty will vindicate the innocent. The question is, rather, "Where lies the culpability for having arrived at this near disastrous condition?"

Every man, a president included, must be accountable for his acts and responsible for his statements. But if the president acts or speaks irresponsibly, those who elected him to office are not free of guilt if the evidence of irresponsibility was available at the time of election. Richard Nixon's questionable ethics have been observable for over two decades. But in those two decades, academic critics and scholars in communication have been more concerned with the technologies of communication than with its ethics. Richard Nixon was and continues to be a "technician" in manipulating public attitudes for self-aggrandizement. Our own publications reflect a preoccupation with Nixon's predictability, his appeals to audiences, his mastery of the television medium, and so on. Few articles, however, have analyzed the ethics or morality of his statements. It is a sad commentary on the state of rhetoric in the academy when we admit that ethical studies of the Nixon rhetoric are more readily available in the press than in scholarly journals. Traditionally, rhetorical critics have, in fact, recognized and accepted their charge as analysts and reporters of ethical conduct. The Fourth Estate, however, and not rhetorical scholars, first alerted the American public to Nixon's special brand of Administrative Rhetoric. Kenneth Burke has used the term "Administrative Rhetoric" to explore the ethical dimensions of Machiavelli's *The Prince*. He contends that:

> Machiavelli's *The Prince* can be treated as a rhetoric insofar as it deals with a producing of effects upon an audience. Sometimes the Prince's subjects are his audi-

ence, sometimes the rulers or inhabitants of foreign states
are the audience, sometimes particular factions within
the State. If you have a political public in mind,
Machiavelli says in effect, here's the sort of thing you
must do to move them for your purposes. And he considers such principles of persuasion as these: either treat
well or crush; defend weak neighbors and weaken the
strong; where you foresee trouble, provoke war; don't
make others powerful; be like the prince who appointed
a harsh governor to establish order . . . : do necessary
evils at one stroke, pay out benefits little by little; sometimes assure the citizens that the evil days will soon be
over, at other times goad them to fear the cruelties of
the enemy; be sparing of your own and your subjects'
wealth, but be liberal with the wealth of others; be a
combination of strength and stealth (the lion and fox);
appear merciful, dependable, humane, devout, upright,
but be the opposite in actuality, whenever the circumstances require it . . . in order that you may get the
advantage of good advice without losing people's respect,
give experts permission to speak frankly, but only when
asked to speak; have a few intimates who are encouraged
to be completely frank, and who are well-plied with
rewards.

Each of us can find specific instances of these administrative rhetorical strategies in the Nixon speeches. They are identifiable as
early as 1948 when, in his senatorial campaign, he goaded the public to fear the cruelties of the enemy and assured the voters that
the fear would end with his election. The strategies are even more
identifiable today with the crumbling of popular respect for the
man and his rhetoric.

As communication critics and educators, we failed in our responsibilities to officially oppose those practices when they became so
blatantly evident. We persist in that failure today. In the ten
hours of deliberations of the Legislative Council at this convention, not a single resolution was introduced to condemn the unethical practices of the Nixon administration for withholding information from the public for political and private purposes; for
deliberately deceiving the public with false statements as in denial
of bombing in Cambodia when, in fact, it occurred; for refusing to
supply tapes, notes and correspondence relating to possible criminal activities; for taping private conversations without the knowledge of the parties being taped; for other acts relating specifically
to the free flow of information and privacy of communication that
should be the central concerns of teachers and scholars in speech
communication.

This timidity in speaking to the corrupt communication practices of the present national administration reveals an abrogation of our role as protectors of ethical communication. If there is one thread that binds together all of the varied interests in our association, it is a dedication to free and responsible speech. Yet, when that freedom and responsibility is abridged or threatened, we fail to act. In this case, the excuse that we must act only in areas of professional competence cannot be claimed as a defense by those who would oppose censure resolutions by this association.

Last year, at this convention, the Legislative Council passed a resolution declaring that "it is the role of the Speech Communication Association, defining itself as a humanistic organization, to be concerned with the communication process and how that process affects human beings; that since those in political power make decisions affecting millions of people, those people have a right both to know those decisions and to offer information and well-considered opinions on them; that in the past it has been apparent that government plays a substantial role in determining the limitations of freedom of speech and the amount of information made available to the public; and that there is a need to study government use of communication, whether it involves abridgment of free speech, failure to communicate to the electorate, or responsible use of communication channels." With this expression of concern for government's use of communication controls, our purpose should be to monitor it and to condemn or praise as the case may warrant.

It may well be true that the moral and ethical permissiveness of the present administration has, as Russell Baker wrote, so accustomed us "to accepting mendacity as a normal condition of life that we assume it is natural for everybody to lie to us, even our best man." But ethical permissiveness, even in a just cause, corrodes the soul; and condoning it can corrode a nation. As Adlai Stevenson once asserted, "Those who corrupt the public mind are just as evil as those who steal from the public purse."

As teachers and scholars in communication, our purpose should be to develop respect for ethical communication and a healthy disdain for deception in and corruption of public discourse. Henry Wieman and Otis Walter wrote in 1957 ". . . Ethical Rhetoric has the promise of creating those kinds of communication which can help save the human being from disintegration, nourish him in his growth toward uniquely human goals, and eventually transform him into the best that he can become." That should be our paramount goal as teachers and scholars in communication.

Politics and the Study of Language

H. Thomas McCracken

At the 1974 meeting of the Conference on English Education, McCracken presented his rationale for the political theme of that meeting: "Our political responsibility is to prepare English teachers who can help students analyze the language of public life—political language." Such a priority is important now, because as he suggests: "By the beginning of the next century, if the present political atmosphere prevails, an inability to analyze political language will affect hearts, minds and bellies far more than in the past." McCracken is a member of the NCTE Committee on Public Doublespeak.

In the twelve year existence of the Conference on English Education, we have not produced any significant changes in the teaching of the English language. CEE has contributed to an increased interest in the use of media and in response to literature. Various conferences, publications and other missionary work over the last decade have provided renewed interest in children's literature, ethnic literature, and the study of dialects, and we are poised to address the problems in preparing community college teachers. One pervasive area of the English curriculum that has not had sufficient airing, however, is politics and the study of language. Some notable exceptions recently have been publications like the Postman, Weingartner and Moran collection of essays called *Language in America* (Pegasus, 1969) and, in another medium, the NCTE Committee on Public Doublespeak.

We have expended so much useless energy and time teaching grammar since the 18th century—and it won't be long before we have equalled that energy and time saying that grammar is a waste of time—that I speak out of near desperation and with a deep sigh when I plead with English teachers to throw away their grammars and use the language of public life as the object of study with their students. The enlargement of American politics on the public consciousness is the reason for such language study.

In these days of Watergate, secret bombings and corporate confessions, we are forced to sharpen awareness of our political responsibilities as English educators. On a peak day of the Watergate hearings last summer, in an unprecedented exposure to the inner sanctum of government, 48 million people watched and listened to serious allegations against a president and his administration. Since then the American people have been required to sift through a massive amount of language subtlety and language pollution. That phenomenon contains an important message for us. For years we in English have delved further and further into finer and finer explanations of grammatical systems and foisted them on high school youngsters. At the time of say the middle 50's, we needed a discipline using scientific method and technology. In that we were reflecting national trends and values, but the national situation has, in some startling ways, changed abruptly. Our emphasis in teaching language must change as well if we are to remain accountable to our students and the public, particularly with respect to language and meaning.

Civic responsibility in the teaching of language

The public has long embraced the myth that the English teacher is the arbiter of language. Allied with that myth is the political mandate to prepare an "enlightened citizenry" for this democracy. Any significant change in the English curriculum, as with other institutional categories, will have to spring from the original well of myth and mandate if we are to keep in touch with the public. As any good politician knows and as the experience of Watergate has taught us, if we lose touch with the public we have lost our opportunity to lead. Our political responsibility is to prepare English teachers who can help their students analyze the language of public life—political language.

Even the most conservative school boards have argued from the beginning that English teachers have a political responsibility to make their students good citizens. Yet they do not see that it can no longer be argued that the teaching of philosophical grammatical systems will provide an enlightened citizenry. It is part of our immediate task to begin revising the myth of grammar-learning as a means for achieving respectability in public affairs.

As an English teacher I must be concerned when a former chief of staff of the Nixon administration claims responsibility for a memorandum which says in part, "We need to get our people to put out the story on the foreign or Communist money that was used in support of demonstrations against the President in 1972. We should tie all 1972 demonstrations to McGovern and, thus, to the Democrats as part of the peace movement" (*New York Times*, August 2, 1973, p. 21). Haldeman's response to the public presentation of that memorandum in the hearings:

> I will accept responsibility for the memorandum, although because of some bad English and other problems in it, I would point out that it is not initialed by me,

which it would have been had I written the memorandum and sent it. . . . Having said that, I am disclaim-
ing responsibility for the English and typos, and accepting overall responsibility for the memorandum.
(*New York Times,* August 2, 1973, p. 21).

Haldeman stated more than once with the first signs of something
like shame and apology that the grammar was bad while affirming
his right to communicate falsehood (he had no evidence for the
link but wanted to "put out the story" anyway). If our job was
to teach grammar, and that has always at least meant to recognize
bad grammar, we did it in Haldeman's case but we didn't do much
more. Haldeman's implication that the memorandum is somehow
cleansed from serious criticism because responsibility for the "English" is denied is absurd. When those in power feel that the *form*
of language is their only vulnerability and that their private *meaning* of that language is inviolable, the teaching of grammatical systems may have been all too successful.

As an English teacher, I must be concerned when a Pentagon
spokesman says, after 3,630 secret bombings of a neutral country
had occurred two years earlier, that words like *falsification, deception* and *cover-up* are not applicable. The same spokesman said,
"It's not a question of trying to set up a system that would falsify
records, it was a question of setting up a special reporting procedure. We didn't want to lose the opportunity to conduct those
operations" (*New York Times,* July 24, 1973, p. 4). Those are
sentences which English teachers can analyze with their students—
sentences which have immediacy and importance. Or students
might treat the full explanation by the Pentagon as a short story,
asking the classic questions: (a) Does the story have unity of time
and place? (b) What is the point of view? (c) Is the protagonist
believable?

It is *not* all the same to me whether my students analyze "Color-
less green ideas sleep furiously" or those sentences above. If my
students don't understand that it is language that moves us, impli-
cates us in vestiges of an American Dream that we share, drives us
to outrage and helps define us, then I can't lead them through the
next decade. If English teachers don't have a mandate to analyze
political language with their students, then I don't know who does.

Grammar clearly is not what our students need to arm themselves
intellectually for survival in the next few decades. At the turn of
the century, homogenization of language was the political responsibility: Immigrants cried out "A man can't get ahead unless he
speaks good English." By the beginning of the next century, if

the present political atmosphere prevails, an inability to analyze political language will affect hearts, minds and bellies far more than in the past.

Political issues in the classroom?

I hear the cries of many colleagues: the schools must be kept pure of politics and English classrooms above all must remain above the mire of political issues. We have, they say, academic responsibilities, not political ones. The myth that the schools are apolitical dies hard. Let me mention some examples. When a State Department of Education attempts to control the content of textbooks used in its state, that is politics. The following is from the Handbook of Policy of that department:

> Textbook content shall not interfere with the school's legal responsibility to teach citizenship and patriotism. Textbooks adopted shall not include selections or works which contribute to civil disorder, social strife or flagrant disregard of the law. (*New York Times*, July 7, 1973, p. 17. The state is Arizona.)

Aside from the problem of whether the statement includes pamphlets, newspapers or paperbacks in its "adoption" system, three implications are striking. First is the almost impossible task of selecting textbooks which are devoid of human conflict. If one were found, it would indeed be apolitical. Second is the presumption of cause and effect between a textbook and what are apparently undesirable acts. Third is that the political view implicit in the statement is quite recognizable: an ultraconservative attempt to define the terms *citizenship* and *patriotism* as if they were the private property of the Department.

When a student teacher in English is allowed to teach *Uncle Tom's Cabin* but not *Soul on Ice*, that is politics in the schools. When high school students are not given permission to have a peace speaker for their assembly on the grounds of possible indoctrination and are given instead a Marine sergeant, that is politics in the schools. And when a teacher is fired for not standing during the "Pledge of Allegiance to the Flag," that is politics in the schools. The point is not so much that politics permeates the schools—of course that is the case because the schools by and large reflect their communities and people are by definition political—and it is no news that the rights of students and teachers are being trampled on. The point is that the language of accusation and defense ought to be analyzed within their political contexts, especially by the very people who are affected. If English teachers are still believed to be arbiters of the language by the public, then they should start making a difference by analyzing the meaning of such political language right in their classrooms. And English educators will have to see that those teachers know what to do and how to do it.

To avoid the language of political issues in the classroom is to avoid the language of "public man." If we could avoid that language, we would produce an absurd state of affairs: we would deny the connection between the literature our students read and the right of their cultural heritage—the right to dissent. We would deny the connection between the language our students need to know and their right to become enlightened citizens. And finally we would deny our political responsibility to students who have a right to expect us to help them understand the meaning of public utterances, particularly those of our leaders and others in power.

Because introspection concerning our political and economic way of life is likely to continue through the next decade and because English teachers have traditionally had prerogatives in the study of the English language, a new urgency presses on English educators. English teachers have an opportunity to regain their effectiveness with a public which is reeling from language pollution. Whether they will have the opportunity to lead in the search for meaning in the language of public life depends in major part on how they are trained, K-Ph.D. Now political responsibility is more than ever on the side of Semantics. I don't see that we have a choice. The Conference on English Education is a bold and resourceful group, and I look for it to meet the challenge.

4

The NCTE Committee on Public Doublespeak

. . . information from within the committee and commentary from outside observers . . . presented as a status report . . .

Beginnings of the Committee

Walker Gibson

In a progress report written for the NCTE journals in spring 1974, Walker Gibson comments on the origin and early activities of NCTE's Committee on Public Doublespeak. Gibson, University of Massachusetts, was one of the cosponsors of the original resolutions, helped establish the committee, gave it support during his presidency of NCTE, and remains on the committee as its liaison officer with the NCTE Executive Committee.

About a year ago, Hugh Rank of Governors State University in Illinois, who was then chairman of NCTE's Committee on Public Doublespeak, conceived a brilliant idea. His idea was to organize an "Insider's Tour" to Washington—an actual excursion by a group of concerned English teachers to the fountainheads of bureaucratic jargon. Accordingly, he arranged appointments for such a group at various federal agencies—the FTC, FCC, Department of Defense, White House Office of Telecommunications. Let their PR men explain themselves to us teachers of English, if they can. And vice versa.

It actually happened. Last November, as part of our preconvention activity, some 40 teachers led by Terence Moran of NYU trooped down to Washington and toured the premises. After three days, they returned to our Philadelphia convention, most of them in a state of exuberant outrage at what they had been told—or not told. "We were lied to steadily for three days," one of them told me happily. "We found ourselves unable," Moran reported, "to penetrate the bullshit barrier." And Neil Postman asked, "Why, after all that's happened recently, should an intelligent person believe anything that comes from the government?"

Whatever its contribution to the improvement of teaching may turn out to be, this invasion of our nation's linguistic capital had one clear consequence: it brought to the Committee on Public Doublespeak its first little touch of national publicity. The exposure began, quietly enough, with a sympathetic article in *The Chronicle of Higher Education* by Malcolm G. Scully, who had accompanied the Washington group on some of its visits. This was followed in mid-December by an editorial, no less, in the *New York Times,* in which the Committee's work was described as "relevant teaching at its best." "If the nation's English teachers sup-

port their colleagues' drive against linguistic pollution," said the
Times, "they will be acting in the spirit of Thomas Jefferson's
statement of faith: 'Enlighten the people generally, and tyranny
and oppression of body and mind will vanish. . . .' "

Immediately thereafter came one of William Safire's nationally syndicated columns, also inspired, evidently, by the article in the
Chronicle. Mr. Safire's piece was not particularly friendly—he
argued, quite rightly, that educators' doublespeak is pretty bad too—
but still, publicity's publicity. (And besides, as many English teachers might protest, who wants unqualified support from the author
of Agnew's alliterations?)   Then in mid-January of this year, a
front-page article in the *Christian Science Monitor,* on misleading
confusion in political language, devoted several paragraphs to the
aims and efforts of our Doublespeak Committee. And a lengthy
interview with Hugh Rank on NBC Radio, a news special called
"1984 minus 10," was taped to be aired during February.

This crest of public notoriety for a committee's work represents a
pretty heady moment in NCTE history. And it affords me an excuse for reviewing briefly the development of the Doublespeak
enterprise, and for defining some responsibilities, not to say difficulties, for the future. We evidently have at hand here a hot issue,
a specific and exciting contribution we might make to education.
Will we, can we, seize this opportunity?

At the Council's Las Vegas convention in November of 1971,
Richard Ohmann of Wesleyan University, then as now editor of
College English, happened to be a member of the Resolutions
Committee. Thanks to Ohmann's leadership, two resolutions on
"public lying" were submitted to the business meeting, and passed.
They are worth repeating here:

> On Dishonest and Inhumane Uses of Language
>
> *Background:* As teachers of English we stress the need
> for clarity, directness, and honesty in the use of language.
> We also try to transmit and evolve a tradition of humane
> culture, of which literature forms a part.
>
> Meanwhile, there is another system of education in lan-
> guage and literature—the media and the commercial
> interests that control them. In this system, too, language
> is not always used lucidly and honestly, but it is used
> with great power. The Council on Economic Priorities
> recently showed, for instance, that many large corpora-
> tions are trying to capitalize on public concern about
> the environment by advertising campaigns that are at
> best misleading, at worst dangerously false. Similarly,
> a lyric poem (a literary form) is being used with musical

accompaniment to suggest that the problem of air pollution had best be left to the corporations. And in other areas of advertising, language and literature have many uses not within our traditional definition of the humanities.

It would be proper for our organization to take an active interest in these matters. Be it therefore

Resolved, That the National Council of Teachers of English find means to study dishonest and inhumane uses of language and literature by advertisers, to bring offenses to public attention, and to propose classroom techniques for preparing children to cope with commercial propaganda.

On the Relation of Language and Public Policy

Background: Most English teachers accept Orwell's point, in "Politics and the English Language," that language is often used as an instrument of social control. At best it is not a "neutral" medium, but reflects and implements the interests of its users. For this reason, the way language is used by those with political power is a matter of concern to all of us.

During the past ten years we have seen public officials in our country use words like "pacification," "free-fire zones," "protective reaction," "incursion," "free elections," "aggression," "defense," and "systems" to mediate and sell a war to the American public.

Although teachers of English do not make national policy, we should do what we can to free public language and thought from manipulation by the powerful. Be it therefore

Resolved, That the National Council of Teachers of English find means to study the relation of language to public policy, to keep track of, publicize, and combat semantic distortion by public officials, candidates for office, political commentators, and all those who transmit through the mass media.

Your Executive Committee's response to these resolutions was, characteristically, to authorize one more committee. It was named, thanks to an inspiration by then-President Virginia Reid, the Committee on Public Doublespeak. As its most outspoken enthusiast on the Executive Committee, I was charged during 1972 with organizing some members, getting things off the ground, proposing various directions. Meeting in Minneapolis that November, a tiny band of founding fathers chose Hugh Rank as permanent chairman. Then things started to happen.

During 1973, Rank, in addition to dreaming up that Insider's Tour, gathered huge piles of assorted information about language pollution from many sources, increased the committee's membership, planned several publications for them to prepare, and arranged a confrontation for Philadelphia between an articulate advertising executive and a representative of the FTC. Not to mention dozens of other activities calculated to bring public lying to public attention. For all this, Rank was rewarded with a series of heart attacks that finally forced him, late in the year, to relinquish the chairmanship.

The present chairman is Dan Dieterich of the University of Illinois, coauthor of a useful ERIC/RCS Report on Doublespeak that appeared in last October's *English Journal*. He tells me that within the year at least four books by committee members will be published in a continuing effort to reach secondary and college teachers with practical materials. The committee plans workshops for teachers in several areas across the country. A journal column devoted to a discussion of Doublespeak, based on specific examples drawn from politics, advertising, the military, and education, will be published in one or more NCTE journals. "Our aim," says Dieterich, "is to expand teachers' philosophy of education. We hope to prepare students in American secondary schools and colleges, not merely to ably produce written and spoken communications, but to critically evaluate the messages they receive each day through the mass media."

My own writing and speaking recently have been addressed to a particular area of the Doublespeak situation—the phenomenon of Euphemism. We are witnessing in our time an expanding effort on the part of powerful leaders in the society to con the citizenry by choosing particular *names* for unpleasant or unjust events, names calculated to make us believe that things are OK when they're not OK at all. Disadvantaged (not black, not poor, not ignorant). Inoperative (not fabricated, not lying, not even mistaken). Air support (not bombing, not murder). Among a thousand wonderful true stories of defensive Euphemism in recent history, there is the one about the American colonel in Cambodia who at a press conference took to task the journalists' reporting on the air war. "You always write it's bombing, bombing, bombing," he complained. "It's not bombing. It's air support."

The incredible display of buck-passing that we enjoyed last summer, in the Watergate hearings, offered an unprecedented opportunity for the English teacher to study Euphemism in the bureaucracy. What do we have to say about a world where illegal acts are uniformly renamed as "inappropriate," where a burglary is an "entry," and where bugging somebody's telephone is referred to as "intelligence-gathering." We had better get ready to say *something* about that world.

Perhaps as never before, a particular activity of the Council is beginning to receive conspicuous and favorable national publicity. Are we, as a profession, ready and able to take up this challenge? It is significant, and alarming, that the Doublespeak Committee's efforts to elicit from teachers some specific classroom approaches and techniques have not so far been successful. Do we believe that one of our responsibilities as English teachers is to alert our students to the facts about public lying in our society? If we do believe that, can we summon the energy and the expertise to put our convictions into action? What kinds of exercises—in reading, writing, listening, looking—are appropriate at various grade levels to induce the kind of awareness we're seeking? What steps are possible to remove some of the gobbledegook from our own educational jargon?

These are some questions that had better be answered, and soon, if we are really going to grasp the opportunity now before us.

Committee Accomplishments and Prospects

Daniel Dieterich

The current committee chairman, Daniel Dieterich, brings readers up-to-date on the committee's work and intentions. Dieterich, University of Illinois at Urbana/Champaign, was an early member of the committee who participated in the Washington, D.C., "Insider's Tour"; he was elected chairman at the November 1973 NCTE Convention.

When NCTE formed the Committee on Public Doublespeak in 1972, its charge to the committee was twofold: (1) to create a series of concrete classroom exercises (lesson plans, discussion outlines) which would focus students' attention on irresponsible uses of language; and (2) to alert the profession generally to the forces that in the committee's judgment are misusing the language: government and its military, industry and its advertisers, educators, you and me.

It has been less than two years since the committee was formed. And yet in that short span of time the committee has taken significant strides toward its goal. One such stride has been to make the American public more aware of the very existence of "doublespeak." At the time the committee was formed, the word "doublespeak" was used rarely and with differing connotations. The committee chose "doublespeak" because it combines Orwell's terms "doublethink" and "newspeak" in an attempt to describe the "dishonest and inhumane uses of language." Since the time of our formation, many have found "doublespeak" to be a fitting description of much of our language environment. Journalists and others have found it so fitting that the eighth edition of Webster's *New Collegiate Dictionary* (1973) gives lexicographical recognition to the term, defining it as "inflated, involved, and often deliberately ambiguous language." Though this definition is obviously a simplification of the nature of doublespeak, the very existence of the term in the dictionary is an indication that the work of the committee has not gone unheeded.

This book represents another attempt to bring the subject of doublespeak before the teaching profession and the general public. It is the first NCTE publication on the subject of public doublespeak. The fact that it is one of three on the subject of doublespeak which Hugh Rank has been working on over the past years is indicative of the zeal with which committee members have approached the task before them.

Our committee is composed of 33 men and women living in every area of the country from Hawaii to New York, from Florida to Washington. Some teach in elementary schools, some in secondary schools, some in junior colleges, colleges, and universities. This variety of backgrounds is matched by a diversity of interests and opinions, a diversity that has often found expression in committee meetings at the NCTE conventions and at regional meetings such as the Berkeley committee meeting held in April 1974. This diversity of opinions was nowhere more apparent than on the committee's November 1973 "Insider's Tour" of Washington, D.C., described in Walker Gibson's preceding essay. But despite their often conflicting views, all committee members are committed to the study of public doublespeak and wish to share their concern and knowledge on this subject with the academic community and with the nation at large.

Many committee members accomplish this by writing and editing books about doublespeak. Neil Postman and Charles Weingartner had published a number of books on the subject long before the committee was formed, among them *Teaching as a Subversive Activity,* in which they outlined their approach to "crap detecting." Terence Moran joined with them in editing a guidebook to American doublespeak entitled *Language in America.* In 1971 Robert Cirino wrote an analysis of bias, distortion, and censorship in the news media entitled *Don't Blame the People.* He followed this in 1974 with *Power to Persuade: Mass Media and the News,* which contained over 150 case studies and questions and activities appropriate for use in secondary schools. Raymond Liedlich's book, *Coming to Terms with Language,* and William Lutz's book, *The Age of Communication,* are designed for use in the college classroom. Books on the subject of doublespeak which are now in process include *Balderdash,* a collection of essays about doublespeak edited by John Black and Bruce Reeves, a college text on doublespeak entitled *The Electric Carrot* by D. G. Kehl, a handbook on *Thinking Clearly about Political Issues* by Donald Lazere, an anthology on doublespeak—as yet untitled—which Terence Moran is coediting with noncommittee member Chris Nystrom, and Hugh Rank's *Liars in Public Places,* an anthology directed to students.

Other committee members attempt to spread the word about doublespeak by writing journal articles. The committee column in *English Journal* this year will feature articles by Howard Livingston,

Richard Gambino, Walker Gibson, and Howard Ziff. The committee column in *College English*, edited by Terence Moran, will contain articles by still others. The editors of *College Composition and Communication*, *Elementary English*, and *English Education* have also called for articles on the subject of doublespeak. Past articles by committee members include "Politics and the Study of Language" (*English Education*, December 1973) by H. Thomas McCracken and "Watergate Lingo: A Language of Non-Responsibility" (*Freedom at Issue*, November 1973) by Richard Gambino.

Still other committee members find that the best way to express their views on doublespeak is through speeches at local, state, and national educational conventions. The committee's Speakers Bureau, established in November 1973, has already provided speakers for several such conventions. In December 1973, Hugh Rank, Donald Lazere, and I addressed a seminar on "The Rhetoric of Doublespeak" at the Modern Language Association Convention in Chicago. Charles Weingartner touched on the subject of doublespeak in his keynote address to the convention of the Conference on English Education in Cleveland in March 1974, a convention which also featured speeches by John Black and Gerald Kincaid on the teaching of language. Hugh Rank spoke about doublespeak at the second general session of the convention of the Conference on College Composition and Communication in Anaheim in April 1974. John Black described the work of the committee at the New England Association of Teachers of English Spring Conference in May 1974. And I spoke and held a workshop on doublespeak at the convention of the Canadian Council of Teachers of English in August 1974 in Saskatchewan.

The 1974 NCTE Convention, held in New Orleans in November, was preceded by a two-day preconvention "Conference on Doublespeak and General Semantics" sponsored by the committee. Co-chairmen of the conference, John Black and Howard Livingston, provided a wide range of activities and speakers in order to familiarize teachers with approaches to the study of doublespeak. During the convention itself, the committee sponsored three sessions: "Teaching Counter-Propaganda Techniques," "Coping with Doublespeak: Secondary Teachers," and "The Language of Watergate." All three featured discussions on doublespeak by panels of speakers. Teachers interested in finding appropriate textbooks and other materials about doublespeak were able to locate them at the committee's convention booth.

To keep the academic community informed about the work of the committee, the *Newsletter on Public Doublespeak* began publication in January 1974. With a circulation of now over 600, the news-letter describes past and future committee activities, lists works on doublespeak which are available either commercially or through the committee, cites media coverage of the committee, and invites cooperation in the committee's work. (To be placed on the news-letter mailing list, write: Committee on Public Doublespeak, NCTE, 1111 Kenyon Road, Urbana, Illinois 61801.)

The committee's work has, recently, taken a number of new forms. In May 1974 the NCTE Executive Committee authorized the com-mittee to sponsor workshops at which committee members and in-terested nonmembers might work to develop instructional materials on doublespeak. At this writing, one such workshop has already been held in Amherst, Massachusetts. Led by Richard Ohmann and Walker Gibson, the workshop concentrated on producing ma-terials for use in the college classroom. A second workshop, to be held in California, is being planned by David Burmester. It is hoped that this workshop will produce materials geared toward the secondary school. Gerald Kincaid of the Minnesota State De-partment of Education is also producing and collecting curriculum materials on doublespeak in order to supplement the workshop materials.

In a recent vote, members of the committee decided to look into the possibility of sponsoring television or radio spots to educate the public about doublespeak in commercial advertisements and in political speeches. Though committee work in this area is still in the exploratory stages, we have been heartened by news of a complaint filed with the Federal Communications Commission which would require that two of the networks provide just such spots in order to enable children to deal with commercial propa-ganda.

Also in the exploratory stages is a committee project to sponsor institutes in which teachers could learn techniques for preparing their students to deal with doublespeak. Directed by Howard Livingston, this project is designed to provide a number of such institutes at colleges and universities around the country, all of them monitored in some way in order to ensure that they would maintain appropriate academic standards.

Perhaps the most encouraging news of all is that in the past few months hundreds of people have written or phoned the committee to express their concern about doublespeak and to learn what can be done to counter it. Some have even gone so far as to es-tablish regional committees on public doublespeak; the Missouri Association of Teachers of English has formed one such committee.

The Canadian Council of Teachers of English is also considering founding their own committee. Teachers of journalism, sociology, English, speech, communications, and consumer education have joined with educational administrators around the country in seeking the means to provide today's students with the critical tools they need to recognize and evaluate irresponsible uses of language. The purpose of the Committee on Public Doublespeak, in the future as in the past, will be to give such teachers and administrators all the help we can.

Relevant Lesson

Editorial from the *New York Times*

Although the intent of the committee had been to keep a low profile until some kind of substantial result could be produced, publicity developed, naturally, without any kind of planned PR campaign. Malcolm Scully, of the *Chronicle for Higher Education*, called, asked if he could accompany the Washington tour of federal agencies, and later wrote a report of it for the *Chronicle*. A few weeks later (December 12, 1973), this *New York Times* editorial appeared—a pleasant surprise, terming the goals of this group "relevant teaching at its best."

About a year ago, instructions went out to all United States Government agencies to eliminate the use of the word "poverty" from all official documents and to replace it with "low-income." The Pentagon made semantic history when it coined the abominable phrase "protective reaction strike." The pronouncement that declared "inoperative" all previous Presidential statements on Watergate will be long be remembered.

The common thread that links these examples is the deliberate misuse of the English language to disguise rather than to communicate facts. Although by no means a new practice, its recent escalation has properly alarmed the nation's English teachers. A group within the National Council of Teachers of English has responded to the linguistic emergency by forming a Committee on Public Doublespeak.

The committee has pledged to "keep track of, publicize, and combat semantic distortions" by public officials, candidates for office, political commentators and others. Eventually, it hopes to introduce its analytical efforts into the schools' English curriculum. Enthusiasts of this timely reform movement even suggest an annual Orwellian Award to the worst example of doublespeak.

The proposal, which seems to us to represent relevant teaching at its best, may not find itself overwhelmed with offers for Federal aid. Few members of Congress are likely to rush to introduce bills for the subsidy of truth in rhetoric. But if the nation's English teachers support their colleagues' drive against linguistic pollution, they will be acting in the spirit of Thomas Jefferson's statement of faith: "Enlighten the people generally, and tyranny and oppression of body and mind will vanish like evil spirits at the dawn of day."

Zieglerrata

Israel Shenker

Long familiar to readers of the *New York Times,* Shenker here writes for *The New Republic* (April 13, 1974) about the growing academic interest in propaganda analysis. Albeit NCTE's stockpile of invectives is rather low, Shenker's tongue-in-cheek survey is rather lively.

Wafflers of the world, beware! An implacable enemy, versed in the ways of language, plots your destruction. For three years now the National Council of Teachers of English—130,000 members who live by the word—has been stockpiling invective to hurl at the specter it calls Doublespeak. The council has a Committee on Public Doublespeak—26 determinedly true-speaking, true-writing teachers of high school and college English, whose aim is to "combat semantic distortion by public officials, candidates for office, political commentators, and all those who transmit through the mass media."

Last November the Doublespeak Committee dispatched a daring suicide mission—under the cover name "Insider's Tour"—to the heart of enemy territory, Washington, DC. Four leaders found that the Federal Trade Commission representative had been unable to define "public interest," the Federal Communications Commission official had difficulties with "controversial," and the Department of Defense man struggled unavailingly with "national security"— though he had no trouble when asked if the Pentagon had lied to the Senate about the bombing of Cambodia. Spokesman Jerry W. Friedhaim replied that the Pentagon hadn't lied, it had merely submitted an erroneous report. This is pure Pentagon Doublespeak.

Back in World War I Maury Maverick defined Gobbledygook as "talk or writing which is long, pompous, vague, involved, usually with Latinized words." Others have contributed State Departmentese, Pentagonese, Strangeloveisms, Bureaucrat, bureaucrack, bureauquack, bureaucratic indirect, bureaucratic amorphous, linguistic pollution, officialese, Nixonese, Ovaloid, Zieglerrata, marshmallow prose, Prosa Nostra, and of course Doublespeak's halfbrother—Doubletalk. Rep. Robert F. Drinan (D, Mass.) calls it unlanguage. He once had such trouble understanding an untext of navy unlanguage that he arranged for navy officials to visit his office and debrief themselves.

To Doublespeak is to polish up the handles on reality. "Things are seldom what they seem/Skim milk masquerades as cream," sang Gilbert and Sullivan. But the past master who damned unlanguage *a cappella* was George Orwell. In "Politics and Language," he wrote: "In our time political speech and writing are largely the defense of the indefensible . . . Defenseless villages are bombarded from the air, the inhabitants driven out into the countryside, the cattle machine-gunned, the huts set on fire with incendiary bullets: this is called *pacification*."

Orwell suggested dealing with political chaos by verbal purification. "If you simplify your English, you are freed from the worst follies of orthodoxy," he wrote. "Political language—and with variations this is true of all political parties, from Conservatives to Anarchists— is designed to make lies sound truthful and murder respectable."

In *1984* Orwell foresaw the triumph of Newspeak, completely re- placing Oldspeak (Standard English) by about 2050. Newspeak would make all forbidden beliefs unthinkable by stripping Old- speak words of unorthodox meanings and diminishing the range of thought: "The word *free* still existed in Newspeak, but it could only be used in such statements as 'This dog is free from lice' or 'This field is free from weeds.'" And: "Ultimately it was hoped to make articulate speech issue from the larynx without involving the higher brain centers at all. This aim was frankly admitted in the Newspeak word *duckspeak,* meaning 'to quack like a duck.'"

James Thurber wrote: "The brain of our species is, as we know, made up largely of potassium, phosphorus, propaganda, and pol- itics, with the result that how not to understand what should be clearer is becoming easier and easier for all of us." As usual his seals were barking up the right tree. Where but in the pea soup of our brain was there a culture for the Doublespeak of Vietnam, where troops were "advisors," where men were not murdered but "wasted," and where the CIA shunned assassination in favor of "termination with prejudice"? Jonathan Schell, who chronicled the terrors of US air warfare in Vietnam, noted that people bombed from their homes began as "hostile civilians" and—in camps—be- came "refugees." When the burden of empiricism became oppres- sive, one US official asked for outside help in thinking up derog- atory names for the enemy.

"You always write it's bombing, bombing, bombing," Col. David H. E. Opfer, air attaché at the US Embassy in Pnompenh, com- plained to reporters. "It's not bombing. It's air support." What might have seemed an old-fashioned invasion of Cambodia turned out to be a simple "incursion."

"It gets worse and worse," said Henry Steele Commager in an interview. "Did you hear Caspar Weinberger, the Secretary of HEW, explain that we have enough medical schools—they are just 'over-applied for'? The Lincolns and Jeffersons and Washingtons and Wilsons didn't use jargon: they found ways of eloquence. 'Make the world safe for democracy.' People can understand it. That doesn't turn the Franco regime into a democratic regime, as this crowd would."

Edward S. Herman, a professor of finance at the Wharton School, put together *The Great Society Dictionary* and *The Great Imperial Dictionary*, and translated Doublespeak into Singlespeak. "Urban renewal" was "Negro removal," "infiltration" was "their movement of troops into the battle zone," "reinforcement" was "our movement of troops into the battle zone." Vietnam talk led straight to Watergate language, and to all-time Orwellian award winner Ronald Ziegler, distinguished for his proclamation that "all previous White House statements about the Watergate case are inoperative." After the President's State of the Union address this year, Daniel Schorr of CBS reported that Mr. Nixon had avoided mentioning the negative income tax because his phrasemakers had not come up with a less negative name for it.

With scholarly discernment H. W. Fowler, in *Modern English Usage,* long ago identified a virus called Sociologese. Daniel Bell, professor of sociology at Harvard, sounded the tocsin for "sociological glossolalia" in an erudite study entitled "Sociodicy: A Guide to Modern Usage." Noam Chomsky sounded the anti-tocsin: "I sometimes think the whole function of the social sciences is to mystify trivial things by putting them into quasi-technical language." Henry A. Barnes, who served as transportation commissioner of New York City, produced a glossary of bureaucratic Western, including "doubtless" (unverified), "interesting fact" (drivel) and "universally recognized principle" (risky proposition).

"A society that cannot speak or understand sense is condemned to live nonsensically," says Prof. Richard Gambino, of Queens College and a member of the Doublespeak Committee. The committee believes in the curative powers of simplicity. To enforce Singlespeak it wields the instrument known as Occam's Razor, the rule in philosophy that entities must not be multiplied needlessly. H. L. Mencken pointed out that the American believes in raising the grandeur of his trade by elevating its name—landscape artist for gardener, podiatrist for chiropodist, which was earlier corn doctor. Evelyn Waugh in *The Loved One* and Jessica Mitford in *The American Way of Death* memorialized the verbal grandeur

founded on corpses, and S. I. Hayakawa analyzed a word's "affective connotations"—"finest quality filet mignon" was another way
of saying "first-class piece of dead cow."

Wesleyan's Richard M. Ohmann, a leading member of the Doublespeak Committee, has analyzed a language he calls Liberal. Speakers of Liberal keep their values tacit and remember that the in-
dispensable word is "problem." "In Liberal," Prof. Ohmann noted,
"one refers to the undesirable consequences of anything—selling
arms to dictators, imprisoning dissenters, burning villages—as a
problem."

Since he knows 25 languages, Prof. Roman Jakobson, who taught
at Harvard, has isolated Doublespeaks all over the place. Talley-
rand, he noted, said language exists to conceal true thought.
Stanislavski passed out promptbooks with the dramatist's words at
right—and at left what the dramatist meant. In *Kultura Yazyka*
(*The Culture of Language*), Grigory Vinokur analyzed what the
Russians call "paper language" and what English teachers recognize
as false phraseology, as in the sacred phrase "Our Great October
Socialist Revolution." Why waste paper and ink? asked Vinokur.
Was there really such a revolution that was not ours? Not great?
Not socialist? What's left is "October Revolution," and—as Profes-
sor Jakobson noted—it wasn't even in October.

The Doublespeak Committee has not yet devised an infallible
guide to the perplexed, or a weapon that would cut the enemy to
the quick, simple word, but Prof. Neil Postman of New York
University hopes to wound the enemy nonetheless. He proposes a
kind of Watergate hearing every month—focusing on public language. Postman also suggests a number of crucial questions that
anyone in danger of victimization should ask: 1) What does this
mean in plain language? 2) What interests or causes are served
by this statement? 3) What avenues do I have to verify the truth
content of the statement? 4) Is it a religious statement to be taken
on faith?

"A taste of truth is like a taste of blood," said Dwight Bolinger in
his 1972 presidential address to the Linguistic Society of America.
Noam Chomsky prescribed "honesty" as the antidote to Doublespeak and warned of an enemy—even more insidious than Doublespeak—which cloaks itself in silence and muffles its aims in secrecy.
Nospeak does not yet have the English teachers aroused, but their
silence may conceal the worst.

In the End Was the Euphemism

Fred M. Hechinger

Former education editor and current member of the editorial board of
the *New York Times,* Hechinger originally wrote this article for
Saturday Review/World (March 9, 1974). "With 1984 a decade away,"
the subheadings proclaimed, "U.S. teachers launch a counteroffensive
against galloping Doublespeak." Hechinger, who has seen educational
"reformers" come and go, recognizes the problems of a group which
"intends not only to bemoan the pollution of language but also to
mobilize a purification drive [within] the classroom." Hechinger believes
that "the committee's success may well depend on its capacity to remain
nonpartisan, avoiding capture by the intellectual New Left. . . ." Thus
far, as informed insiders can testify, this nonpartisan capacity has been
sustained by the diversity of the group.

It was George Orwell's grim prediction that by 1984 the official
language of Newspeak would persuade the populace that "ignorance is strength" and "war is peace." To assure a continuous revision of history, Orwell wrote in 1949, the "day-to-day falsification
of the past, carried out by the Ministry of Truth, is as necessary
to the stability of the regime as the work of repression and espionage
carried out by the Ministry of Love."

With ten years left until the target date of Orwell's political-science
horror fiction, some observers of the American language scene are
afraid that the horror was not entirely fictitious and that the
United States is ahead of schedule on its way to Newspeak. Since
they consider this more than a matter of semantics, they have begun to organize a linguistic counteroffensive.

The rebels are part of a normally unobtrusive organization, the
National Council of Teachers of English (NCTE). An alarmed
group within the council has formed the Committee on Public
Doublespeak, which intends not only to bemoan the pollution of
the language but also to mobilize a purification drive, with the
classroom as the basic decontamination unit.

Examples of Doublespeak—the sometimes unwitting but more often
deliberate misuse of words to cover up, rather than explain, reality—
are easy to find almost everywhere. Government bureaus, for instance, have been instructed to eliminate the word *poverty* from
official documents, replacing it with *low-income,* a term not nearly
as alarming as *poverty.* For similar reasons, the unpleasantness of

slums or *ghettos* has long given way to *inner city.* Instead of *prisons,* there are now only *correctional facilities.*

U.S. State Department employees are not *fired* but *selected out,* a term that sounds like an award for excellence. Other government types tend to be *terminated.*

In each instance, the aim is to make things appear better than they are or, in the case of *correctional facilities,* actually to seem what they decidedly are not. If all this were only a matter of semantics and style, there would be little cause for concern. Unfortunately, the truth is that the linguistic cosmetics are often used to create the impression that nasty problems have already been solved or were not really too nasty in the first place. The result: smug lack of concern. Inaction. A comfortable rest on political—or even pedagogical—laurels.

Some of the new committee's members have cited such post-Watergate Doublespeak as calling *inoperative* something that the President had said earlier but later turned out not to have been true. Others have aimed their fire at even more troublesome semantics, such as the explanation by American bombers—after having struck the enemy first—that the maneuver was a *protective reaction strike.*

When "the other side" sends its troops into neutral territory, it is characterized as *aggression* or *invasion;* when "our side" does the same, it is an *incursion* to protect the lives of American soldiers. When a Watergate witness admits, under pressure, that he ought not to have done what he did, he describes the action, not as *wrong,* but as *inappropriate* and then only in *the particular time frame.*

Although the immediate suspicion is that the new committee may be excessively political in its own right—a number of the members probably fall into the category that Spiro Agnew, himself a master of Newspeak, called *radiclibs*—there is clearly much room for semantic recycling in totally non-political areas. For example, public utilities and other commercial interests tend to announce new procedures that result in higher rates or less service with the explanation that they are doing so *for your convenience.*

When an airline tells you that there will be *a change of equipment* in Chicago, it means nothing less than that you have to get off the plane and onto another one, if and when it is available. When a recorded voice over the telephone informs you that your call will be *answered sequentially,* it means simply that you had better wait your turn, buster.

Schoolchildren might examine—for classroom analysis is the committee's ultimate goal—the meaning of *free gifts* offered by savings banks in return for new deposits. Strictly speaking, if a gift is not free, it is not a gift. The bank's gifts, however, are not really free: If the deposit is withdrawn before a minimum period, the gift, or an equivalent amount of money, is taken back. The free gift thus turns out to have been a conditional gift all along.

Walker Gibson, until recently NCTE president and professor of English at the University of Massachusetts, whose brainchild the Doublespeak group is believed to have been, feels that official statements and commercial advertising ought to be read as critically as Shakespeare.

Professor Gibson said his antennae first sent out an alarm when, quite a number of years ago, the War Department renamed itself the Department of Defense. The use of euphemisms subsequently became one of his scholarly interests. "Watergate itself is a spectacular example of euphemism," Professor Gibson said. He added that educators might have been slow to do battle against Doublespeak because "they are themselves so blatantly guilty of their own gobbledygook." He seemed encouraged, however, by a special factor of timing: English departments, he pointed out, are in a state of depression and they may welcome the opportunity to get into a broader field of activity and impact.

Professor Gibson said in his presidential address to the NCTE last November: "If we are to survive as a profession, if we are to serve our society in a useful way, it will not be because we've refined our teaching of Walter Scott or even William Faulkner. It will be because we've directed our attention . . . to the ways language works in the society."

The academic brunt of the counterrevolution is currently being borne by Daniel Dieterich, the Doublespeak committee's chairman, at NCTE headquarters in Urbana, Illinois. Intended as the anti-Doublespeak group's primers, several publications for English teachers are nearing completion. They will deal, in Mr. Dieterich's words, with verbal "card-stacking." Essentially, their goal is to provide a system of language analysis for all age groups, from grade school children to teachers.

One of the books in preparation will probably be titled *Liars in Public Places,* a collection of essays for students edited by Prof. Hugh Rank of Governors State University in Illinois. Also on the way is *Balderdash,* co-edited by Bruce Reeves and John Black.

Mr. Dieterich is also involved in working up curriculum guides as well as a column for professional journals that will contain up-to-date examples of Doublespeak and new methods for exposing it.

There are plans for a special Speaker's Bureau to spread the word on words, hopefully in plain English, as well as for workshops and seminars.

Mr. Dieterich expects soon to be ready to distribute a pamphlet on the problem, for use in high schools, tentatively titled *The Language of Politics,* to be followed later by *The Language of Advertising.* But, he added, there is no need to wait for new publications. Among those already available, he said, are: *Language in America* by Neil M. Postman, Charles Weingartner, and Terence Moran; and two more recent volumes by Mario Pei, *Double-Speak in America,* published a year ago, and *Words in Sheep's Clothing.*

The concept itself is not entirely new. Some twenty years ago, an English professor at Antioch gained a measure of notoriety when he asked every freshman class first to write a *Time*-style cover story about a close friend and, this done, demanded that the piece be rewritten to make the same person appear as a thoroughgoing heel—without changing a single fact, only adjectives. This traumatic exercise came at the height of Henry Luce's "*Time*-speak"—an earlier assault on the language.

In a more recent approach, our older son's fifth-grade class two years ago produced a play composed entirely of fragments of nursery rhymes and TV commercials. And our seven-year-old, like masses of his contemporaries, is a dedicated collector of Wacky Packages, those irreverent cards that play havoc with the labels and extravagant claims of hundreds of commercial products.

Mr. Dieterich reports that the response from teachers has been highly favorable, but he is not unaware of the campaign's high potential for controversy and for counterattacks by conservative political and commercial interests. The committee's success may well depend on its capacity to remain nonpartisan, avoiding capture by the intellectual New Left and letting the euphemisms fall where they may.

Perhaps the best safeguard against retaliation would be reliance on a sense of humor rather than on outrage. The first opportunity to make schoolchildren laugh the enemy into verbal retreat could be the committee's first annual "Orwellian Award" for the worst example of Doublespeak. The choice will not be easy, but it is worth the effort, particularly if the judges keep in mind Orwell's 1945 warning about "Politics and the English Language." The language, he said, "becomes ugly and inaccurate because our thoughts are foolish, but the slovenliness of our language makes it easier to have foolish thoughts." And, to commit foolish, and perhaps even dangerous, acts as well.

Thistlebottomism

William Safire

Safire, speech writer for Spiro Agnew and responsible for the famous alliterations, left the White House staff before the Watergate crisis (and before it was revealed that he was one of the "trusted" aides whose phones were being bugged) to join the *New York Times* editorial staff. The following article first appeared in his syndicated column (December 24, 1973); when this editor pointed out some of his errors, Safire replied (in a letter to me): "O, my offense is Rank!" (Despite such puns, I still recommend his *New Language of Politics* as one of the best books one can read to gain an insight into political language manipulation today.)

"Miss Thistlebottom's Hobgoblins" was the name of a delightful book about word usage written by Theodore Bernstein of the *New York Times* two years ago.

"Miss Thistlebottom" was a mythical English teacher, and her hobgoblins were fussbudget rules that—rigidly applied—obfuscate rather than clarify meaning. It was a Thistlebottom who insisted that Winston Churchill not end a sentence with a preposition, to which he thundered, "This is an impertinence up with which I will not put!"

Recently, a group of Thistlebottoms has been formed by the National Council of Teachers of English into a "Committee on Public Doublespeak," charged with finding and exposing what the teachers call "lying in public places," which could mean reclining in libraries but probably refers to the use of euphemisms by public officials.

"We need to point out to kids," says Walker Gibson, president of the teachers' council, "that they are being conned in many ways by powerful, rich forces." (The use of "rich" in that statement tends to foster class hatred; as used by some teachers today, "rich" has a pejorative connotation, like "political.")

The Public Doublespeak committee will "combat semantic distortion," it says. An example of the distortion it will expose: "protective reaction," a Pentagon term for air strike, which is a dragon that has frequently been slain.

But where does "semantic distortion" begin? In the halls of academe, that's where, as malleable little minds are worked over by pretentious Thistlebottoms.

Who took a chubby little boy named Ronny Ziegler, bombarded him with computer terminology at a tender age—even to the point of using "program" as a verb—until, years later, "inoperative" sprang unbidden to his lips?

Who took the words "contemporaries" and the words "equals"— that convey honest meanings—and cast them into the ashcan, to be picked up by garbage men now called sanitation engineers, semantically distorting them into the harsh and pseudoscientific "peer group"? The pedageezers, that's who, not the politicians.

Physician, *spiel* thyself. In spoken discourse, who has elevated the verb "to orient" to the acme of academic vogue, and not by occident? The "peer-group-oriented" child hardly knows where his head is at, and one Far East expert at the State Department described himself as "Orient-oriented."

Have you ever tried to pin a Thistlebottom down to specifics without getting back a fistful of Pablum he or she calls an "overview"? How come the "underview" is not part of academic jargon? Bel Kaufman, in "Up the Down Staircase," defined "interpersonal relationships" as a fight between kids, and a request for "ancillary civic agencies for supportive discipline" as a frantic academic euphemism for "Call the cops!"

Wading through the meaningless "meaningfuls," the irrelevant "relevants," the cancerous "viables," and the madness of "methodology," it is not hard to see how the jargon-fed graduates of our school systems turn into the jargoneers of the Pentagon, cranking this in and phasing that out, exacerbating, quantifying, proliferating as they were taught to do. They were weaned on hegemonized milk.

The scenario-oriented General, gruffly barking "What are the options?" is the pupil who started to say "choose" one day when his teacher came back with the voguish "opt"; that child swore never to be one-opt again.

I'm not really angry at English teachers; I was started on my way with words by Miss Ruth Goldstein of the Bronx High School of Science, and hardly a typewriter clicks whose pounder does not owe a debt to some Miss Thistlebottom somewhere.

And it is a great idea to combat semantic distortion, so long as one begins at home and never pretends that an "Orwell Award"— named after the essayist who held that political speech was "largely the defense of the indefensible"—is limited to men seeking political power.

For with all the doublespeak spoken by teachers and politicians who would like to consense us, we can also hear the vivid phrases that inspire, inflame or infuriate: from the apt appellation of leak-pluggers as "plumbers," to the cruelly evocative "twisting slowly, slowly in the wind," to the use by John Mitchell of Joseph P. Kennedy's immortal line: "When the going gets tough, the tough get going."

That enlivens and bespirits the discourse, and calls for toppers, not stoppers: Teachers of English should not just be pointing to the manipulative use of language but hailing the birth of colorful phrases.

Examples are everywhere. Sprayed on the side of a New York subway car was a Latin student's social comment: "Gloria mundi is sick of transit." And across a table in a Washington restaurant, Presidential counsel Leonard Garment summed up the Administration's energy policy with a paraphrase of St. Matthew: "Many are cold, but few are frozen."

Tell that to your peer group, Miss Thistlebottom.

Doublespeak Committee Uses Double-Talk

Kenneth J. Rabben

Not all critics were as lighthearted as William Safire in his admonition of "Physician, *spiel* thyself." Here Kenneth Rabben, writing for the Copley News Service (July 17, 1972), responds to the original NCTE announcement of the resolutions concerning political and commercial propaganda. He views NCTE as a "frequent purveyor of educationese and similar nonsense," and makes a rather scatter-shot attack: some points (I would concede) as valid; others, debatable; but, *in toto*, some very broad generalizations and innuendoes.

Most Americans are familiar with double-talk from many sources and few groups use more of it and confuse more people with it than "educators."

So it was amusing to learn that the latest organization to enter the fight against obfuscation is the National Council of Teachers of English, a frequent purveyor of educationese and similar nonsense.

In a statement that calls for virtual censorship to cloud its anti-intellectual goals, the council announces formation of an Orwellian Committee on Public Doublespeak "to scrutinize the language of public officials, campaigning politicians, military leaders, advertisers and educators themselves—and expose those who employ language to pull the wool over the public's eyes."

The committee also will collect examples of "public lying" and teach pupils to recognize it. This may come as a surprise to taxpayers who thought and have been told that pupils have been learning this all along.

An organization whose policies indicate its belief in collectivism and use of the schools as the nation's social problem solver and whose stock in trade is language, complains that "language is often used as an instrument of social control," a use long practiced by schoolmen and the council.

According to resolutions passed at its annual convention last year, the major council target is identified as "large corporations," their advertising practices and politicians who tailor words to their own definitions. The council believes most people are unable to separate fact from fiction. It must lead them by the hand down the path to truth.

The first statement the doublespeak committee should investigate is this one from a council resolution: "And in other areas of advertising, language and literature have many uses not within our traditional definition of the humanities."

A second resolution dealing with language "as an instrument of social control . . . by those with political power . . ." and "manipulation by the powerful," uses that very resolution to advance its political opposition to the Nixon administration and the Vietnam war. "During the last 10 years we have seen public officials . . . use words like 'pacification,' 'free-fire zone,' 'protective reaction,' 'incursion,' 'free elections,' 'aggression,' 'defénse' and 'systems' to mediate and sell a war to the American public."

The committee certainly has its work cut out. The "education establishment" and teachers have become one of the nation's most potent lobbies, wielding immense political power in municipal, state and federal legislatures. The National Education Association and its affiliates, including council members, for example, boast of their political muscle and increased political involvement. Their special political action committees at all levels come dangerously close to jeopardizing their tax-exempt status.

As its investigations continue, the doublespeak committee should define "inhumane uses of language," a phrase from a council resolution and include schoolmen, politicians they support, and office-seeking teachers in its premise "to keep track of, publicize and combat semantic distortion by public officials, candidates for office, political commentators and all those who transmit through the mass media." This is particularly important when considering the captive audience of more than 52 million pupils.

The committee also should explain this double-talk in its press release and resolutions: "degradation of candor," "a tradition of humane culture," "to mediate . . . a war to the American public" and encouragement through their use of such creations as "co-opted," "sexism" and "classism."

215

The Teacher-Heal-Thyself Myth

Hugh Rank

Here, the editor makes some personal reflections, not necessarily shared by NCTE or by members of the Committee on Public Doublespeak. In fact, at times, he rather rudely insinuates that some of his English teacher colleagues are sometimes *wrong-headed, witless dullards,* or *snobs*; and actually calls some of his fellow reformers *Preachers* and *Puritans, Assassins* and *Cuddlers*; reserving, for advertisers, the terms *seducers* and *child molesters.* In the midst of all this name-calling, Rank also speculates about the errors in some current myths and assumptions, and recklessly predicts some future propaganda crises.

1

When NCTE announced it had formed a Committee on Public Doublespeak to combat language abuse by politicians and advertisers, one of the immediate responses—from both within and outside the profession—was "Teacher, heal thyself." Columnist William Safire was witty about it ("Physician, *spiel* thyself"), but others, such as journalist Kenneth Rabben, were more sarcastic: "Most Americans are familiar with double-talk from many sources and few groups use more of it and confuse more people with it than 'educators.' So it was amusing to learn that the latest organization to enter the fight against obfuscation is the National Council of Teachers of English, a frequent purveyor of educationese and similar nonsense."

Letters sent in to the committee expressed the concern of teachers. "Clarity begins at home," said one; "Let's put our own house in order, first," said another. Other colleagues made profound observations about people living in glass houses, and people throwing first stones. Most negative reaction was on this level, a knee-jerk response of clichés and adages.

Some were more thoughtful, more extensive analyses. One distinguished teacher wrote: "[Newsmen] are more aware of their responsibilities and conscious of the slipperiness of language than college professors. If professors plan to guard the uses of language and other forms of communication, I think (I am not being sarcastic or coy) they must begin with their own communications. They are among the chief agents teaching dishonesty. I can't conceive how an NCTE commission or committee could do the things these resolutions encourage."

Another well-known teacher and writer responded: "Sure, English teachers and faculty types generally are quick with deceptive rhetoric, especially when we talk about what *we're* doing. . . . I don't think we can do much more than call the kettle black. But that kettle is so much more dangerous than our pot. . . . We should be talking to the public about Pentagonese even if somehow we fall into self-righteous jargon while doing it. This is clearly not a time to wait for someone without fault to come along and cast the first stone."

Many teachers recognize their own language manipulation and that of their colleagues. Because they do not want to be hypocrites, any sense of moral outrage they may have against the language of the Pentagon or Madison Avenue is countered from within, from their own sense of personal guilt that they, too, manipulate language. So their call for reform is usually very personal: "Let's reform ourselves first, then, once pure, we can go after others."

Thoreau, speaking about reformers, observed: "There are a thousand hacking at the branches of evil to one who is hacking at the root." In my judgment, the root cause of much of our confusion about language today is the implicit assumption, seldom recognized or articulated, that language manipulation is intrinsically bad. Those who unconsciously accept this premise are condemned to feelings of guilt, frustration (due to their call for impossible conditions), and possibly even misanthrophy, because it can be observed that all people, in all eras, in all lands do this "bad" thing of language manipulation. Indeed, most of the reformers, the critics of advertising, the texts and the teachers I've encountered have assumed this premise that language manipulation is bad. In contrast, let me state a premise that language manipulation is a neutral, natural human activity, and that any "goodness" or "badness" depends on the context of the whole situation.

By "language manipulation," I mean the process of *intensifying* or *downplaying* elements of human languages. Language, here, is being used in a broad sense to cover verbal language, both written and spoken; mathematics; and all nonverbal ways by which humans communicate information or attitudes: facial gestures, body movements, spacial relationships, and so on. I believe there is no "neutral" transfer of information; all communication involves a basic selection/omission process by which we intensify or downplay. We intensify some things simply by selecting them; we downplay others simply by omitting them.

To clarify this intensify-downplay activity, consider how we manipulate the elements of verbal communication; for example, a *word.* Words are intensified by adding modifiers (adjectives or adverbs), by using synonyms (substituting other words which have greater connotations), by adding a prefix (patriot/*super*patriot; liberal/*ultra*liberal) or a suffix (beat*nik,* peace*nik*), or a dozen other ways. We can intensify writing with CAPITALIZATION, with underlining, or with punctuation—add quotation marks, for example, and we can supercharge a word: "intellectual." We can even play around with spelling and the alphabet: Amerika, U$A, Nixon with a swastika for the x. In our speech, we can intensify or downplay an individual word by the stress, the pitch, the tonal qualities we choose to give it. In brief, we do thousands of things to words, the basic building blocks of our verbal language, which are designed either to intensify or downplay.

Most English teachers spend their days involved in some aspects of working with the manipulation, the intensifying-downplaying process, of verbal language. In teaching syntax, we know the thousands of patterns which can be generated from a few core ideas, the deep structure of a sentence. We know we can intensify by certain devices and patterns within a sentence—by repetition, by positioning, by association, and so forth. In fact, the very earliest studies of language in ancient Greece gave us long lists of the classical *tropes* and *schemes,* those patterns by which groups of words can be ordered. We know also, as we consider larger segments of writing, the architectonics, the structure, of whole speeches, whole essays, whole novels. Many English teachers are rather expert at analyzing the structure of a piece of writing, pointing out the basic mechanics of how transitions are made, how coherence is achieved, and so on. Yet, if one were to ask their opinion on *euphemisms,* for example, it's quite likely the answer would be prescriptive: "Don't use euphemisms." There's an almost instinctive reaction, an uncritical accepting of assumptions, that this kind of language manipulation is "bad."

To illustrate the dilemma of those who assume that language manipulation is intrinsically bad, let me use an example from Mario Pei's book *Words in Sheep's Clothing* (New York: Hawthorn, 1969). This book is an extensive collection of contemporary examples of what Pei calls *weasel words:* "The term can be legitimately extended to cover any word of which the semantics are deliberately changed or obscured to achieve a specific purpose, or which is used in a given context for the sole purpose of impressing and bamboozling the reader or hearer. Weasel words are shifty, tricky, dishonest."

Note here this premise, rather explicit, that language manipulation is bad. Later in the introductory chapter as Pei begins to explain and qualify, he forgets that value judgment ("shifty, tricky, dishonest") made in his first premise. He concedes that "semantic change is as old as language itself," but asserts "most semantic changes occur accidentally" and hedges, "The process of deliberate semantic change is largely modern. Still, there are historical examples." Finally, he qualifies: "It is only partly true that most of these deliberate semantic changes occur in the realm of politics and administration. As we go over the rather large lists we have accumulated . . . we find that weasel words appear in all fields of human endeavor. . . . Full treatment of the subject calls for a book that will never be complete, because each year sees a bumper crop of new weasel words."

In the 20 chapters that follow, Pei gives almost equal space to each of his selected categories: weasel words from advertising, the movies, the arts, cocktail parties, education, politics, the military, hippies, race relations, etc. In some chapters, the reader can sense that Pei has greater enthusiasm for attacking the weasel words used by certain groups; and, at times, Pei drifts away from his listings and begins to preach—in favor of Loyalty Oaths, or against "relativism." Pei, as preacher, warns us: "We have largely forgotten our moral sense, our sense of right and wrong. Relativism is rampant among us. Things, deeds, patterns, or behavior are no longer regarded as intrinsically good or bad, but only in relation to existing circumstances. The moral code has become elastic. Worse yet, it has been conveniently forgotten. There is no absolute honesty, no absolute honor. There is only what you can get out of the world, the government, your fellow man" (p. 132).

Pei reveals his own absolutist position, but I believe he misrepresents the position of those who would stress the importance of the *situation* or the *context* in making moral judgments. Formal, logical, syllogistic differences separate the two positions. Some people, including Pei, place the value judgment ("language manipulation is bad") in the major premise. Then, after collecting the evidence—the widespread, ubiquitous examples of all kinds of people manipulating language—that "everybody does it," they conclude that everyone is guilty of this bad thing. And commonly end up in the same situation as Pei, who gives almost equal treatment: one chapter to artsy talk at cocktail parties, one chapter to the language of thermonuclear war.

In my judgment, in my moral code, thermonuclear war is a hell of a lot more important, more significant, more dangerous, more deserving of attention than chitchat at a cocktail party. My major premise: language manipulation is a natural, neutral human activity. I expect *everyone* to intensify, to downplay, to manipulate languages for their own benefit and advantage. This is what human beings do. This is what they've always done, always will do. If you start with this as a major premise, then any moral judgments are made in the minor premise.

Value judgments concerning the ethical or moral aspects of language have to be made in context with the whole situation: who is saying what to whom, under what conditions and circumstances, with what intent, and with what results. Because such judgments are demanding, complex, and often tentative, they are much less emotionally satisfying than the "certitude" afforded by relying upon an *a priori* judgment that language manipulation is bad in and of itself.

Some people in our society desire a rigid, well-defined set of rules, a list of dos-and-don'ts, an absolute certainty. Sometimes we label these people as *absolutists,* perhaps even as *authoritarians.* We may disagree with their rigidity. However, they do exist in our society; they are "well-intentioned"; and frequently, among other certitudes, is their sense of "being right," of being the embattled defenders of Truth and Virtue.

Such people, I believe, are likely to react negatively to any attempted revision in the English curriculum that is based on the premise that language manipulation (the intensifying/downplaying of elements) is a neutral, natural human activity. Such language education can be as potentially explosive as sex education has been in the past in American schools.

In the sex education controversy, one side usually argues that students need some kind of basic sex information as an essential survival skill for the individual and society and contends that this basic information can be presented as neutrally as possible, without moral judgments—which they hope would be supplied by either home or church. The opposition attacks either premise, insisting that schools should not teach sex education, *or,* if taught, that the program should be didactic and moralistic, one that implants values and norms. (But in our pluralistic society, an immediate problem emerges: whose values? whose standards? whose norms?)

In one sense, parents would be less likely to protest a new approach to language education (especially after Watergate!) than they would be to complain about sex education. But opposition could occur; we need to be prepared to explain to hostile parents that when we, as teachers, describe or discuss certain techniques of language manipulation we are not endorsing immorality.

Certainly in my own graduate courses I do not have any trouble teaching Aristotle's Rhetoric to my adult students. But I can imagine, and sympathize with, the problems faced by my students who go out into the local schools and teach in the 5th and 6th grades, the 11th and 12th grades. Can you imagine some 5th grader running home to gleefully tell mommy that "teacher said" the emotional appeal was more effective than the rational appeal? Some mommys and daddys would be off to the local school board, irate at the evils being taught. Can you recognize the potential problems if we try to inform our kids about the real ways languages can be manipulated?

Rhetoricians have always worried over the problem of teaching the realities of language manipulation. Dwight Bolinger of Harvard, for example, in his Presidential Address to the Linguistic Society of America, recently stated: ". . . what if enough [linguists] were to turn their attention to truth and falsehood for it really to make a difference? It is a risky business when scientists start developing tools that are capable of misuse. To bring to light the mechanisms of Machiavellianism may be to provide future Machiavellis with easy access. But I doubt we can teach today's Machiavellis much that they do not already know. This is one game where the con men have less to learn than their victims." Bolinger and many others today are echoing the anguish of Aristotle who worried over this same problem in the opening pages of his Rhetoric, his treatise on the art of persuasion. Aristotle was an extremely moral person and he was very concerned with the problems of teaching people the possible techniques and ways of persuasion. But he did describe in detail the methods by which people could be persuaded. Aristotle's motive was not to train future evildoers, but to alert and train citizens how to recognize and to counter such techniques: "Further, we must be able to employ persuasion, not in order that we must practice it in both ways, for we must not make people believe what is wrong; but in order that we may see clearly what the facts are, and that if another man argues unfairly, we, on our part, may be able to confute him." (In my terms, a defensive rhetoric, or counter-propaganda.)

Our professional persuaders already know how to persuade and manipulate. Our educational system has provided intensive training to a small segment of our society in universities and business schools, with courses and programs labeled *Salesmanship, Public*

Relations, Advertising, Market Behavior, Consumer Behavior, and
Marketing Strategy. Various on-the-job training programs (such
as the Dale Carnegie courses) also have done a rather effective
job of training persuaders how to persuade.

But of the 60 million young citizens now in our schools, only a
few thousand will be trained in these techniques of persuasion—
in the use of the emotional appeal, associative techniques, image
building, etc. The great majority of our future voting citizens,
and future consumers, will have little or no training in identifying,
naming, or analyzing such persuasion techniques.

I'm not overstating the case. Simply check the available texts:
of the 19 leading college textbooks I analyzed for their treatment
of "propaganda analysis," however labeled, all of them gave it but
a few pages, and most of them concentrated on the fallacies of
formal logic. At the high school level, more than half the texts
and related materials I've seen have been based on the old Institute
for Propaganda Analysis list of propaganda techniques, a list
created pre-TV, pre-World War II, pre-Pentagon, pre-computer,
pre-etc. Unfortunately, in addition, the list has internal errors of
cross-categorization.

To recap: there's a widespread common assumption that language
manipulation is bad in and of itself. Letters to the committee,
editorial comments, textbook prescriptions, and so on, over-
whelmingly seem to be based on this assumption, usually not
articulated. I used Pei's book as my main example primarily
because it's easily available in order for readers to check my
commentary on it. (*Why* there is in America such a general
attitude which favors this kind of "linguistic Manicheanism" is not
my concern here. I'll suggest that it stems from our Ramist
tradition, our Puritan rhetorical tradition, and from the historical
development of English departments and speech departments in
the U.S. during the past century. But, regardless of cause, I think
it's accurate to state that such a phenomenon, such an attitude
toward language, does exist.) Secondly, I believe that once we
begin to introduce into our textbooks and classrooms a more
descriptive attitude toward language manipulation, we are likely
to incur the wrath of defenders of Virtue who will charge that
such attempts are subversive and corrupting.

One of the most revolutionary things which can happen now is
simply for teachers of language to teach *how* language operates,
to teach what can be done with words and numbers and images
and other human languages, not what should or shouldn't be done.
To teach, not to preach. To teach our young how languages can

be manipulated by anyone, to describe what is possible, to teach children to recognize their own manipulating and the manipulating done by others. At present we have a lot of English teachers acting more like preachers, more concerned with making their moral pronouncements about a particular politician or a particular commercial than with giving their students a good grounding in understanding language techniques. Students may be impressed, at least temporarily, with the particular bias or enthusiasm of a favorite teacher, but students may not carry with them the life-long ability to recognize language manipulation coming from all different directions. We've already seen students totally wise to and jaded by the Madison Avenue con game yet at the same time unaware of their own parroting of counter culture slogans and clichés.

Certainly one goal of any counterpropaganda campaign would be to immunize, to inoculate, students in advance of any particular propaganda blitz—from Left or Right, from Establishment or Counter Culture. Most critics and reformers usually react afterwards; the teacher's job should be to prepare students in advance. This is best done, I think, by being very honest with our young and telling them what we really know about language manipulation. Because such frankness is not common in texts today, and is apt to provoke a response, I believe one of the major emphases of any effort here should be to assure parents, and fellow citizens, of our own moral standards. If we are going to remove a moral judgment from the *major premise,* we had better emphasize it in our *minor premise.*

In our pluralistic society, where diverse standards are obvious, it seems that equality and mutuality are the most commonly accepted standards. Our legal system, our public rhetoric, our common sentiments all agree on the ideals of equality, fairness, justice; ideally, our laws are established to protect people from inequality, injustice, and exploitation. However much reality differs from these ideals, these ideals are still the structural framework of our society.

In a classroom, even if a teacher concentrates on what *can* be done with language, it's quite probable that students will seek advice about what *should* be done: "Should we use euphemisms?" "Is it immoral to do something like that?" The teacher faces a difficult situation. Instead of replying with the euphemisms-are-bad bit, the teacher has to explain the general problem of making a value judgment in context and then is expected to offer some analysis of a specific case, using specific criteria for a moral judgment. In our society, I would suggest that an acceptable criterion would be equality.

Our moral sense is outraged by inequality. In sexual matters we already have a sophisticated vocabulary to describe situations of equality and inequality. For example, we speak of *seduction* when there is not an equality, a mutuality of exchange, when the knowledgeable or crafty seducer takes advantage of the innocent or the naive; we speak of *rape* when force or violence creates a situation of inequality; we speak of *child molesting* when age is concerned, when the young are abused. Using this analogy, it is clear that in language situations today many of our advertisers are *seducers* and *child molesters,* taking advantage of the young, the innocent, the naive, the gullible. At present there exists in our society great inequality in the ability to persuade. When a kid sits down in front of a TV set to watch the cartoons, we seldom realize that at the other end of this language situation there is a large group of adults—sophisticated in persuasion, well-paid, well-equipped, well-advised—who are targeting in on this little consumer. On one side, a $26 billion language industry with advertising blitzing us day and night; on the other side, a few random gestures by the schools.

I think the major thrust of any counterpropaganda campaign should be directed at a balance, at a situation of equality. To make the situation equal, we must make the persuadee more sophisticated; we must teach the student that which the persuader already knows. I'm not advocating confrontation tactics, in which the dominant metaphor is the ever-ascending escalator; I'm not advocating an attack on advertising, on particular products, or on political policies being peddled. I am advocating a counterpropaganda effort in the schools in which the dominant metaphor is the *teeter-totter,* the *seesaw,* and our work is directed toward creating a more balanced, a more nearly equal situation, between persuaders and persuadees.

If you grant that language manipulation is a natural, neutral process, that moral judgments must be made in a context, and that equality is a useful criterion here, let me illustrate how one can talk about our much maligned technique, the euphemism.

Many people and texts condemn the euphemism: "You shouldn't use euphemisms. . . ." But the fact is, people *do* use euphemisms all the time; we manipulate language in these instances to downplay certain things. In many situations it seems to me perfectly polite, kind, and moral to use a euphemistic phrase to express sorrow or to avoid insulting someone or injuring their feelings. The morality, the goodness or badness, depends totally on the situation and context. In one of Jacques Cousteau's undersea

adventure books, he spends a page telling about the many euphemisms his crew uses for "shark." They never use that word; the
dreaded monsters are always referred to in some euphemistic way,
such as "friendly visitors." Now it's perfectly acceptable for the
crew to use these phrases among themselves, in a situation of
equality: "Hey, Pierre," someone says, "there's some friendly visitors
below." Both the sender and the receiver of that message know
the referent out there and all that implies. But if I were a visitor
aboard the ship and a crewman told me, as I was getting ready
to dive overboard, that there were some "friendly visitors" below,
I'd probably have a mental picture of picturesque pink-and-purple
Angelfish swimming around. If I thus placed myself unknowingly—
and unwillingly—into that dangerous situation, it would be a most
immoral use of euphemisms because of the inequality of the
language situation. To use such in-group euphemisms, or technical
jargon, with an audience that doesn't comprehend the reality of
the referent can be a most immoral act if it places the audience
unknowingly into a dangerous situation.

When the Pentagon uses euphemisms, or technical jargon, such as
"low yield, clean thermonuclear device," most people do not get
an accurate mental picture of the reality because the words sound
rather pleasant: it's *low* yield, *clean,* and only a *device.* By words,
the military has concealed the reality that what they're talking
about are bombs that are more powerful, more devastating, more
horrible than the A-bombs dropped on Hiroshima and Nagasaki,
more catastrophic than any weapon ever used before in human
history. Such a use of language, I believe, is immoral. In a
democratic society, for the military to deceive its own citizens
seems to me to be a gross, illegal abuse of power. I don't know
what can be done about the "system" here; it's certainly more
complex to indict the Pentagon or the CIA than it is to impeach a
President. If you accept the concept that everyone manipulates language to benefit their own position, then it's not likely that the
Pentagon will reform itself. To equalize the balance, journalists,
broadcasters, and teachers of language have a special obligation to
translate military and political jargon, euphemisms, and circumlocutions into language that citizens can understand and
comprehend.

Note that the NCTE committee is focused on *Public* Doublespeak.
Assuming that everyone manipulates language, in private and in
public, here the focus is on the public sector. There are many
possible public speakers worthy of critical attention (including
educators and clergymen), but I'm working from a rather solid
old-fashioned idea that one ought to focus first on the most

important and the most powerful persuaders in our society. In 1974, Madison Avenue will spend $26 billion dollars to persuade Americans to buy this or that; the Pentagon will continue to mount the most intensive, most expensive propaganda blitz—on its own country—in history; and, soon, the politicians will be in high gear trying to persuade us of their policies or their presidential choices.

Priorities need to be established; value judgments need to be made in any counterpropaganda campaign in order to determine which of the many possible persuaders are the most significant to watch, analyze, and bring to public attention. In my own writings, you may recognize that I place higher values on life-and-death issues and health-and-safety issues than on various cosmetic and parity product issues. How our military and political leaders manipulate language, what they conceal and omit, and how they blitz or censor or confuse seems to me to be of greater significance, worthy of more attention than most commercial advertising. Within the realm of commercial advertising, I also see a hierarchy of priorities: certain health-and-safety issues (automobile safety, tires, drugs, foods) are more important than worrying about whether someone wastes a few dollars buying some cosmetic dreams or loses a few cents buying a parity product.

2

Looking to the future, it's possible to predict at least some of the propaganda crises. The advertising industry, for example, forecasts an even greater expansion during the next five years; their optimism might be a bit inflated, but obviously advertising is not going to be less sophisticated than it is in 1974. The political campaign in 1976 is quite apt to be the most technically adroit ever; before Jeb Stuart Magruder went to jail for his Watergate activities, he bewailed the fact that no one really appreciated the "good" work that the Committee for the Re-Election of the President had done. Magruder believed (and rightly so) that the direct mail, computer, and telephone techniques which had been integrated into the GOP 1972 strategy to persuade specific types of voters would be models for all future political campaigns. One can reasonably expect that all candidates in 1976 will be very concerned about their image of sincerity, credibility, and trustworthiness; we'll get what Arthur Herzog calls "the Candor Con."

The mass image-making campaign generated by the Bicentennial won't be a crisis, but will be certainly a nuisance. By 1976, we'll be so supersaturated with Bicentennial co-opting we'll be ready for another Revolution—this one to be touched off by a symbolic dumping into Boston Harbor of all the plastic American eagles, Early American furniture, and patriotically peddled Red-White-and-Blue knickknacks and doodads. We'll wince everytime we hear the words "heritage" and "tradition" or see Liberty Bells, Franklins, Washingtons, and Jeffersons in the ads. (For more information, write the Peoples Bicentennial Commission, 1346 Connecticut Avenue NW, Washington, D.C. 20036, a group of motley youths who have done a brilliant job of exposing the crass commercialism of the "official" Bicentennial groups.)

Language manipulation during the past two decades has concealed one of our key housing problems. Under the romantic imagery of the covered wagon, metaphors of wanderlust, and euphemisms of "mobile home" and "parks," a significant change has occurred in housing patterns. By 1970, "mobile homes" accounted for 34 percent of all new single family units, and there were estimates that 94 percent of low income housing was such "mobile homes," usually crammed a few feet away from their neighbors in rows in such "parks." We are building new ghettos throughout the country, but few Americans are concerned, partially because most people have bought the PR phrases of the industry and accepted uncritically the glamourized idea that "mobile homes" are really mobile. To provide adequate, humane housing for 100 million new Americans in the next 25 years is a problem of great concern; thus any language manipulation which tends to conceal or obscure reality here must be exposed, must be countered so that citizens can make judgments in a situation of equality in which facts are not masked by deliberately maintained illusions.

In the next decade, I believe we will see one of the most serious propaganda campaigns ever encountered: on food and diet. Judging by the past—by the problems involved in the cigarette smoking issue (see Thomas Whiteside's *Selling Death: Cigarette Smoking and Advertising*) and by our ongoing controversy (with the FTC, FDA) about the various drug pushers on TV—the forthcoming argument about food and diet patterns in America will be an even more lopsided propaganda blitz.

In the cigarette issue, for example, only a few companies and a few Southern states were involved directly in losing money. Yet their fight for personal profits, despite the solid evidence of health hazard *(cancer)*, still continues. A current cigarette ad (from a company which spent $85 million in advertising in 1973) has the chutzpah to claim: "If you don't smoke nobody is urging you to start." For this blatant lie, I lodged a "deceptive advertising" complaint, as yet unanswered, with the FTC. But I guess I must be patient: the FTC has been going after Bayer and Anacin and Bufferin and Excedrin for more than a decade, and the ad agencies and lawyers for these drug pushers are still finding loopholes in the laws, still rephrasing lies. But neither the cigarette issue nor the drug issue have the potential for controversy that we're going to see in the near future over some basic "American ways of life" concerning food and diet.

Granted, there are fanatics, faddists, and health nuts with dire predictions about food and diet. But there are also serious scientific researchers now sending out warning signals based on probable conclusions of current studies. As traditional scientists they are not making premature claims, but evidence is accumulating that our American diet (really a post-1945 American diet) of hamburgers and hot dogs, steaks and snack foods, pizzas and soda pop, candy and ice cream, is having a devastating effect on the health of our citizens. In the past generation, the American combination of advertising and abundance has created an environment harmful to our health which we have taken for granted; in other words, the cumulative effect of millions of ads for food products and food sellers has been a "conditioning propaganda." Americans are quite likely to scoff at, scorn, and reject any medical advice which points out that we are literally eating ourselves to death. As these medical reports are issued in the future, we are apt to see a propaganda blitz from those who profit by selling us certain foods and who stand to lose money if Americans change their eating and snacking habits.

"Every major food company today," said E. B. Weiss (*Advertising Age,* January 29, 1973, p. 54), "is getting more than half its income from products that weren't on the market 10 years ago." Obviously, any medical advice to stay away from greasy foods, snack foods, and the like because they are strong contributing factors, or even causal agents, to the epidemic of heart attacks affecting the American population is going to be countered by a massive advertising campaign confusing the issues, discounting "rumors," intensifying themes of personal "freedoms," focusing on here-and-now pleasures. Such advertising and such attitudes are going to come not merely from the major corporations peddling snacks and sweets (1973 ad expeditures: General Foods, $180 million; General Mills, $74.2 million; Kraftco, $74 million; Coca-Cola, $76 million; Nabisco, $69 million; Pepsico, $58 million; McDonald's, $46.5 million, etc.) but also from the thousands of small food companies, local restaurants, and farm groups such as the beef industry and the milk industry (which as we found out in 1973–74 has a rather large expense account and lobby).

In August 1974, for example, the FTC sought an injunction against the National Commission on Egg Nutrition, which had been placing ads claiming that "there is absolutely no scientific evidence that eating eggs, even in quantity, will increase the risk of heart attacks." This claim directly contradicts the advice given by the American Heart Association. If readers knew that the National Commission was a front for the industry, the American Egg Board, which was spending $2 million on this campaign, readers would be in a more nearly equal situation to judge the bias and source of the ad. The egg industry is indeed in trouble: per capita consumption of eggs has dropped from 389 in 1950 to 292 in 1973. A complex economic and moral question is posed: do we "save" the egg industry, or do we risk the possible premature deaths of millions? Today's egg industry is no longer a folksy chicken-coop-in-the-backyard business; it's primarily modernized into sleek rows of buildings, "egg farms" where the hens never touch the ground. But it is not a big industry in comparison to the corporate giants whose toes are going to be stepped on in the future, who are going to be launching propaganda campaigns in defense of their interests.

A great deal of "conditioning propaganda" has already been going on for some time now, under the name of public relations or public service campaigns, with the purpose of making citizens feel very friendly toward our corporate giants. In some cases the intent is a bit obvious, for example, the PR campaigns for oil, coal, and electric corporations that suggested specific "solutions" for the Energy Crisis (sic). In other cases, institutional public relations campaigns for non-consumer or non-retail companies are designed to create a favorable public atmosphere in order to ward off demands for trust-busting, control legislation, or other governmental action that citizens might seek. Remember, after World War I the public was very angry at the "merchants of death," the corporations that had profited from the war. But who today can be mad at U.S. Steel or DuPont after they've been telling us week after week that they're involved in doing good things for better living?

Some conditioning is even more subtle, and a great deal of this is getting into the classrooms, almost unnoticed, making some teachers innocent co-agents and "volunteers" for corporate PR campaigns. For example, check the sources in the "Free Films for Educators" books. Last year, McDonald's provided thousands of classrooms with excellent kits and teaching aids about taking care of our external environment ("don't litter!"); I wonder if next year Ronald will give us some nutritional advice?

I'm not saying that we should be advocates of a particular cause—for example, a specific diet. Or that we should necessarily get involved in confrontational tactics—for example, in devising counter-commercials ("You deserve a Stroke today!" "Pimples Today! Coronary Tomorrow!"). Or that we should in any way impinge upon others' free choice to do what they wish. But any meaningful freedom of choice means knowing the alternatives, the options, the other sides of an issue.

Rhetoric, as the art of persuasion, deals with issues in which there is doubt and disagreement; rhetoric is concerned with the probable, not the certain; rhetoric is concerned with complex choices—the lesser of two evils, etc.—the real dilemmas in human affairs which are not easily solved. Any professional persuader, any advertiser, knows this and also knows that scientists and doctors are going to be extremely conservative and slow in making definitive statements because their whole training and approach is focused on a search for rules and laws, predictable reproducible results. One should not attack this scientific quest for certitude, but one should recognize that in the interim period, public arguments will be rhetorical ones debating probabilities. Teachers can help future citizens be aware of this, so that citizens know what the issues are in a complex argument, where the money is, who the speakers are. Above all, we should recognize the basic inequality that exists: not only is the money, media, and manpower to defend vested interests concentrated heavily on one side, but in addition the environment in which we have grown up has been so conditioned by advertising to certain norms and lifestyles that we find it difficult even to conceive that things could or should be different.

3

Teachers can help "do something" about the current and future propaganda blitz. English teachers especially have a good opportunity because they are directly involved in language at all levels of our educational system. However, in my opinion, many of the kinds of reformers I've observed in the past few years are not very useful, effective, or coherent. Let me oversimplify by pointing out some "types":

Potshotters are those people with an eclectic enthusiasm, a random zealousness, who take potshots at everything with little concern for relative importance. Such people are outraged one day by a Pentagon communique, the next day by a hand-lettered sign in the local grocery store window. Targets are chosen not by significance but by proximity, perhaps even by whim. Without order or coherence, such randomness often wastes the energy, drains the enthusiasm, and exhausts the zeal of good, well-intentioned people who have not coherently established their goals and priorities.

Assassins could label those reformers with traces of paranoia or megalomania. Every Cause has its share of people whose motives are intensely personal and often a bit irregular or peculiar. Although extreme cases are relatively rare ("General Motors is out to get me!"), a much larger percentage of reformers can be classified simply as rivals for power. They damn the existing situation or Establishment, but they would be damned eager to impose their way, to substitute their ideas, if only they had the power. Underneath the selfless slogans of many reformers, underneath the veneer of idealism, lies a submerged strata of authoritarianism. The "If-I-were-King" fantasies are not limited to those poor souls who are institutionalized; all reform movements have their share of would-be tyrants.

Single-issue people concentrate on one aspect of a problem, ignore the context, or exaggerate the part in relationship to the whole. Frequently, single-issue people focus on a narrow subject matter and have a short-term, one-shot existence as reformers. (Some distinctions must be made here, because it is valid and most useful for a specialist in a particular area to analyze or to criticize specific situations within the area. It is also reasonable for reformers to use a "task force" approach, a brief intensified attack on one specific aspect. But such valid approaches should be considered as tactical maneuvers within a wider, broader strategic context.) "Single-issue people" as used here suggests those narrow specialists whose scope and vision have been so restricted or distorted that they do not see the broader implications of problems.

Ivory Tower Dwellers are the non-reformers within the teaching profession, those specialists who are totally blind to the problems of language and society. In the discipline of English, they are the technicians of literature or linguistics who plead they have no training, no interest, and no time to get involved in "someone else's specialty." Such an attitude is a gross abdication of responsible citizenship, of humane scholarship, of the intellectual life.

Thus far most observers would agree: the *potshotters,* the *assassins,* the *single-issue people* and the *ivory tower dwellers* contribute little to the cause of reform. Yet these types can hinder, delay, and obstruct change because they represent inertia, vested interests, emotional commitments to their own specialties, defensive reactions to anything which would seem to threaten their turf. But often the inert hostility or the misdirected effort of these "types" of teachers is easier to deal with than some other commonly seen attitudes: the *Preachers,* who use the podium as their pulpit, to instill their own political views or moral judgments; the *Puritans,* who hold that language manipulation *per se* is "bad" (called Puritans here because I think their "linguistic Manicheanism" derives from a Puritan, Ramist rhetoric) ; the *Rousseauists* and *Luddites;* and the *Cuddlers.*

Rousseauists and *Luddites* are those reformers more common in colleges among younger teachers who are "with it" or "right on" (or whatever this semester's slang is) and whose classroom discussions are lively conversations about current events and pop culture. In theory, most of the modern Rousseauists may grant the concept of persuasion; that is, they will accept the idea that persuasion *is* legitimate. But they fear an organized, institutionalized persuasion. For them, it's allright for one person to try and persuade another person, but when it comes to an organized institution (i.e., the advertising industry) persuading the public, the Rousseauists deny commercial advertising the right to exist. They share Rousseau's fear of institutions and organizations. During the 1971 FTC Hearings, Alvin Achenbaum (vice-president of J. Walter Thompson Co. advertising agency) correctly rebuked the recklessness of many of the anti-advertising zealots: "Critics rarely define manipulation or back their charges with hard evidence. It is hard to know whether they are against advertising as such, or the misuses of advertising, or against selling in general."

Some teachers even share the Luddites' fear of machines and glamorize those inhumane revolutionaries today who literally want to destroy the existing urban-industrial system with the mad dog tactics of a savage anarchy. In reality, such destruction would cause death and suffering to millions of human beings. Relatively few teachers are so extreme, but more than a few who see themselves as "reformers" in fact romanticize the pastoral sentimentality of the counter culture, pandering to the wishful thinking and the self-centered luxury of the weekend Whitmans and the summertime Thoreaus. Henry David Thoreau is a dear friend of mine. But I'd hate to have this Henry as one of our strategic policymakers today, concerned as I am with the very real problem that in the next generation we have to feed, clothe, and house 100 million more people in this country and perhaps several billion more in the world.

Cuddlers characterizes those sincere teachers who do not want "to corrupt" the young, who want "to protect the innocence" of the children and act as a shield for their students. These teachers may know a great deal about language; they may know a great deal about human duplicity. But they hesitate to pass these items on. They don't want "to hurt" the children or "to destroy their illusions." They want children to remain forever innocent, to be trusting, to be believers. One such teacher wrote to me: "Isn't it a shame there's such a credibility gap now. I think our job is to restore our children's confidence in their government."

No. I disagree. Teachers should *not* act as the press agents or the public relations staff of any administration, any government, any corporation. If a democratic society is to remain free, young citizens should *not* be trained to be docile, trusting, and naive. Governments and their functionaries, corporations and their products, are always asking for our trust, our confidence, our belief in them. "Trust me" is the standard pitch of every politician and practically every product peddled. At a recent FTC hearing, an advertising spokesman cogently noted that "Advertisers realize that when consumer confidence deteriorates, the value of all advertising deteriorates."

In a capitalist economy, corporations have a vested interest in promoting trust and confidence as great virtues. In America, for example, "responsible" corporate groups (Chambers of Commerce, Better Business Bureaus, etc.) sponsor "self-regulatory" rules and agencies to discourage the abuses by fly-by-night frauds so the reputation of established business is not threatened and consumers remain confident. In both capitalist and socialist spheres, governments spend enormous amounts of time and money building confidence, faith, and credibility not only for external propaganda but also for home consumption. Today, both modern corporations and governments have an enormous amount of sheer power—in money, manpower, media access, laws and lawyers, rules and regulations—compared to the individual citizen.

Throughout human history the problem of innocence and experience has been a central theme of moralists, philosophers, teachers, and, in a very personal sense, of parents. We are aware of the danger of "corrupting" the young; Christ, for example, warned against such corruption by using the powerful metaphor of the millstone drowning those who would corrupt youth. But, the Bible also gives us the injunction: "Be ye as wise as serpents and as innocent as doves."

If teachers in a free democratic society do have certain moral obligations, it would seem that their efforts should be directed toward providing individual citizens with survival skills in a society of sophisticated persuasion techniques, and not in endorsing or advocating trust and confidence in any particular politician, administration, government, corporation, or product. Foremost among our survival skills must be a healthy skepticism, a realistic attitude, and an ability to make critical judgments.

All of these attitudes, these reformers, exist now within our schools, within our society. But which of these attitudes do we wish to encourage for the next generation? The 100 million more children who will be in American schools in the next 25 years will be exposed to a more intensified and sophisticated propaganda blitz from a larger advertising industry and a larger government and will live in a society even more organized and institutionalized. Shall we encourage the *Rousseauists?* The *Puritans?* The *Potshotters?* The *Assassins?* Shall we go back into our Ivory Tower, ignore the problem, and hope that it will go away? Or shall we attempt, once again, to reform, to create some kind of coherent, organized, thoughtful, reformation of our attitudes toward education? If we are to be reformers, let us reform that for which we are most responsible, the teaching of language.

But where, specifically, shall we start? Without being trite, we must start with ourselves. But not in the hand-wringing spirit of "teacher-heal-thyself" from your indulgence in that "bad" thing of language manipulation. Let us start in a simple, realistic acknowledgment that most of our previous training and attention has been directed toward literature and classroom methodology and that we are generally ignorant about rhetorical techniques, nonverbal communication, and basic information on the media, advertising agencies, regulatory agencies, and so on. This means that, as individuals, we have to devote attention and make time for personal reading and research in these areas. Obviously, we must sacrifice other priorities or other items which now consume our time.

Instant results cannot be expected. It takes time, patience, a long-range view. But imagine if only a few thousand of the several hundred thousand people who teach language in the schools today were to decide now to focus their interest on these issues, to expand their readings, their research, and their writing. If you can imagine this, I can imagine that five years hence, we'd start seeing some very visible results.

It would be reasonable that, much like a series of widening, concentric circles, after such "self"-interest, one would be concerned with articulating these ideas in the classroom, the department, the school system or school district, and in the various regional and national organizations. There have to be some comprehensive curriculum changes, but I can't foresee this happening very soon, and certainly not without a broad base of support from alert, informed teachers.

"Do you really think," a voice inside me says, *"that any of this can really happen? That any of these words you've written, or any of the words so eloquently written in some of the other essays here, can really have any influence? Aren't all of you simply putting off your roles as Mr. Chips and Miss Thistlebottom for a chance to put on your Don Quixote clothes and encourage others to do the same?"*

But words count. Well-written sentences have lasted longer than corporations, nations, or empires.

Public Doublespeak: A Personal Reading List

Hugh Rank

1

"I am planning to teach a course. . . ," the letters usually began, "please send me a reading list about Doublespeak." Other letters began, "What do you *mean* by Public Doublespeak?" Reasonable requests and reasonable questions. For over a year, I served as chairman of the NCTE Committee on Public Doublespeak, a committee assigned to the vague, omnibus task of "doing something" about the misuse of language in political propaganda and commercial advertising today.

When I joined the committee, my main interest was in trying to help sort out, to classify, and to categorize the various things which might fall under the general heading of propaganda. I thought the word "Doublespeak" had a nice Orwellian connotation, and that it served as a useful "umbrella" term to suggest the general interest of the committee in propaganda analysis, semantics, rhetoric, persuasion, and other related studies.

In one sense, I saw myself as a "typical" or "representative" English teacher: that is, practically all of my formal training had been in the study and analysis of *literature*. What I knew about rhetoric and composition, I had generally picked up by experience, over a period of years of teaching. (In another sense, I was to find out that my own "traditional" education at Notre Dame probably provided me with a more extensive background in philosophy than most of my contemporaries; and that my own interest in Jonathan Edwards led me, via Peter Ramus, back to Aristotle's rhetoric; and Ed Corbett's *Classical Rhetoric for the Modern Student* helped me to make many links between the traditional study of rhetoric and the modern analysis of propaganda.) Nevertheless, I was not a "propaganda expert"; I saw myself as a "typical" English teacher, and sought to seek out materials useful to my colleagues who had the same traditional, literary-oriented background, and to provide them with readable materials and references for their use if they wanted to do something about propaganda analysis.

For months, I gathered books and articles from our own library, plus received incoming suggestions from other English teachers, until my office began looking like a branch library, books stacked high on all the shelves. In one of my committee reports, I told the members, "You recognize the problem: aspects of our omnibus concerns are discussed in journals from many disciplines (English, speech, journalism, sociology, psychology, media, etc.) using different terminology. . . . Our first goal is to sketch out some of the possibilities, and the optimums; the final goal is to come up with some practical realistic proposals. I am aware that the Speech Communication Association is also working on a list of the "10 best" and "50 best" books in their eight divisions; their system is simpler and probably more workable than what we are attempting; yet we may be able to achieve some more results. If you have special interest in IS&R, systematics, taxonomies . . . let us hear from you." And to those correspondents who still demanded a reading list *right now*, I suggested, "O.K., then read: Artistotle, Allport, Bruner, Burke, Chase, Cirino, Corbett, DeMott, Ellul, Hayakawa, Johnson, Katz, Lasswell, Lazersfeld, Lee, McDougall, Miller, Mills, Minteer, Moran, Ong, Orwell, Packard, Pei, Piaget, Postman, Safire, Smith, Weingartner. . . ."

Basically, one can see that the problem has the dimensions of the "information explosion,"—or, in old-fashioned terms, the Tower of Babel. For example, *Ulrich's International Periodical Directory* lists, according to my count, 33 abstracting and indexing services which would be relevant to the study of propaganda: e.g., *International Abstracts, Language and Language Behavior Abstracts, Marketing Information Guide, Psychological Abstracts, Social Sciences and Humanities Index, Sociological Abstracts*, etc. Here, one must not only identify which abstracting services to use, but also identify those *descriptor terms* used in these various indices. Some items are already computerized; but, generally speaking, there has been little organized input concerning propaganda items. For example, ERIC/RCS has a few listings, and is adding more under the leadership of Dan Dieterich; but it is restricted by its goal to index only those items which are directly related to classroom teaching.

The most encouraging factor, as I see it, is that there is a great deal of expertise available, many books and articles, many people working in specialized areas. But the main problem is to synthesize and to translate this material about propaganda analysis into a language, or into a program, geared at a wide popular audience. There is no shortage of *experts;* there is a dire shortage of *translators*. Much more could be done, but, as the *New York Times* editorial about the NCTE Public Doublespeak Committee put it, no federal agency is going to break its neck funding a project which has such political implications.

Reluctantly, I present this "recommended reading list." To me, it's still unsorted; it still needs a lot of work, which I am doing, slowly. But both Walker Gibson (1973 NCTE President) and Dan Dieterich (1974 Chairman of the Public Doublespeak Committee), who have visited my book-infested office, have asked me to itemize, very simply, the material which I do have on hand. Despite all of the inconclusiveness, it still represents a reasonably good collection of material for the average teacher.

Another lesson learned is that no matter how much reading you do, there'll always be someone to point out your ignorance in "their" speciality: "Oh, you haven't read *so-and-so*. Well, he's absolutely the *key* to the whole subject." The antidote to this kind of put-down is to read the FTC Hearings on Modern Advertising Practices and find out just how ignorant (lacking in *knowledge*) the professional persuaders and the professional regulators are about matters which are not directly germane to their own speciality. I would anticipate that the publication of this informal bibliography will bring in scores of letters pointing out that I missed "the most important" thing in X, Y, or Z. Fine. Such suggestions will be most useful; they'll be collected by the committee, kept on hand for future use. My intent here is to help other teachers, not only in building their libraries, but also in building their egos. If you start out as a "typical" English teacher, you're quite apt to feel insecure among these diverse experts, until you begin to realize that no one yet has pulled together a "perfect" synthesis; nor will there be a panacea. Hopefully, this list will be a shortcut for you in making your own synthesis and in passing it on to your students.

2

Advertising, Rhetorical Analysis. Any study of contemporary advertising, marketing, consumerism, and the federal regulatory agencies must begin with *Advertising Age*—the weekly newspaper of the industry. Of special interest is the "overview" issue (November 21, 1973) "The New World of Advertising," the annual surveys (in August) of the 100 major advertisers, the yearly forecasts (in December), and the periodic special issues devoted to particular segments of the industry. *Advertising Age* is published by Crain Communication, Inc. (740 North Rush, Chicago), which also produces a quantity of technical books on advertising. Most important to the "outsider" is *Advertising and the Public Interest: A Staff Report to the Federal Trade Commission,* by John A. Howard and James Holbert ($10), a vital reference work for libraries because it is the most authoritative, most available summary of the 1971 FTC Hearings on Modern Advertising Practices. (The full testimony of these important hearings runs through scores of volumes and is "officially" available only in the Washington office of the FTC.)

If advertising terms confuse you, try Ayer's *Glossary of Advertising & Related Terms* (Philadelphia: Ayer, 1973), a brief, highly technical lexicon, useful in a college reference collection. For a good introduction to the hidden side of advertising—marketing research—start with the special *Ad Age* issue of July 15, 1974, then consult such standard reference works as *M.A.M.E.* (Robert Schiller's *Market and Media Evaluation: The Association of Industrial Advertisers Handbook of Advertising to Business, Industry, Government, and the Professions*, Macmillan, 1969) or Daniel Starch's *Measuring Advertising Readership and Results* (McGraw-Hill, 1966), or brief survey texts, such as Boyd and Levy, *Promotion: A Behavioral View* (Prentice-Hall, 1967). By now you get the drift of my message: certainly titles are going to change, but if an English teacher wants to keep up with developments in advertising, then instead of using "our" descriptor terms, such as *persuasion* or *rhetoric*, we have to think in the terminology of the advertisers: *consumer behavior, market behavior, marketing research, public relations, salesmanship, etc.*

For general reading about advertising, perhaps the best place to start is still Martin Mayer's *Madison Avenue, U.S.A.* Although somewhat dated (1958) in its details and names, this informative survey of the basic structures and operation of the industry remains readable because of its clear, lucid style. For a more recent analysis, I'd recommend E. B. Weiss', *Marketing to the New Society* (Chicago: Crain, 1974), a collection of over 80 articles by Weiss which have appeared in *Advertising Age:* a potpourri from an insightful prophet of the industry.

After reading these books, one can then go back to read (or re-read) the granddaddy of all of the "New Muckrakers"—Vance Packard's *The Hidden Persuaders* (1957). Parts of Packard, too, are outdated: his dire predictions about "motivational research" never materialized. Ernest Dichter, for example, has much less influence and credibility today than he did back in those early days of psychoanalytical experimenting with "consumer motivation." From Packard's book one might want to go to a recent issue of *Psychology Today* (February 1974), for Berkeley Rice's "Rattlesnakes, French Fries and Pupillometric Oversell," for a succinct history of recent attempts and failures of the industry to analyze consumer behavior.

Advertising has produced a mass of novels, exposés, and autobiographical success stories—books which are almost polarized in their admiration or damnation of the industry. If you want to sample some of the advertising ego trips, try David Ogilvy's *Confessions of an Advertising Man* (Ballantine Books) ; these "confessions" lack the originality of a Rousseau, the intelligence of a Newman, and even the humility of a Ben Franklin, but they do give an insight into the mentality of some of advertising's greatest "geniuses." Another autobiographical scrap is Jerry Della Femina's *From Those Wonderful Folks Who Gave You Pearl Harbor* (Pocket Books) — a witty title (that contains 99 per cent of the book's humor) referring to an in-joke about Sony TV ads. From this successful entrepreneur one can learn such pearls of wisdom as "once you arrive at the problem, then your job is really almost over, because the solving of the problem is nothing. The headache is finding out what the problem is" (p. 159). Such profundity is matched only by the humorous anecdotes about selling sewing machines to impoverished Indians in Peru, who do not have electricity, but who now have time payments to make. Other, recent, gossipy books, which are filled with facts, insights, and anecdotes about Madison Avenue today, are Edward Buxton's *Promise Them Anything;* Samm Baker's *The Permissible Lie;* Carl Wrighter's *I Can Sell You Anything;* and Nicholas Samstag's *Bamboozled.*

Closely related to advertising are those books concerned with the official regulatory agencies and the unofficial consumer movements which function as the watchdogs of advertising. Here, one could start by reading the yearly *FTC Reports;* even these bare, antiseptic abstracts provide a litany of horrors as they dryly itemize the offenses and illegal acts committed by America's major "reputable" corporations, those found in the *Fortune* 500 list. When Ralph Nader raised the question, "Who watches the watchdog?" the result was *The Nader Report on the Federal Trade Commission* (New York: R. W. Baron, 1969) by Edward Cox, Robert Fellmeth, and John Schultz, the original "Nader's Raiders." This report read today still makes a lot of sense, despite the improvements and changes which have gone on within the FTC in the past six years. While some of the names and situations have changed, the basic problems still remain: systematic detection of violations; establishing priorities; using existing enforcement power with energy and speed; and failing to seek adequate authority to make its work have real effect. The Nader Report is no neutral document, but it will long remain a landmark of informed exposé writing. Susan Wagner's *The Federal Trade Commission* (New York: Praeger, 1971) is a useful, available survey of the FTC's history and operations; bland, at times it almost seems as if it were an FTC "approved" guidebook. Despite my warnings here about the weaknesses of the FTC, it would be best to close by emphasizing the strengths: the accomplishments the FTC has made, despite the opposition of powerful pressure groups; the written materials and consumer aids it does provide. The list of FTC publications, free or inexpensive, is available from them on request.

Closely related to this is the work done by the Office of Consumer Affairs, working directly out of the Executive Office of the president. Two useful books published here are: *Guide to Federal Consumer Services* and *Consumer Education Bibliography*. This latter publication is a bargain bibliography ($1.00, from USGPO), but must be handled with care: it's a hodgepodge of items including genuine consumerist and reformer critiques, mixed together with an odd assortment of juvenile-interest books (e.g., *Gerbils, Better Football for Boys*, etc.) and much self-serving propaganda material from various commercial and industrial groups. Most of the "free films" and "free charts" offered for classroom use make the teacher an unwitting propagandist in the public relations campaign of some special interest group.

Other useful consumer-oriented books are Robert Rosefsky's *Frauds, Swindles and Rackets* (Chicago: Follett, 1973). Rosefsky, a syndicated financial writer, provides a complete course in the various "hardcore" frauds, how to spot them, and how to avoid them. Mail fraud is still a major industry, bilking Americans out of an estimated $500 million a year, despite the old-fashioned gimmicks (chain letters, get-rich-quick schemes, phony contests, etc.) ; for an informative insight into this little-known "word" industry, see E. J. Kahn, Jr., *Fraud* (Harper, 1973). Most books concerned with consumer fraud are subject oriented (medical frauds, insurance, land sales, etc.) ; one of the best ways to enter this whole field is by reading *Consumer Reports*, the original consumerist magazine dating from the 'thirties. Although some reformers have complained that *CR* can get too petty, too mundane, too tied to middle-class penny pinching in its detailed reports on consumer products, I think the overall impact of *CR* has been significant. Now that "consumerism" is a good word, a dozen other magazines of varied quality are on the bandwagon, using the term "consumer" in their title. One excellent but little-known consumer newspaper is *Media & Consumer* ($12.00 yearly, Box 850, Norwalk, Conn. 06852), a well-edited synthesis of consumer information, a publication originally bankrolled by Consumer's Union and worth ordering for your school's library. Finally, a newsletter which is probably already in most high school libraries, *The Consumer*

Educator, a brief monthly fact sheet published by the National Association of Secondary School Principals, in cooperation with the Better Business Bureau (1201 16th Street, N.W., Washington, D.C.). Not too many radicals hanging around the BBB, but this little journal is still worth investigating.

In the academic world, any interest in the language manipulation of the "real world" usually was located within speech departments (competing there with elocution lessons, drama, speech therapy, *et al.*) or within the vague domains of the "social studies." English departments were not in the forefront in analyzing the social implications of language; more attention was being given to the minor 19th century authors than to the major 20th century developments in language. Such an ivory tower attitude was encouraged by the dominance of the "New Critics," with their emphasis on the work of art itself and their dictums against the mortal sin of the "affective fallacy." But if literary critics ignored the reader or the audience, the professional persuaders did not; they were extremely concerned with audience, with response, and with public opinion.

Academic interest in propaganda analysis probably started with Walter Lippmann (*Public Opinion,* 1922), but developed most rapidly in the early 1930s, more or less as a response to Hitler's propaganda blitz. The basic guide to this early work is Harwood Child's *A Reference Guide to the Study of Public Opinion,* originally published by Princeton, 1934, but now available in reprint from Gryphon (Ann Arbor, Michigan); but probably a more comprehensive bibliography is Harold Lasswell's *Propaganda and Promotional Activities: An Annotated Bibliography* (University of Chicago Press, 1969).

Public Opinion Quarterly began publication in January 1937. The Institute for Propaganda Analysis started in 1936 and lasted for a few years, producing among other things its famous list of the "seven major propaganda techniques" (Glittering Generalities, Name-Calling, etc.). Curtis McDougall in his book *Understanding Public Opinion* calls this the period of "panacea hunting." McDougall states, "too many social scientists have been too eager to get on any bandwagon which might possibly be heading in the direction of something statistically valid. First, propaganda analysis was all the rage, and many who should have known better acted and talked as though all the riddles of collective social behavior would be solved if it became possible to pin the proper labels on every word spoken or written intended to influence the thought or behavior of anyone other than its originator. As a result . . .

skepticism became so widespread that every persuasive argument, no matter how valid, was suspect."

Most English teachers have had some encounter with the General Semantics movement, and recognize that it has fervent supporters (and detractors, too, who argue against the "cult"). If one hasn't been introduced to General Semantics, the best entry is S. I. Hayakawa's *Language in Thought and Action* (3rd ed.) or *The Use and Misuse of Language,* his anthology of articles drawn from *ETC.* (the GS journal). From these, one can get a good bibliographical lead into the other basic works in this area: Stuart Chase, Wendall Johnson, Irving Lee, etc. People associated with the movement have produced many valuable books, reaching both a popular audience (e.g., Neil Postman's and Charles Weingartner's *Teaching as a Subversive Activity*) and a student audience via texts and audiovisual materials which are inspired by the language analysis techniques of this movement.

Much of what we call "propaganda analysis" or "rhetorical analysis" is done within speech departments, and frequently appears in speech journals and in learned societies such as the Speech Communication Association (SCA) and the International Communication Association (ICA). Much is available here, but perhaps some useful introductions are Barker's and Kibbler's *Speech Communication Behavior: Perspectives and Principles* and Bitzer and Black, *The Prospect of Rhetoric: Report of the National Development Project* (both Prentice-Hall, 1971). College level texts which focus on problems of contemporary persuasion also appear more frequently in speech departments than in English departments. Notable among these texts would be Jeffery Auer's *The Rhetoric of Our Times* (New York: Meredith Corporation, 1969) and John Bower's and Donovan Och's *The Rhetoric of Agitation and Control* (Reading, Mass.: Addison-Wesley Publishing, 1971). Both of these are excellent in themselves, but also provide many further leads to follow. Other speech texts worth examination are Thomas Scheidel's *Speech Communication and Human Interaction* (Glenview, Illinois: Scott-Foresman, 1972); George Borden's *An Introduction to Human Communication Theory* (Dubuque: Brown Publishing, 1971) and William Thompsen's *Media and Communication* (New York: Harcourt Brace Jovanovich, 1972).

Another related movement developing in the late 1940s was the sophistication of polling techniques, especially by Gallop, Roper and others, with the application of mathematic probabilities and demographic studies. A decade earlier, polling techniques had been discredited by the famous Literary Digest Poll which had predicted that FDR would lose the 1936 election; but after the war pollsters were confident of their newly-developed skills—until once again, in 1948, all the polls were wrong when Truman beat Dewey. The polling techniques of that innocent age seem outdated now that the computer has entered the scene; Americans today are accustomed to the seeming infallability of the computer-controlled polls. In the past decade the computer pollster has become the Delphic oracle for Americans and currently enjoys a credibility rating higher than the government or the press. The search for objective statistical methods to analyze communications continued in the early 1950s and one of the most significant contributions was Bernard Berelson's *Content Analysis in Communication Research* (1952) ; in one sense, the speculative analyses of early thinkers such as Walter Lippmann and Harold Lasswell were being replaced by the statistical surveys of the funded research teams. Robert Lane's and David Sears's *Public Opinion* (1964) is a readable introduction to the subject, but perhaps the best place to start is simply reviewing the back issues of *Public Opinion Quarterly.*

Such analysis of audience is not confined to sociologists and political scientists; one is likely, within business schools, to see the same concerns expressed in different terminology. Here one seeks the books and the journals which are concerned with "consumer behavior" or "marketing behavior" or "marketing research." Important journals are *Journal of Marketing Research, Journal of Marketing, Harvard Business Review,* and the popular business magazines: *Fortune, Forbes, Business Week,* etc. Some of the sample titles, listed in the *Consumer Education Bibliography,* indicate the range and interest of the marketing research people: *The Psychology of Consumer Behavior, The Psychology of Pricing, Research in Communication Behavior, Why People Buy, The Strategy of Desire, Knowing the Consumer, How to Predict What People Will Buy, Consumer Behavior of Children and Teenagers.* Rest assured there is no lack of publication, nor financial support, for those who are able to analyze the audience, the consumers' motivations for purchase. This is an extremely saleable kind of research scholarship and many of our behavioral science brethren are breaking their necks to do such work. My own bias, you see, is on the side of the consumer, the *persuadee,* and there has been very little work done in the academic world to protect the consumer's interest. Most of the consumerists' heroes have been the lone wolves, the Ralph Naders and the Vance Packards, standing outside the academic world.

If *business* is interested in what makes people tick, in what motivates people, in how to persuade people, it also might occur to you that *governments* are now starting to get into this. One such major effort is the Human Resources Research Organization (HumRro), a "non-profit research and development corporation" whose purpose is "to improve human performance, particularly in organizational settings, through behavioral and social science research, development and consultation." Such noble, idealistic work is carried out by your federal government, funded primarily through the Department of Defense and concentrating mainly (thus far) on military and para-military activities. While some of their work, naturally, is classified "secret," HumRro has an active public relations department and is willing to send its catalogues of research activities and publications to those who are interested. Write: Research Information Coordinator, HumRro, 300 North Washington Street, Alexandria, Virginia 22314.

American Politics. If I had to restrict myself to three recommendations, I'd vote for David Wise's *The Politics of Lying* (Vintage, 1973) for its chapter-and-verse description of the realities of our political word manipulation during the past decade; William Safire's *The New Language of Politics* (Collier Books, 1968, 2nd edition), a basic and extensive (800 pp.) dictionary of political language and political savvy; and, finally, William Fulbright's *The Pentagon Propaganda Machine* (Vintage, 1970), a most important analysis simply because the Pentagon is the most important, best organized, and most potentially dangerous propagandist in the world today. Other than this first team, I would recommend some very enjoyable reading in American political propaganda with Joe McGinniss's *The Selling of the President 1968,* that detailed exposé of the packaging of Richard Nixon's image by the Madison Avenue boys in order to sell us a president as they would sell us a box of soap powder. Two scholarly books closely related to this are Gene Wyckoff's *The Image Candidates: American Politics in the Age of Television* (Macmillan, 1968) and Dan Nimmo's *The Political Persuaders: The Techniques of Modern Election Campaigns* (Prentice-Hall, 1970). College level textbooks on this general subject would include Thomas Brockway's *Language and Politics* (Boston: Heath, 1965), a brief sampler (Orwell, Machiavelli, Lasswell, DeTocqueville, Art Buchwald); Nick Aaron Ford's *Language in Uniform: A Reader on Propaganda* (New York: Odyssey, 1967), another brief sampler (J. S. Mills, Jonathan Swift, Thoreau, Milton, Hutchins, etc.). Better yet, in my judgment, is *Language in America,* edited by Neil Postman, Charles Weingartner, and Terence Moran (Pegasus, 1969), a lively and more diversified reader with a more contemporary focus; and Raymond

Liedlich's *Coming to Terms with Language* (John Wiley & Sons, 1973).

If you read all of these horror stories about political manipulation of language and if you've endured an almost daily diet of Watergate and White House chicanery, then you're entitled to a few moments of relaxation with Art Buchwald's collected columns (*The Establishment Is Alive and Well in Washington; Have I Ever Lied to You?; And Then I Told the President*, etc., periodically released in Crest paperbacks) or with G. B. Trudeau's "Doonesbury" collections (*Still a Few Bugs in the System; The President Is a Lot Smarter Than You Think*, etc., published in paper sporadically by Holt, Rinehart and Winston). Or with the *National Lampoon*. Or with *Mad*. With satire, we can preserve our sanity.

International Propagandists. In this age of detente in the 1970s, we often forget the intensity of emotions aroused by the "Cold War" propaganda battles fought during the past 20 years. Although it might not be fashionable today, one must admit that a lot of money has been spent by both major and minor powers during the past few decades on propaganda activities: to persuade others, and their own populace, of their own merits and their opponents' demerits. Rather than start from scratch, (i.e., the Hitler/Goebbels era) let me recommend just three books of more current vintage and more contemporary interest (i.e., nuclear gamesmanship, etc.); these three books not only contain a variety of viewpoints but also have ample bibliographies in international propaganda activities: Ervin Whitaker, Jr., *Propaganda and International Relations* (San Francisco: Chandler, 1962); Herbert Schiller, *Mass Communications and American Empire* (New York: Kelley Publishers, 1970); Thomas Franck and Edward Weisband, *Word Politics: Verbal Strategy among the Superpowers* (New York: Oxford University Press, 1971). For further suggestions, try visiting your local political science department, mass communication department, etc. Few requests for advice have ever been turned down.

Media. Television, naturally, is the critical mass media of our era. Where to start reading about it? Again, for a good informal introduction, I'd recommend Martin Mayer's *About Television*, (Harper, Row, 1972); Mayer's graceful style, his ability to synthesize and to produce readable prose make this book a good starting point for student and teacher. From there, one can go in many directions. For an "action book," for example, Nicholas Johnson's *How to Talk Back to Your Television Set* (Bantam, 1970) is the best consumer-oriented book available today; Johnson is the advocate for the audience.

If you are concerned with bias and slanting in the media, a whole range of attitudes will be found in books such as Robert Cirino's *Don't Blame the People* (Vintage, 1972); in Edith Efron's *The News Twisters* (Los Angeles: Nash Publishing, 1971), a content analysis charging that the networks are biased ("elitist-liberals"); Efron's sequel *How CBS Tried to Kill a Book* (New York: Manor Books, 1973) is interesting, but perhaps she confuses opposition with "bookburning" (p. 134). Among other such fascinating, lively, and provocative books are Fred Friendly's classic *Due to Circumstances beyond Our Control* (Random House, 1967); Sig Mickelson, *The Electric Mirror: Politics in an Age of Television* (Dodd, Mead, 1972); Joseph Keeley, *The Left-Leaning Antenna: Political Bias in Television* (New Rochelle: Arlington House, 1971); William Small, *To Kill a Messenger: Television News and the Real World* (New York: Hastings House, 1970); S. Freidin and G. Bailey, *The Experts* (Macmillan, 1968). Some of these books are uneven and cannot be recommended indiscriminately to wide audiences, but they (and their bibliographies) are reasonable entries to subjects not frequently taught to fledgling English majors in college. For a good listing of books about the press, newspapers and periodicals, I'd suggest reading the appendix to Cirino's *Power to Persuade* (discussed below).

Of special interest to teachers (and parents) are those books which focus on the impact of TV upon children. Most important here is Evelyn Sarson's *Action for Children's Television* (Avon, 1971); the most recent significant analysis is Charles Winich's *Children's Television Commercials: A Content Analysis* (New York: Praeger, 1973), which itemizes sales persuasion techniques, characters, story elements, language, etc. See also *Advertising Age* (circa April to June, 1974) for the running news reports and commentary on the FTC hearings on children's television codes.

Ethical considerations of the mass media have received increased attention from the churches. For example, the National Council of Churches supported the excellent study by William Rivers and Wilbur Schramm, *Responsibility in Mass Communication* (Harper, Row, rev. ed., 1969). A brief, interesting, but essentially inconclusive analysis is the symposium report issued by the Toronto School of Theology: *Truth in Advertising* (Harper, Row, 1972). Readers interested in the moral issues involved in contemporary advertising and propaganda may do well by keeping current with those literate religious periodicals concerned with such matters: *Commonweal, America, Christian Century,* and *Commentary.*

Texts. Most of the books sampled here have been directed at adult audiences and have useful readings for teachers, college students, and advanced high school students. Obviously, teachers are also concerned with texts available geared to younger students. Here the pickings are rather slim; although many texts have good, brief sections within them which deal with semantics or propaganda analysis, there are few which deal extensively with these subjects. Other reviewers from the committee would probably be more explicit in their analysis of what is available, but right now if I were asked what books I want my own children (in junior high) to use, I'd answer, rather enthusiastically, for the McDougal, Littell series *The Language of Man* (Box 1667, Evanston, Ill.), a series distinguished in its approach, attitudes, and graphics. (I was delighted recently when my children told me that these were the "new books" they were using in their school this year.)

If I were teaching in high school, I'd probably use Philip Roden's *The Elusive Truth* (Scott, Foresman) for younger students—it has good sections on logic, advertising, and peer pressures—and David Riley's *Freedom of Dilemma* (Scott, Foresman) —a solid collection of essays and critical readings in the mass media for older, more sophisticated students. And *everyone* would have to read Robert Cirino's excellent new text, *Power to Persuade* (Bantam, 1974) —a collection of 150 brief case histories concerning media and government censorship, bias, news management, advertising, etc. This is an exceptionally strong text: cheap ($1.25), complete with hundreds of "Questions" and "Suggested Activities" geared for the classroom (yet fascinating for an adult audience), and well-balanced: Cirino spares neither Left nor Right, and his extensive bibliography covers the whole spectrum. Four stars!

There are other books I'd like my kids to read, especially to make them more aware of persuasive techniques used in television. Here I'd recommend Sister Ann Christine Heintz, BVM, *Persuasion* (ComEd, Chicago: Loyola University Press, 1971); William Kuhns, *Exploring Television* (ComEd, Chicago: Loyola University Press, 1971); and *Why We Watch Them: Interpreting TV Shows* (New York: Benzinger, 1970). A useful text for teaching critical reading of the newspaper, especially for younger students, is Ruth Smith's and Barbara Michalac's *How to Read Your Newspaper* (Harcourt Brace Jovanovich, 1970). American Education Publications (AEP/ Xerox, Middleton, Conn.) publishes a useful series in semantics, edited by Thomas Born, titled "Understanding Language"; although these four brief (33 page) unit books are well edited, the layout and newsprint leave much to be desired. When kids are a little older, they may be ready for *Rudy's Red Wagon: Communication Strategies in Contemporary Society* by Irving Rein (Scott, Foresman, 1972), a sophisticated and entertaining tour of persuasion strategies seldom discussed elsewhere: the put on, the hussle, graffiti, the rhetoric of AM rock radio, used car lots, etc. You have to read it; I'm not putting you on.

In the future, more texts will be available. I know other writers—including Walker Gibson, D. G. Kehl, Terence Moran, and John Black—are now working on books; from the outlines I've seen, there's very little overlap. Let a thousand flowers bloom: the examples of doublespeak are so numerous, and the approaches to it so varied, that we need to encourage more scholars and analysts (and publishers) to get things in print, into the hands of teachers and students. My own textbook, *Liars in Public Places,* is an anthology for high school and college students on language manipulation in politics and advertising; it will be published by Scott Foresman in 1975.

Nonverbal Communication. For introductions into nonverbal communication, one can start with Edward Hall's *The Silent Language* and *The Hidden Dimension* or with Ray Birdwhistell's *Introduction to Kinesics* or *Kinesics and Context.* Other books related here would be Erving Goffman, *Behavior in Public Places;* Julius Fast, *Body Language;* Stephen Baker, *Visual Persuasion;* parts of Robert Ardrey's *The Territorial Imperative.*

Propaganda. Perhaps the most important books for a teacher to read are those studies not designed to be texts, but written to provide an underlying theory or approach to propaganda. Included here would be Jacques Ellul's *Propaganda: The Formation of Men's Attitudes* (Vintage, 1965); J. A. C. Brown's *Persuasion: From Propaganda to Brainwashing* (Penguin, 1963); George Gordon's *Persuasion: The Theory and Practice of Manipulative Communication* (New York: Hastings House, 1971); George Miller's *The Psychology of Communication* (New York: Basic Books, 1967).

Although I violently disagree with his analysis, Mario Pei's two books *Words in Sheep's Clothing* (New York: Hawthorne, 1969) and its updated sequel *Double-Speak in America* (New York: Hawthorne, 1973) are extremely valuable collections of word manipulation today. The merit of the books is their scope, bringing together jargon and euphemisms from more than 20 different fields: the arts, journalism, education, politics, the military, advertising, etc. In such scope also lies the weakness of these books: Pei gives as much attention to artsy-craftsy talk at cocktail parties as he does to Pentagon and White House manipulation of language which masks the realities of war and thermonuclear bombs.

P.S. Don't forget Aristotle. The Rhetoric. *De Rhetorica.* It all started there. And it's surprising how well those lines have held up and how meaningful they are today.